Arrow of Chaos

Edited by

Sandra Buckley

Michael Hardt

Brian Massumi

THEORY OUT OF BOUNDS

...UNCONTAINED

BY

THE

DISCIPLINES,

INSUBORDINATE

PRACTICES OF RESISTANCE

...Inventing,

excessively,

in the between...

PROCESSES

OF

HYBRIDIZATION

Arrow of Chaos

Romanticism and Postmodernity

Ira Livingston

Theory out of Bounds *Volume 9*

University of Minnesota Press

Minneapolis • London

"Gains" and "Composition," from Bei Dao, *Old Snow*, copyright 1991 by Bei Dao, are reprinted
by permission of New Directions Publishing; Wallace Stevens, "Of Mere Being," from *Opus Posthumous*,
copyright 1957 by Elsie Stevens and Holly Stevens, and lines from "Notes toward a Supreme Fiction,"
from *Collected Poems*, copyright 1942 by Wallace Stevens, reprinted by permission of Alfred A. Knopf, Inc.,
and Faber and Faber, Ltd.; William Tay's translation of Gu Cheng's "Curve," from *After Mao: Chinese Literature and
Society, 1978–1981*, edited by Jeffrey C. Kinkley (Council on East Asian Studies, 1985),
reprinted by permission of Professor Tay and the Council on East Asian Studies, Harvard University;
and W. B. Yeats, "Second Coming," from *The Poems of W. B. Yeats: A New Edition*, edited by Richard J. Finneran,
copyright 1924 by Macmillian, renewed 1952 by B. G. Yeats, reprinted by permission of Simon & Schuster and by
permission of A. P. Watt, Ltd., on behalf of Michael Yeats.
Chapter 6, "Traffic in Leeches," appeared in *American Imago* and is reprinted in revised form
with permission of the Johns Hopkins University Press.

Published by the University of Minnesota Press
111 Third Avenue South, Suite 290,
Minneapolis, MN 55401-2520
Printed in the United States of America on acid-free paper

LIBRARY OF CONGRESS CATALOGING-IN-PUBLICATION DATA
Livingston, Ira, 1956–
Arrow of chaos : romanticism and postmodernity / Ira Livingston.
p.   cm. — (Theory out of bounds ; v. 9)
Includes bibliographical references and index.
ISBN 0-8166-2794-0 (hardcover : alk. paper)
ISBN 0-8166-2795-9 (pbk. : alk. paper)
1. Literature, Modern—20th century—History and criticism.
2. Chaotic behavior in systems in literature.   3. Romanticism.
4. Romanticism.   5. Postmodernism (Literature)   I. Title.
II. Series.
PN771.L588   1997
809'.04—dc20
96-21764

The University of Minnesota
is an equal-opportunity educator and employer.

Contents

Preface

To begin, I'll try to indicate punctually what I think this book is about, and in the process to suggest why punctuality is to an extent inimical to what this book is about.

Arrow of Chaos is a "chaology of knowledge" insofar as it is a study of chaos as a logic at work in epistemological processes. "Romanticism" and "postmodernity" name the blurry beginnings and ends of a modernity that is forever chasing its own tail.

In what sense do the historical and cultural formations of Romanticism and postmodernity cohere in or between themselves, or as appropriate objects for a chaology? In what sense does "chaos" (or "chaos theory") itself cohere as a paradigm or logic? While I sometimes address these questions in the chapters that follow, I do so less to resolve and more to sustain and/or displace what I hope to show are generative ambiguities and constitutive contradictions in formations for which discombobulation is as definitive as coherence.

Chaologies often identify certain thresholds (sometimes called "singularities") at which occur "spontaneous self-organization" or "emergent behavior" or "order out of chaos." This last formula is misleading since what follows a singularity may be more like another *kind* of order (or chaos) more or less at odds with the order/chaos that precedes it and that may be *ongoingly necessary to sustain it*: this contingency is why "*self*-organization" is also misleading if construed as simple autonomy. Romantic ideologies of "self" and "organism" continue to be involved in generating these constructions and misconstruals.

Manuel De Landa, in *War in the Age of Intelligent Machines*, rounds up some of the usual suspects to illustrate one form of self-organization, so-called "spontaneous cooperative behavior":

> *The individual spin of atoms in a metal "cooperate" to make the metal magnetic; the individual molecules in a chemical reaction "cooperate" to create the perfectly rhythmic patterns of a chemical clock; the cells making up an amoeba colony "cooperate" under certain conditions to assemble an organism with differentiated organs; and the different termites in a colony "cooperate" to build a nest. (7)*

It would be possible to assert that these phenomena are related *metaphorically* insofar as metaphor proposes a similarity between essentially different realms. Here, though, De Landa puts the word "cooperate" in scare quotes to indicate that it is only *apparently* an anthropomorphizing metaphor, but also that metaphor cannot simply be dispensed with: the question of how a certain human intentionality (e.g., "cooperation") has been attributed to nature should not assume the difference between them; rather, we would have to look at how certain practices (ideologies, technologies, and so on) differentiate "human" and "natural" by establishing various correspondences and oppositions between them, and also, then, to use this inquiry to question *how human intentionality has been attributed to humans.*

The notorious unscientificity of metaphor may enable the "gotcha" effect of showing the absolute reliance of science upon metaphor, but at what points does this dialectic begin to compromise the distinction between metaphor and science? Taking another tack, would it be possible also to maintain that metaphor is a process in nature, that "poetics" also has purchase on the world typically thought to be monopolized by science, and not exclusively by critiquing science as a second-order simulation? These are open questions.

Unfortunately, it is against metaphor that De Landa casts "recent advances in experimental mathematics" as finding "deep" similarities between the only apparently very different processes he assembles (7). In other words, De Landa claims his examples as cognate epiphenomena of a single and definitive abstract law (or "gene" or "machine"), more like an identity among members of the *same* realm (dubbed "the machinic phylum" after Deleuze) and thus *not* metaphorical. Clearly, De Landa doesn't want military historians to find that they're reading a book on poetics. But setting aside De Landa's revamped Enlightenment masternarrative of scientific progress, and even allowing the "depth" of the "family resemblance" he remarks, what the resemblance *means* in practice—how it can be lived—remains an open question: it *may* mean that some reconfigured discipline (probably not poetics, but I'll do my best) could claim partial authority to study termite colonies *and* magnets, but what opportunities and constraints does it offer for those who are organized only partly by the "emergent behavior" in question? Do termites and magnets enjoy some special intimacy? Affiliations always sprawl across categories, and if an organism is always a provisional (and high-maintenance) affiliation of multiple and contradictory constraints and reducible to no single one of these (i.e., a "fuzzy set"), why talk about an underlying *identity*? "Singularity" comes into question in turn; metaphor opens up into a catachrestic and centerless orbit—a tail-chasing—which is the kind of *about* that this book is about: less referentiality (*about* as "in regard to") and more of a "strange attractor" (*about* as "around; by a circuitous way; here and there").

Returning, then, to De Landa's assemblage, what does it mean that the apparently scientific phrase "spontaneous cooperative behavior" seems to be a roughly precise description of the effect of a kind of power (a typically modern and postmodern power) already described in cultural theory as "hegemony"? To begin with, looking at how scientists are "constructing" nature (and mathematics) in the image of postmodern power may be a necessary—politicizing—step in correcting the aestheticizing and scientizing that are rampant in the discourse of fractals and chaos. I get tired of hearing the mandate that humanists must learn to engage scientists on their (the scientists's) terms and to fight for a piece of the high ground of "objectivity" and "truth," but maybe this mandate is better received as a performative imperative (whose meaning is its always partial and selective recruitment function) rather than a totalizing edict. In any case, it seems important to demonstrate to one's own satisfaction that one who believes he has discovered an objective fact of nature is only looking through the wrong end of an epistemological telescope at his own cultural navel; however, as everyone knows, scientists are mostly licensed to care almost nothing for such a "gotcha"—or may even laugh with you, as they say, all the way to the bank (where you've got an account, too). In frustration, one may be driven to engage a more difficult double mandate: neither/both to cop a certain authority by scientizing, nor/and to show how scientific claims are driven and shaped—or at the very least thoroughly inflected—by economic and political logics. At least, a historical truth-effect may be recognizable in its characteristic doubling back onto itself: to study the "emergence of emergence" must be to throw the paradigm back into its historicity. As in poetic self-reference, this doubling back constitutes more and less than a referent or self: it is an opportunity, a relative "freedom" in that the more a message is about itself, the more its content is up for grabs: it partially encloses or semiautonomizes itself (as a "self-organizing system"), but it thereby also extends its implication with other phenomena (like a hurricane or a termite colony in the wood of the paradigmatic Master's House).

To follow this double mandate is not necessarily to gain more direct purchase on scientific discourse (perhaps the reverse) and also to risk spinning one's wheels, also disabling one's engagement in literary or cultural discourse. This is a necessary and definitive risk of contemporary cultural studies, subject to many permutations. I would not go so far as to say, as the driver of a big-wheel pickup truck once boasted to a friend, that "when I spin my wheels, the earth moves," but the leverage of wheel-spinning is still a crucial—although partial—aspect of the logic of self-organization.

De Landa defines as his object the "machinic phylum": "the set of all the singularities at the onset of processes of self-organization—the critical points in the flow of matter and energy, points at which these flows spontaneously acquire a new form or pattern" (132); these are the grains around which the pearls of nature/culture are secreted. One can then go on to trace how humans have "tapp[ed] into the resources of self-organizing processes in order to create particular lineages of technology" (7); to investigate the emergence of certain "logics" as they come to be maximally embodied in various machines, architectures, social relations, and so on—and maximally abstracted, in the forms of paradigms, theories, mathematics, poetics, and the like—and to consider how "portable" these logics may be, how far they may stray from their original conditions of possibility and how they mutate as they do so, and to what extent they carry with them or are obligated to reproduce their conditions of possibility as they go, like Count Dracula with his boxes of native earth. This is a common predicament of bodies, cultures, and texts. If it is imperative/impossible to steer a course between the unity/multiplicity and materiality/ideality of these logics (it is), one can begin by acknowledging that "the" machinic phylum can be a kind of *Other* or *unconscious* insofar as its agency is neither separable from nor reducible to our own but an interface or *hinge* that both binds and separates us from others (and from "ourselves," since we are multiple, too). Romanticism and postmodernity are treated here as such thresholds, not events that have already happened but ones that are constituted through recursive repetition ("iteration")—as ongoing reperformances—and thus continually open to mutation in the process. There is various discursive pressure to hype these thresholds as historical "ruptures" or radical "discontinuities"—or, on the other hand, to sing a lullaby of "continuity through change." The story I would like to tell opposes and depends on this opposition. It is the story of a *conservation* of chaos, against which modernity has always been a reaction formation. If "things fall apart" defines the implacable direction of thermodynamic time as a foil to both the eternal return of the Same ("reproduction") and the heroic integrity of Romantic Difference ("production"), things are always falling apart and together in the drift of the Arrow of Chaos; how they are allowed to do so is where all is at stake.

Perversity dictates ongoing betrayal of the no-doubt scientistic will to power that makes me want to claim the conservation of chaos as a kind of natural/cultural first principle, or rather, like De Landa, I want to keep my friends (they're just different friends). The same perversity dictates betrayal of the epistemological reek of literarity that hangs around phenomena defined by what I earlier called "generative ambiguities." If you're asking how a *reek* could intelligibly be *betrayed*, then you have a sense of the thorniness of the problem. In any case, the pride of place accorded to poetry in this study is justified at least insofar as, throughout Romantic modernity, "poeticity" has typically been identified with recursive self-reference. The narrative whereby "science" (not to mention politics, journalism, and so on) has increasingly of late learned to practice various forms of the self-referential trick is related to the account (in chapter 3) of how *irony*, a leading trope of self-reference, became a privileged marker of literariness in European Romanticism and continued to explode, with capitalism, toward a global and molecular discursive horizon, becoming a privileged marker of postmodern culture generally. Formerly among the touchstones for the Romantic-modernist project of New Criticism, irony—along with the "close reading" that traced its arabesques—used to work in the service of establishing the fundamental distinctiveness, integrity, and autonomy of the literary text. As time goes by, following several generations of critics engaged in displacing the hegemony of New Criticism, one finds increasingly that the fundamental things no longer apply (and never really did); that the more "closely" one reads, the more the literary object breaks apart, dissolves, shifts polarity, or turns against itself; that the literariness of literature no less than the genricity of any genre is seen to be both undermined and/or supported at every moment by molecular code-switchings and figurative flux (If You Can Read This, You're Not Close Enough). Disciplinary boundaries are fractal interzones: this makes them peculiarly recalcitrant as much as it makes them peculiarly malleable; it does start to suggest various constraints and possibilities in engaging them. This book implicates chaos, Romanticism, and postmodernity and traces relations between them at several scales (e.g., across the spans of the book, its chapters, and their sections), and by cycling through several kinds and dimensions of texts, sometimes by hypertextual "asides," tangential illustrations, and assorted uncomfortably overelaborated "metaphors." The book thereby works to install a "recognition device" for fractal logics while leaving mostly open the question of what uses this device can serve (e.g., in implicit injunctions to "study this" or "intervene here" or "produce meaning at this intersection").

The first, introductory, chapter winds up some of the paradigms to be spun out in what follows. Chapter 2 describes the emergent hegemony, in Romanticism, of a power that works by orchestrating fluxes, inducing resonances and variations across scale and discipline, and by "chaotizing" through mutual "Horrors of Order and Disorder." The next three chapters take as general headings figures and processes affiliated with studies of chaos and fractals. The significance of these figures is not primarily how they derive from or attach to the phenomena-in-question or to disciplinary turf, but how they drift and sprawl across each other and their terrain; that is, if there is no capital-T Theory here (The Cultural Physics of Romanticism; or, A Fractal Poetics of Culture?), there are T-cells (theorems, termites, machines with "local intelligence") whose engagements include partial recognitions, camouflages, accommodations, incorporations, rejections. Both specific and indiscrete, among them, fractal logics reconfigure but not necessarily in their own images.

Chapter 3 describes a paradigmatic trajectory that moves repeatedly from figures of concentricity to spirals and "strange attractors," a movement rehearsed as a kind of implosion whereby the ongoing collapse of the concentrized romantic/modern subject leaves a surprisingly stable kind of wobbling around a vacant center (i.e., an attractor). Romantic prolepses or prefigurations include, here, explicit figures (the "wheel within wheel" of Blake's utopian physics), spiraling figures of the figure of irony, and concentrically embedded narratives in Wordsworth, Coleridge, and Mary Shelley, among others.

Chapter 4 traces several kinds of "binary decomposition," here a rough term for the process whereby an ideological gestalt is made to follow in the wake of an infinite breakage and sliding of categories that implicates real and textual time-space. This process is made to account for how subsequent editions of *Frankenstein* reperform the play of Gender-as-Double-Bind enacted in Mary and Percy Shelley's collaboration on the novel; and for how a "crossed" Keats letter functions throughout its history to engender itself along a fractal boundary between poetry and science. The final section follows fractally scaling structures into Romantic modernism through the equivocal branchings that bind the texts and works of a Wallace Stevens lyric.

Chapter 5, "Rhythming," takes off from the story of how Romanticism disciplined complex chaotic rhythms from kinds of order and of disorder. From Romantic poetic figures of chaotic rhythm, the chapter moves on to "real" chaotic cycles that run through the shifting economies of William Blake's relationship with his employer, William Hayley, and through private and public texts of Dorothy and William Wordsworth as they negotiate among them ongoing contradictions of gender and class around the problematic of "dependence." The final section follows the construction of "Parkinsonism" from its Romantic patriarch to one of its postmodern popularizers to question how a changing framework of "pathological knowledge" situates accounts of the ways rhythms inhabit and animate the body.

The "Postmodern Postscript" picks up the story of parasitism and professionalism that began (in the previous chapter) with Wordsworth's "leech-gatherer" and continues here — with a vengeance and a difference — in David Cronenberg's 1976 film, *Rabid*, suggesting altered semiotic protocols in the process. The next two sections follow these protocols as they wind through snakily citational sequences of texts: "The Ends of Dreams" show how what Freud called the "dream-work" can be pursued as ongoing ambiguation or a "conservation of otherness"; the figure of an octopally extensive disciplinary power (first examined in Blake) is displaced by some of its postmodern mutations. The final section follows the ways in which China's "Obscure Poetry" movement of the 1980s enacts the simultaneity of Romanticism and postmodernity so as to shift the definition of Romanticism (e.g., as an "opposition to capitalism in the name of precapitalist values") toward postsocialist and postcapitalist formations.

Acknowledgments

I finished much of this book as a fellow of the Oregon State University Humanities Center during 1993–94, and my thanks go to its director, Peter Copek, and staff. I'm also grateful to those who have commented on, or contributed to, parts of this book at various stages (Nancy Armstrong, Mark Bedau, Sandra Buckley, Mary Byers, Elizabeth Cook, Nikki Crook, William Flesch, Barbara Gelpi, Wlad Godzich, Pat Gonzales, David Halliburton, Michael Hardt, Herbie Lindenberger, Brian Massumi, Diane Middlebrook, Greg Laugero, Arkady Plotnitsky, Adrienne Rich, Anne Running, Steve Shaviro, Cliff Siskin, Susan Squier, and Liam Walsh), and to my students and colleagues in the English and history departments at SUNY–Stony Brook, and to many others who have kept and keep me alive in various ways (such as Elizabeth Bohun, Shay Brawn, Mary Jean Corbett, Ann Christensen, Miranda Joseph, Amitava Kumar, Rachel May, Clayton Sankey, Lang Walsh, and Sarah and Phil Winterfield).

All illustrations were designed and produced by the author unless otherwise noted. Special thanks to Liam Walsh, who produced the figures on pages 10, 11, 27, 36, 92, 105, 111, 140, 150, and 151; to Professor Scott Sutherland, who produced the figures on pages 29, 65, 81, 123, and 226; to Eugenio Rivera and Professor Fred Walter, who produced the diagram on page 6. Other illustrations are courtesy of Craig Reynolds (page 28); Kirk Borne of STSI/NASA (page 16); Professor David Bella (page 29), from the *Journal of Professional Issues in Engineering*

113.4 (1987); the Museum of Fine Arts, Boston (pages 82 and 83); the Houghton Library, Harvard University (pages 137 and 166); Ralph M. Siegel and Oliver Sacks (page 189); and Joseph Grigely (page 219).

This book is dedicated to my friends Alexandra Chasin, Joseph Grigely, Judith Halberstam, and Michael Sprinker, and (excessively) to Iona Mancheong.

O N E

Introduction

Romantic Machinery

I consider several ways of approaching Romanticism in what follows, but the tendency here is to investigate it/them as a loose species of machinic organisms that reproduce themselves in language. In chapter headings I call them "logics" to emphasize their status as embedded or "black-boxed" protocols for generating statements. Black-boxing, according to Bruno Latour, refers to how the active role of scientific theory in shaping fact is effaced, often by being *embodied* in laboratory equipment: the use of such equipment then constitutes an inertial operating assumption (Bachelard's "reified theory") allowed to remain unexamined (Latour and Woolgar 1986, 66, 259n). The converse is more germane here: black-boxed assumptions in discourse operate as machines by being transformed from *message* to *code*. To say that such logics operate as machines is not simply to make a metaphor except insofar as Latour allows us to understand an actual laboratory machine as also a metaphor and metaphor-maker, in its operation displacing and condensing a series of assumptions. This circulation of referentiality between machine and metaphor allows black-boxing to be investigated—not just to "demystify" it but to deploy it. If the typically postmodern "revelation of the mechanism" (i.e., "I can show you how I do the trick and still fool you") shows the ineffectivity of demystification *as demystification*, it also shows the power of black-boxing and metaphor-making as exemplary forms of embodiment, of the production of agency. Bodies and texts, like black boxes, operate by (partially) "rendering items of knowledge distinct from the circumstances of their creation" (Latour and Woolgar 1986, 259n).

In the course of this study, a long list of terms may be substituted for what I've called "logics" and "machinic organisms": patterns, tricks, episteme engines, ideologemes, programs, protocols, genes, dynamos, mantras, paradigms, metaphors, metonyms, symbols, strategies, technologies, topoi, moves, artifacts, tools, theorems, poems, orbits, trajectories, fetishes, truths, scenarios, stories, codes, relays, and so on. No doubt some subtle ecology influences the distribution of these terms, but there are also reasons for some indiscrimination in naming a set of objects that themselves function as "a regulated, continuous, immanent process of variation" (Deleuze and Guattari 1987, 103). The logics engaged here are relatives of what Latour (after Michel Serres) calls "quasi-objects, quasi-subjects" (1993, 51–59). Not so total or integral as to be called a "system" nor so local as an "internal logic," they function by repetition, saturation, mutation. They are not "deep structures" that can simply be reified, located, and then accommodated or intervened in. Their coherence is not such that they present a convenient Achilles heel; it is more like the shape-shifting liquid-metal man from the film *Terminator 2*, who can be pierced or blown to bits any number of times and still re-form. This shape-shifter (a morph) nicely gothicizes the equivalence, in psychoanalytic "object relations" theory, of the much-sought-after "indestructible object" and the "object that can be destroyed" (e.g., I can hate Daddy and make him "go away," but he still comes back), or, in Lacanian theory, of the uncastratable and the always-already-castrated. Appropriately, *Terminator 2* provisionally redivides its objects (reprogrammed "terminator" robot and morph) into "good father" and "bad father" finally only to dissolve both. The logic of "quasi object" performs another crucial twist on both these equivalences and oppositions: it thrives on ambivalence; it emerges and conserves its place at the borders of presence and absence, of word and thing, of discombobulation and coherence; it resists being either articulated or disarticulated; and it sometimes operates both as "that which cannot be spoken" and "that which cannot *but* be spoken." These mandates do not describe a sublime object, abject mush, null set, or paralytic double bind but a generative contradiction. Neither power nor resistance nor the body nor discipline has a monopoly on the chaotic logic of the "someness" of the quasi object. Provisionally, then, for my purposes, this logic serves just as a recognition device: all that is of interest here partakes of it.

The persistence-through-change of Romantic ideologemes — the way they've taken a licking and kept on ticking — is explicable by their extension and saturation—their participation—in ongoing formations of capitalism and disciplinarity. Neither their coherence nor their mutations can be referenced back to an origin except insofar as origins are continually under construction. Machines, we are told, have mutated dramatically in two hundred years, from the machine comprising discrete parts articulated to perform a specific task to the (ideally) reconfigurable, multifunctional device represented by the computer (or the brain or the poem). Of course, the Romantic opposition between machine and poem is what enables the simple perversity of treating poems as machines or machine-phenotypes (as I often do in what follows) to have some ontological effectivity, not as a metaphor or truth claim but as a potential deformation of the terms involved (Romantic, opposition, between, machine, poem, simple, perversity, and so on). A deformation of this kind always falls short of its goal, but in order to accomplish it at all, *care* must be taken to avoid the circuit breakers (damage-control devices) wired into the disciplinary mechanism; for example, the stipulation that a mechanical poem is simply a bad poem, end of story.

Another word for *care* in this instance is *perversity*. Perversity dictates that no single term be allowed to foreclose an ambivalence that operates as an ongoing foreclosure of foreclosure. Any theory (e.g., "chaos theory") that seems to legitimize categories of phenomena otherwise excluded from consideration also opens up, by this validation, new realms to disciplinary penetrations; this dynamic of simultaneous liberation and colonization informs Keats's account of Romanticism as a "thinking into the human heart." Part of the intent of this project, then, is to compensate for widespread use of terms such as subversion, rhizomicity, dialogism, chaos, nonlinearity, fluidity, and performativity as progressive or even messianically liberatory moments or movements. To hold such terms and moments in question does not so much represent a grumpiness about hype or cautionary gesture; it does insist that it is with suspicion in pleasure and pleasure in suspicion that significant objects be engaged, that to particularize and to theorize are mutually interruptive acts, and that the life of the objects at hand follows the trajectory of this mutual interruption.

"The master's tools will never dismantle the master's house" (Lorde 1984, 112), but can another turn of the machine ever make it something different as well as driving it in deeper? After how many turns does a dialectical machine produce not only a new synthesis or antithesis but also a nondialectical machine? When or where does literary canon change produce not only a new canon but also a new relation or nonrelation between canonicity and disciplinarity? The logic of feedback loops isn't circular. Moments of mutation are not in themselves liberatory but they are moments of possibility, openings onto other machines; moments not of prediction and control but where the future is actively uncharted.

The "best" literary text, by canonical or disciplinary standards, may well be the one that is most intertextually implicated—*thickest*—with other literary texts that come before, around, and after it. Looking instead for where poems are thickest with *other* discourses is to reengage them with what makes any given landscape an interdisciplinary thicket—a gauntlet or "a wilderness of turnpike gates," as Thomas Paine put it (1973, 305)—but it still does not tell us how to get through or around without discipline taking its toll either way.

Foucault imagined a history of discourse in which "the meaning of a statement would be defined . . . by the difference that articulates it upon the other real or possible statements, which are contemporary to it or to which it is opposed in the linear series of time" (1975, xviii). If statements and discourses have meaning only insofar as they are made to perform mutations on other possible statements and discourses, we are left with a discursive ecology of interzones-without-interiors (a predicament that comes as no surprise to those who have found no safety in what are supposed to be cozy interiors—academia or America or family or their own heads). To remain neither in nor out of this economy of meaning is to speak *to and from* the interzone between discursive self-difference (how statements within a given discourse are allowed or mandated to differ from each other in order to count) and difference-from-others (how categories of statements are sanctioned to differ from others). This interzone between what could be called "colloquial" and "alloquial" discourse is not a metadiscursive phenomenon (since it operates immanently, always both within and between), nor does it operate by "interdisciplinarity," that is, within disciplinarity as an even heuristically self-contained system, since by definition it is also implicated in the way discourse or language differs from something of a different order. The next turn of the expansionist hegemony of "language" in (post)structuralist thought, after "language invades the universal problematic" (Derrida 1978, 278), brings the acknowledgment that "even language, we might say, isn't really 'structured like a language'" (Shaviro 1993, 34). The mechanicity of language is a way station to the nonlanguageness of language (its condition of possibility); the turbulent double trajectory of becoming itself and becoming other is its modality.

This project comes of age in the *wake* of Romanticism as a receding origin "borne back ceaselessly into the past," whose ripples continue to disperse across the present; its *wake* as a celebration of its death and an opportunity to contest its will. I am often stunned by how hard it is to say certain things that seem fundamental for survival and pleasure; Romanticism continues both to make possible and to render unintelligible much of what matters to me. When I listen, in the late-twentieth-century United States, to political speeches or to the accounts artists or scientists give of their works, it has seemed that the always-provisional coherence of Romantic power-knowledge is drifting on a historical ice floe: stretched between irreconcilable positions, huddled with incompatible bedfellows on an eroding base, jumping frantically among positions. For amphibious discursive creatures—for the "quasi objects, quasi subjects" among us—this is, as it has always been, a parodic and dangerous spectacle.

Romanticism and Postmodernity

Romanticism is one of the names assigned to a constellation of discursive changes that emerged in late-eighteenth- and early-nineteenth-century Europe, a.k.a. "modernity." For many of us now in its wake (since its coherence is radically contingent on historical position), the constellation turns on the new sways of capitalism and the disciplinary forms of power that accompanied and enabled it; that is, on processes specified partially by E. P. Thompson as *The Making of the English Working Class* and by Foucault as *The Birth of the Clinic.*

Romantic power and knowledge were *horizontalized* (the vertical self-similarities of the Great Chain of Being becoming the collusive play of difference and similarity between disciplines), *pluralized* (disciplinary autonomy being predicated on multiple triangulations between disciplines), *miniaturized*, and *put into circulation* so that, in the new regime of "micropower," the smallest and most motile unit—the "episteme"—becomes also that which most defines the totality.

Postmodernity is one of the names assignable to a cusp of discursive change two centuries later. Postmodern transnationalization of capital and the redoubled saturation of disciplinary technologies represent the breaking of the wave that swelled in Romanticism. Characteristically, postmodern power-knowledge has not merely been horizontalized, miniaturized, and pluralized but rendered *viral*. This change cannot adequately be described in terms of degree (everything gets "smaller" or "more plural"), since the scale of comparison as well as the meanings of "scale" and "comparison" change in the process. The virus is an episteme with a vengeance: globally dispersed but at a microscopic scale, it is "big-little." Pluralism "squared" in postmodernity (where pluralities are not just sets of units but sets of pluralities) does not simply reproduce a more elaborate "scaling" universe like that of the premodern Great Chain of Being, characterized by isomorphisms between macrocosm and microcosm. Rather, it entails a new protocol of assemblage I sometimes

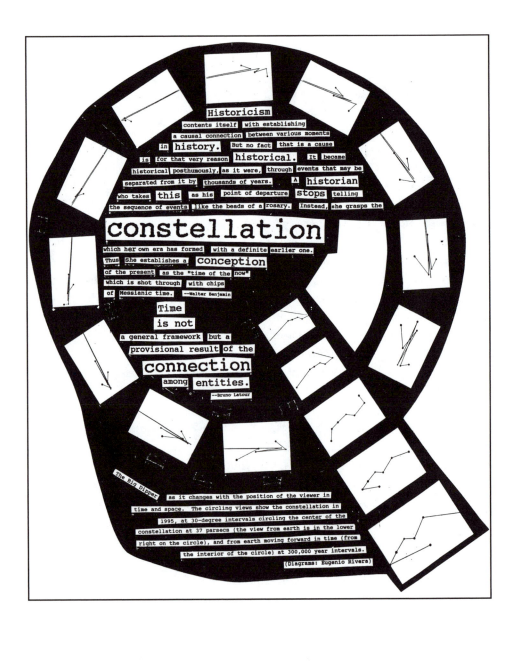

Historicism contents itself with establishing a causal connection between various moments in **history.** But no fact that is a cause is for that very reason **historical.** It became historical posthumously, as it were, through events that may be separated from it by thousands of years. A **historian** who takes **this** as his point of departure **stops** telling the sequence of events like the beads of a rosary. Instead, she grasps the **constellation** which her own era has formed with a definite earlier one. Thus She establishes a **conception** of the present as the "time of the now" which is shot through with chips of Messianic time. --Walter Benjamin

Time **is not** a general framework but a provisional result of the **connection** among entities. --Bruno Latour

The Big Dipper as it changes with the position of the viewer in time and space. The circling views show the constellation in 1995, at 30-degree intervals circling the center of the constellation at 37 parsecs (the view from earth is in the lower right on the circle), and from earth moving forward in time (from the interior of the circle) at 300,000 year intervals.

(Diagrams: Eugenio Rivera)

call "someness" (Halberstam and Livingston 1995, 8–9), in which axes of one/many or big/little are not meaningful, where pluralities between (for example, between disciplines or cultures) and pluralities within (for example, within "split subjects") are *subject to fractal realignments and interferences*. Discursive space-time oriented by cleavages across scale is the subject of a fractal history that tells the story of the conservation of a chaos recognizable by its characteristic *intrigue* across various sets of relations.

Romantic Chaos

Prior to what came to be called Romanticism, Dr. Johnson characterized the "romantic" by its *wildness*, defining *romance* as "a tale of wild adventure" and *romantick* as "resembling the tales of romances, wild," or "full of wild scenery" (1963, 349). The word "wildness" is one of those that can be its own opposite, denoting on the one hand superabundant proliferation (the wildness of the rain forest), and on the other barrenness, waste (the wildness of the desert). In either case, the association with uncultivated nature as opposed to culture, with chaos as opposed to order, with female (as either fertile or barren) as opposed to male is explicit. Those who came later to be called Romantics assigned the two kinds of chaos differently. For example, Blake's chaos (like Blakean nature in the absence of culture) is always barren—and Blake, as the pages of his illuminated books demonstrate, abhorred a vacuum. Wordsworth, on the other hand, associates the excrescent "thickening hubbub" of London street culture with the "universal hubbub wild" of Chaos from *Paradise Lost* and reacts in horror (1979, 238, 238n), just as he does to "frantic novels" and "deluges of idle and extravagant stories in verse" (1969, 735). The reactionary Wordsworth recoils to contain proliferating chaos by enforcing an antithesis between figure and ground and between high and low culture; Nathaniel Hawthorne's famous outcry against the "damned mob of scribbling women" (Mellow 1980, 456) employs the same image of chaos and makes its implication in masculinist gender anxiety explicit, as well as—in the specter of the chaotic "mob"—confirming its classism.

       Arthur Lovejoy's famous 1924 call for "the discrimination of Romanticisms" follows Wordsworth's strategy of chaos management. He argues, for example, that the difference between English and German Romanticism can be characterized as the difference between "a fundamental preference for simplicity—even though a 'wild' simplicity—and a fundamental preference for diversity and complexity; between the sort of ingenuous naiveté characteristic of 'The Enthusiast' and the sophisticated subtlety of the conception of romantic irony: between these," he asserts, "the antithesis is one of the most radical that modern thought and taste have to show" (quoted in Gleckner and Ensoe 1975, 75). Lovejoy set Romanticism up as a set of once-distinct currents that had become muddled into a "thickening hubbub"; he prescribed rediscrimination to restore a healthy plurality, to recultivate the academic garden in which monstrous hybrids had been proliferating.

Lovejoy engraves fractures between Romanticisms without noticing—perhaps in order not to notice—that the same pattern of fractures inheres in each of them and is in fact the echo of his own Romantic conceptual framework. Lovejoy's distinction between the sophisticated irony of German and the naive enthusiasm of English Romanticism, for example, also inheres in the cultural space of English Romanticism. Blake's works (to pick an easy example) are continually crazed by embrace/rejection of both highbrow Enlightenment skepticism and the lowbrow "enthusiasm" of inner-light religion. This binarity also structures temporal scenarios: naive revolutionary seems to give way to sophisticated reactionary, pantisocracy to clerisy, ironic young man to earnest authoritarian, *Sartor Resartus* to *Heroes and Hero Worship*, Romanticism to fascism. But temporal fractures between phases are in turn spatial fractures within phases; fascism was always waiting in the wings. Any lines we draw between Romanticism and some previous or subsequent phase seem also to divide Romanticism from itself, and ourselves from ourselves. However cut up or pinned down, Romanticism is a voodoo doll that oppresses and empowers its handlers with its own fractures and fixations.

M. H. Abrams asserted that "the Romantic enterprise was an attempt to sustain the inherited cultural order against what to many writers seemed the imminence of chaos," an enterprise he characterizes as "a display of integrity and courage" (1971, 68). Thus a culturally reactionary pro-Romantic congratulates Romanticism for resisting a chaos that reactionary anti-Romantics (such as Yvor Winters) condemned them for promoting. These seemingly mutually exclusive views of the Romantic enterprise belie a shared politics: cultural chaos is to be feared and resisted, order is to be sustained. After sparring in the academic ring, the "two-handed engine" that operates these Punch-and-Judy Romanticisms retires to toast law and order. But Abrams's assertion amounts to a tautology; to attempt to sustain order is to be by definition—albeit a finally counterproductive definition—on the side of integrity (intactness, wholeness). The irony whereby the desperation and meanness of high-cultural damage control can be called courageous is also that whereby the opening of the cultural canon can heroically be lamented as a "Closing of the American Mind," echoing the depressive and hysterical cry of Burke over "learning, cast into the mire and ground down beneath the feet of a swinish multitude" (92). To the subject of a closed system, entropy always seems to be increasing: disorder is the continual result of the project of defending intactness.

Still more recently, the debate over Romanticism as a rhetorical and figurative system turns again on a chaotic axis. De Man values in the Romantic ironist his realization of "the rocky barrenness of the human condition" (1983, 225), while Anne Mellor, opposing Abrams, values the subversiveness of Romantic irony, which she associates with Schlegel's "chaos" that "is abundantly fertile, always throwing up new forms" (1980, 4).

Now, as chaos itself is being redefined in opposition to both order and disorder, computers generate Blakean arabesques out of simple deterministic functions and polymathematicians use this mechanical imagination to "manufacture intuition" about real and symbolic systems. Western science is learning to simulate a nature more to Romantic specifications: "I think of recent mathematical research; . . . I can recognize that the limit has itself become a new dimension, that this ever-hidden thing which makes us fold our hands has begun to press down upon multitudes" (Yeats 1966, 300).

Romanticism and Romanticism

Ever since it gained academic currency, then, Romanticism has been a contested category. Even when the term is used to denote a period reasonably discrete in time and place, it is ambiguated by questions of where, when, and how it begins and ends; whether it can best be studied as the Spirit of an Age, a historically contingent superstructure, or a maximally embedded episteme; whether it includes only certain kinds of works (such as "literature") or describes a total discursive ecology; whether it is a single movement or a congeries of irreconcilable phenomena. When the term is not so narrowly periodized, ambiguity increases by several orders of magnitude, ranging from the transhistorical binary opposition between Romantic and classic, popular since the early nineteenth century (see Gleckner and Ensoe 1975, 19–25, 184–85), to de Man's crypto-autobiographical "remembering of a failed project that has become a menace" (1984, 59), to Sayre and Löwy's ongoing world-historical struggle of "opposition to capitalism in the name of pre-capitalist values" (1990, 26). If this lack of consensus has become a conventional feature of accounts of Romanticism, it at least indicates that problematization of identity is an identifying feature of both Romanticism (the putative phenomenon) and Romanticism (study of the phenomenon).

Still, no surprise in spite of this apparently radical contestation, over 90 percent of professors confine their Romanticism courses to the discrete period 1789 to 1832 and focus largely on the "big six" poets (Linkin 1991, 550). Romanticism is to this extent characterizable, in its historical operation, as the ongoing reduction and elevation of a diverse, internally contradictory and contested discursive field to a discrete and exclusive pantheon. As such, Romanticism (the phenomenon or its study) exemplifies disciplinarity itself as a "continuous, individualizing pyramid" (Foucault 1984, 209).

Romanticism is, in this sense, not just a category but a categorization system: Romanticism generated and continues to reproduce the disciplinary category of English Literature before it could be named (always retroactively) within it. This trick resembles the operation of the Romantic "symbol," "always part of the totality that it represents" (de Man 1983, 191): Romanticism camouflages not itself but the landscape in which it operates.

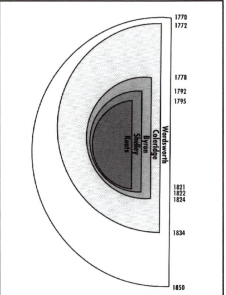

The Tupperware Model. This old student trick for remembering the life spans of five of the "big six" poets (Blake is odd man out) marks a Romanticism still concerned to preserve the "author function" in the form of a pattern of relations between individual "masters." The diagram suggests a normatively neat concentric gradient of intensity between two caricatures: Wordsworth's long slow poetic deterioration and Keats's maximal intensity.

As such, Romanticism cannot be redefined but only displaced by other categorization systems or nonsystematizing strategies. Unless Romantic categories of literature, science, and politics are reconfigured, it doesn't really matter where "Romanticism" is placed within them. Unless Romantic periodization is relativized by studies that do more than put literature "into historical context"—that instead serve histories of the present—Romanticism is falsely monumentalized into an intricate network of fixations since "outgrown." Such monumentalization is counterproductive (precisely its ongoing function), since the outgrowing of fixation and supercession of Romanticism (like the decline of family values and so on) are themselves Romantic masternarratives, whether nostalgic or celebratory; ontogenetic or phylogenetic; Romantic, Victorian, or modern. To avoid this scenario, I follow here the provisional tactic of considering Romanticism as a set of temporal or spatial patterns formed through *interactions* between the synchronic distribution of differences within Romantic discourse and the diachronic (or syntagmatic) fraying and braiding of discourse across post-Romantic history.

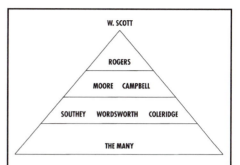

An Individualizing Pyramid. Byron sketched out this ranking of his contemporary poets in his journal for 1817. The hidden ground and point of the pyramid is the metaindividual who sketches it out but does not appear in it.

Metastibility and Metastability

This account moves toward a Romanticism that is not only a set of changes, but a change in the form and status of change itself. This metachange could in turn be retemporized into a sequence of metachanges, but not without leaving an active remainder that appears as a formulaic but irreducible quandary: if change first took the form of x and then took the form of y, which form (x or y?) should characterize the change? This process (Derrida called it "a *rupture* and a redoubling" [1978, 278]) produces another kind of change, or to take it out of a productivist model (itself part of the y-mode in the two-stage Romantic equation), it disturbs the x-ness of x, the y-ness of y, and their relation; that is, it alters the order of time structured around the relation. Metachange is *metastible*, capable of infecting and altering a range of both synchronic and diachronic relations.

But how could we assert that in Romanticism change became significant, mandatory, or valued as it never had been before, when, merely by selecting the status of change as a significant feature, we participate in a valorization of change that we were meant to describe? To focus instead on stability and identity across time is no way out, since stable identities may in a given instance be by-products of changes (changes that take ontological priority over identities) rather than their raw materials. To identify something according to how it changes is, in fact, the signature of a Romantic ideology that seems to situate mobility and transformability as socioeconomic origins, means, and ends. Identity based in kind of change is *metastable*, that is (by the chemical definition), it stabilizes when it contacts even the smallest particle of its stable form (as in the sudden crystallization of a supersaturated solution). Thus, otherwise fluid, unrelated, or nonteleological sets of changes are subject to fixation by Romantic masternarratives of development and growth, the smallest particles of which can be called "epistemes" or "ideologemes." The story of the rapid crystallization of modern class and disciplinary structures (the takeoff of modernity) in the Romantic period is one such partial account.

On the other hand, to imagine a timeless "becoming" or a kaleidoscopic and nonteleological *play* is to fall back into a Romantic valorization of pure process that would be neither possible nor intelligible except against a simultaneous valorization of product, an increased capacity to turn process into product, and vice versa. One might as well say that "pure" play is a by-product of capitalist work discipline.

History Moves like a Snake

The most succinct and ambitious recent definition of Romanticism may be Sayre and Löwy's formula, "opposition to capitalism in the name of pre-capitalist values" (1990, 26). As such, Romanticism is allowed to emerge and mutate with capitalism and modernity, assuming various avatars—for example, in Fascism and Nazism (with their militantly nostalgic appeals to a prealienated, organic society), in modernist "culturism" (where culture is located as the privileged site of resistance to commodification), in desperate appeals to home and family as happy feudal fiefdoms still holding their own against the encroachments of modernity, or (in one of its most virulent postmodern forms) in assertions of the integrity of dominant ethnic or religious nationalisms against the disintegratory thrust of transnational capital and culture.

But Sayre and Löwy's formula yields another kind of value when its apparently one-directional and one-dimensional scenario is deconstructed.

Of course history, even Western European history, does not simply cross, in its forward march, a line dividing a uniform and monolithic capitalism from a previous mode of production, and then look back to reevaluate where it has been. This one-way scenario may remain intact even as it allows that various semiautonomous but interdependent entities (e.g., the state, the family, the body, certain nations, and certain economic or cultural sectors) cross the line at various speeds, leaving assorted stragglers ("survivals") to dig in their heels or to be pulled violently across. The linear scenario begins to break down—and in so doing, to achieve an even more thoroughgoing hegemony—in the subsequent assertion that such various entities, by crossing the line at various times, enter a different world, and thus change that world and are changed by it in ongoingly different ways—ways that the assertion allows to amount to nothing more than iridescent wavelets in the wake of the end of history.

We might consider instead that, rather than being stretched along the time line like a train on a track, history sits perpendicular to it, pushing various features to either side as it goes, like players in a chess game. "We have always actively sorted out elements belonging to different times. . . . *It is the sorting that makes the times, not the times that make the sorting*" (Latour 1993, 76; emphasis in original). In this view, since time is an ongoing artifact under construction by history, "precapitalism" must always be produced retroactively. Romanticism works "in the *name* of precapitalist values," a name always articulated by capitalism itself. But because this new paradigm, by putting the historical players perpendicular to the time line, tends to reify time rather than history, a third— "diagonal"—movement emerges in which "time is not a general framework but a provisional result of the connection among entities" (Latour 1993, 74).

What, then, if time/history moves like a snake, by its insinuations, by torque and friction across its whole length, moving by virtue of its multiple diagonalities to the directions in which it is moving (as a sailboat "tacks" against the wind)? Then we could not speak of the present deriving from the past, or the past being revised by the present, but rather understand that historical movement entails (or comprises) coordinations and oppositions, articulations and reorientations—at once con-

How Snakes Move. A 1970 *Scientific American* article titled "How Snakes Move" (Gans 1972) identifies four types of snake motion: lateral undulation, rectilinear locomotion, concertina progression, and sidewinding. However, "these categories are somewhat artificial. Most species of snakes can move in more than one of these patterns; indeed, a snake moves in more than one pattern at a time" (40). Curiously, although the categories may be "somewhat artificial," their slippage against and into each other seems to reproduce the movement of the snake quite rigorously. Unwittingly or not, the author describes the predicament of the would-be historian of chaos in a moving passage:

> An exact description of slithering requires that the position of each element at any given instant be specified. It is easily seen that investigators who seek such a detailed description must solve a truly staggering number of simultaneous equations. The task is complicated by the fact that as the snake travels its parts move and accelerate at different rates. The solution gains several magnitudes of complexity when one wants to know which of the snake's thousands of muscles are actually exerting the forces that induce and maintain motion. (38)

But what if we want to know how the snake is not simply moved by itself or by its muscles but by the heat of the rocks, the twist of its genes, or the twitching of its prey? What if the snake itself is a kind of slithering between snakiness and nonsnakiness?

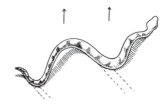

A Sidewinding Viper. Arrows indicate overall direction of movement; dotted lines show the trail of the snake's body.

tinuous and discrete—between past, present, and future; that history *really* moves across its whole length at once or doesn't move at all.

This is very different from weaker assertions that our "perspective" on the past and future change, or that we "reinterpret" events as we will come to be reinterpreted. These assertions are simply damage-control maneuvers to preserve the notion of an objective reality, even (especially) by perpetually deferring access to it. Nietzsche's "uncertainty of the future" or Derrida's "future as pure danger" are better models for *all time* than the falsely retroactive uncertainty of the past. History is a slithering-in-limbo between what may never have happened (such as Romanticism or modernity), what may or may not be happening, and what may never happen (such as postmodernity). A history that slithers means that present changes really change what happened in the past, and what happens in the past really changes the present, and the future really changes what is happening now, because each of these changes pulls the others into new sets of relations.

Instead of situating time or history as either untranscendable horizons or reified objects, the historical snake deconstructs the either/or opposition into a volatile middle ground of history as it is lived. Like most or all metaphors, though, this one dies like Moses on the brink of the Promised Land. The snake can only take us so far before its terms become a hindrance. Does history move against a ground of some kind, the also shifty ground of "meaning," if not the supposedly stabler ground of "nature"? Doesn't history's movement also move the ground against which it moves? Doesn't it also move immanently, by torque and friction against itself, like a zero-gravity orgy? We are led to consider not merely a slithering history, but a history of wrigglings and frottages, a Medusa's head that can only be viewed obliquely.

Worlds in Collision

A thought experiment: imagine the collision of several galaxies. Because galaxies are such dissipated structures (a feature we share), the collision would be more of a mutually transformative *interpenetration* than a simple impact discrete in space and time. Some stars would collide, fuse, and/or explode; these events might be local or have "ripple" effects. Some stars or star systems might pass in close enough proximity to enter into orbital relationships, which could be torn apart by continued galactic movement; or could serve as new centers or gravitational catalysts for larger systems, pulling other stars or star systems into their sway; or could simply become part of one galaxy or another; or could sheer off from their parent galaxies because of their newly combined motion. The galaxies themselves might pass through each other almost unchanged; one might subsume another; they might fall into some kind of galactic orbit; they could be mutually reconfigured into *n* galaxies more or less resembling their predecessors; or they could cease to be galaxies at all: their gravitational interaction might be so turbulent that they would go off every which way, or so resonant that they would implode into a gigantic mass or black hole. The subsequent effect of *any* or *all* of these events could in turn have various effects on individual stars, on surrounding galaxies, or on the local microstructure of space-time, ranging from negligible to drastic.

Given the motion of galaxies relative to each other, could such a range of events happen? Is a galaxy a very fragile ecology? Are individual stars, planets, or solar systems relatively imperturbable and autonomous, or are they sensitive to minute changes in the web of forces in which they are always involved? I've chosen this example because I don't know the answers to these questions, and not in order to find the answers but to preserve and economize this indeterminacy.

What happens when cultures collide? What reconfigurations can result from interpenetrations between languages, discourses, powers, systems, and subsystems in a "single" culture? What happens when people become friends or lovers or enemies, or some configuration of each of these? Are people or cultures or discourses or languages more like stars or solar systems or galaxies, or like the space in which galaxies collide?

What has happened or is happening or is likely to happen in a very particular instance; for example, this particular cultural interpenetration, this particular reading of this book, right now? No amount of particularity and specificity can eliminate the indeterminacy. Finally, then, there is a sense in which the maintenance of indeterminacy (or conservation of chaos) is what constitutes success for a living system or a given interaction.

Imagine galaxies colliding: at the leading edge of this collision, disorder (defined against the coherence of each galaxy as an autonomous system) is increasing, but order (defined against the previous nonrelation between galaxies) is also increasing. The leading edge is not, of course, an edge at all, but an *interzone* that may in fact be dispersed throughout each of the galaxies so thoroughly that their own variegated structures may be indistinguishable from it, may extend beyond them to implicate surrounding events, may be played out in numerous scales of time and space from subatomic oscillations to cosmic expansion and contraction. To make the space and time of their interaction coextensive with the galaxies themselves is to suggest that the galaxies may have been interzones all along.

The thought experiment began with discrete galaxies that came together to form an interzone: lines leading into a kind of "black box" from which

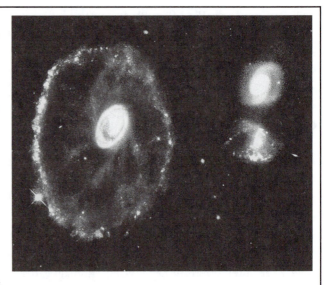

Galactic Collision. The "Cartwheel Galaxy" seems to have assumed its current shape when another galaxy crashed through its core, sending out a ringlike ripple of gas and dust 150,000 light years wide, in which billions of stars are forming and/or exploding in the wake of the collision. The pinwheel-like spokes beginning to form between the core cluster and outer ring indicate that the galaxy's original spiral shape may be reemerging. Either of the two smaller galaxies to the right may have been the interloper: a recent collision is suggested by the disrupted shape and clusters of newly forming stars of the bottom galaxy; however, the "smoothness" of the galaxy above it may indicate that its gas has been stripped away in a collision. As it turns out, some astronomers believe that collisions may have been an important factor in the original formation of galaxies.

any number of results issue. It might have begun instead with interzones and described discretion, stability, and autonomy as effects of certain relations rather than as givens, in which case we would have to consider the dependence of autonomy or instability of stability. This reversal may be a very subtle one in terms of what other possibilities for interaction it allows, but it is dramatic in moving from what could be called a *truth* protocol (which assumes the autonomy of autonomy and discretion of discretion, if only as defining limit-cases) to one of *meaning* (in which the contingency of autonomy or instability of stability not only can never be factored out, but also may be defining moments). This move between regimes strangely resembles the collision of galaxies insofar as it describes a simultaneous falling together and apart. If it seems to appear as a second stage in the argument, it is also clear that the example of colliding galaxies was dependent on it from the beginning: the severalness of the galaxies (as an indeterminacy awaiting specification) was proposed only with an eye to their future *someness* (indeterminacy as ongoing condition).

This reversal is similar to the maneuver by which Barthes found or founded the condition of *intertextuality*, whereby texts only exist at all through their participation in an intertextual matrix that precedes them and from which they can never be extricated (see Barthes 1977, 160). Thus a text or a word or a discourse is never a discrete node in a network; text, word, and discourse are multiple nodes in multiple networks, the trajectories of which may be oblique or aberrant with respect to each other (e.g., the use of a single word may be implicated in its multiple meanings in several disciplines, each of which may mutate or grow apart or drop out or fuse). Like anything else that signifies, a text is always a destroyed/indestructible quasi-abject quasi object, a shifting cleavage of cleavages together and apart.

Celeste Olalquiaga associates the priority of intertextuality with a postmodern valorization of simulation: "Simulation will be understood here as the establishment of a situation through intertextuality instead of indexicality. In other words, rather than pointing to first-degree references (objects, events) simulation looks at representations of them for verisimilitude"(1992, 6). This account of postmodernization via simulation bears a suspicious resemblance to the inaugural *modernist* movement of structuralism (which studies language as a system unto itself rather than by reference to things outside it), or, as I argue later in this book, the advent of Romantic disciplinarity itself, insofar as it emerges as an always-already-interdisciplinary collusion that produces truth-effects by cross-reference.

Olalquiaga's formula allows both a binarity and a telos between truth and verisimilitude, a movement from a first to a second degree, from "reality" into "representation," from fixed to floating referents, from reference to self-reference ("poeticity"). Even if this movement is structured primarily in order to authorize various interpenetrations between its phases, it does so only by fixing the difference between fixation and floating rather than by floating it. In so doing, it appears as a kind of *Romanticism* insofar as its own mode of differentiating phases (i.e., fixation) belongs to what it implicitly identifies as a superseded phase.

Thomas Kuhn's scenario for the progress of science is based on a similar distinction. Kuhn differentiates sharply between the way "normal science" operates after controlling paradigms have been established and the way science operates in a "pre-paradigm" phase (1970, 10–22). But this simple two-stage temporal structure entails another distinction *within* the paradigm phase, namely between paradigm-driven science and other (non-paradigm-driven) discourses against which science has now apparently distinguished itself. Further self-differentiation is also produced within paradigm-grounded ("normal") science, since the wild proliferation of theories that characterizes the preparadigm phase for Kuhn returns echoically into the paradigm phase in the "structure of scientific revolutions": the moment *between* paradigms (83, 91). The eventual consequence of this "binary decomposition" is to call into question the paradigm of the paradigm and with it, the scientificity of science.

What if the point at which a given paradigm or disciplinary category (such as literature or science) becomes a player is not simply the moment that it differentiates or autonomizes itself but the point at which its own internal resonances and fractures can come into play with the resonances and fractures between it and its various "Others," which include not only other disciplines but also pre- and post-, non- and antidisciplinary forms of knowledge and power?

Posthumanities

One more (brief) thought experiment: imagine that earth has been secretly infiltrated by aliens (just as the collision of galaxies can be described as a cross-infiltration), but that the aliens are neither localized in bodies nor extended in space and time the same ways that humans are. In fact, the aliens have been able to infiltrate secretly because they are *articulated* so differently. They inhabit a register that overlaps with human perception, but events or phenomena disparate and unconnected for us cohere intelligibly for them. Let's say that an ensemble (or, for us, an assemblage) of certain aspects of various textual, biological, and technological phenomena (e.g., snake motions, telephones, heterosexuality) together constitute the alien bodies, the movements of which are complexly articulated between them. If we were able somehow to map these features together (like connecting the dots to make a constellation) and to show their movement through the discursive time-space manifold of their mapping, we could make a kind of animated cartoon of alien history. But how do we know what to select as features (since they may not be as punctual as stars) and how to connect them? Or perhaps the aliens have *homeorrhetic* bodies (Serres 1982, 74); that is, stable patterns (such as waves) that maintain themselves although the media of which they are constituted and through which they are propagated may change. Such aliens might be even harder to locate since they could move (constantly, or at will, or in response to stimuli) among various media. Or perhaps both the shape and the structure of the alien bodies as well as their media are subject to change.

If these aliens existed in disparate dimensions, we could coexist in the same time and space without knowing of or interfering with each other (we would be blind horses to their nods and winks); after all, multiple dimensions can exist in the same time and space. But would it count as the same time and space if, for example, the aliens were articulated in events that occur a hundred years apart, like the curves of a sea serpent emerging from the surface of our time? After all, multiple times and spaces can exist in the same time and space. And what if our worlds and lives constituted merely a ground or landscape for them, one against which they move, and upon whose surface they leave their (to us) ambiguous or disarticulate marks, as garbled for us as a movie is to an ant walking across the big beach of a silver screen? Does this count as the same space-time?

How might we unknowingly wound these aliens (or vice versa) and what would be the consequences for them or us? How would they engage in sex, war, or politics (ours or theirs)? How could they become manifest to us, or how could we become known to them? Let's say that the aliens are not *completely* unintelligible for us, that they can be detected—or if not detected, felt—at certain points where phenomena in which they are involved seem to have a certain implacability or logic or desire of their own (resistant to being changed or to being discretely articulated), or a certain curious ambiguity or elusiveness, and not just to our reason or will or desire, because the aliens may be involved in all of these as well. What if these points are not marginal or inconsequential but in fact the ways we orient ourselves: our anchors, our synapses, our genes, our cultures? What if we are semiautonomous Siamese twins joined at these points, where we share certain vital organs?

Intimate Alienation. Once I was talking with a friend on the phone. I told her about the letter I had just gotten from a Korean student looking for books unavailable in Korea: he had introduced himself as "a non-swimmer in English," and closed with "thanks for hearing my awkward voice." She told me she had just been swimming with some friends in a lake where schools of little fish would nibble at their body hairs, darting out of the way of any hand that moved into their midst. I told her how I had, many years before, visited a conservatory with a friend, and how we had watched a child squatting next to a fishpond, pointing to the bright carp swimming in the murky water and (because he wasn't quite able to say the word "fish") delightedly exclaiming over and over, "FEEE.... FEEE...." (a nebulous word for a nebulous shape somewhere between absence and presence, between "fort" and "da"); and how years later I told my lover this story, and how years later still she remembered that *she* had been there with me and that we had seen the child together.

There was a lot of intermittent background static in the phone connection. After a while it seemed to get louder and its rhythms became discernible as those of a phone conversation, although it remained only almost (but not quite) intelligible. We wondered if they could hear us. We tried to hail them with shouts, but their garbled conversation just continued. At one point it seemed to us that they may have paused to listen or wait for our disturbance to pass, but it may have been just a lapse in their conversation: an angel passed. It was very disconcerting to address them: we had begun talking to each other, assuming, as usual, that we were two endpoints of the phone line between us. Then the line changed dimensions; in trying to talk to it, we changed with it. It estranged and intrigued us, rendered our own conversation ambiguous, as if the phone line had broken up into our body hairs nibbled by fish, or rendered us flesh or fish in turn, or the water in which alien species swim. We liked it, but we had to stop talking. (N.B.: This vignette conflates two actual phone conversations.)

What if certain people or kinds of groups of people, known and/or unknown to each other, willy-nilly or not, come into various relations to certain of these aliens: lover, midwife, symbiote, parasite/host, master/slave, medium?

What if the parties to this ongoingly negotiated reconfiguration could be called language, science, literature, family, nation, class, sex, body, nature, culture, humanity? Reconfiguring humanity as posthumanity means recognizing the priority of *betweenness,* of a continuous fractal relation with otherness that necessitates and equates both care and perversity.

Panopticon and Pi: The School of Mirrors

What now constituted the unity of the medical gaze was not the circle of knowledge in which it was achieved but that open, infinite, moving totality, ceaselessly displaced and enriched by time, whose course it began but would never be able to stop—by this time a clinical recording of the infinite, variable series of events. But its support was not the perception of the patient in his singularity, but a collective consciousness, with all the information that intersects in it, growing in a complex, ever-proliferating way until it finally achieves the dimensions of a history, a geography, a state.

—Michel Foucault, *The Birth of the Clinic*

The exemplary irrational and "transcendental" number, pi, represents the ratio between a circle's circumference and its diameter. Mathematicians have calculated its value to some millions of digits and have determined that no repeating pattern exists. So while the circle seems succinctly definable for us, the order of pi remains unintelligible.

Imagine creatures for whom the order of pi is succinctly definite but for whom the circle is unintelligible. The two are too intimately related to go their separate ways. Is pi an excess produced by the tyrannical rigor of the circle, condemned to meander forever, the irrational creature of a primal repression that founds Euclidean consciousness? But this formula only gives all agency and priority to the circle. Or is the circle just an overrated bubble in the froth of a chaotic universe? Priority and agency are beside the point here, since the question is how the coordination and opposition between the two deform the field in which they operate.

Between them, pi and the circle roughly describe two faces of disciplinary logic. The circular function of discipline establishes a center and a normative distance around it, divides the field in which it operates into an inside and an outside (just as it more intimately cleaves a Euclidean self to and from its irrational other). But the failure of the model of center-and-margins or inside-and-outside to account for either the effectivities or vulnerabilities of disciplinary power is also obvious. What is liminal or marginal in one sector may not be in another, but even where it is liminal, it possesses a kind of power to define, a kind of centrality. Once we take the first step away from the regime of truth to consider the centrality of marginality, how can we stop? Must we then proceed into an endless morass of unwieldy paradoxes? Would this infinite exercise render the distinction between center and margins meaningless—or extend its hegemony everywhere? The infinite exercise represents the pi-face of disciplinary power: "a continuous process of variation." To look into this face, a familiar example of disciplinary structure will serve nicely.

One of Foucault's paradigms of Romantic discipline is the late-eighteenth-century prison proposed by Jeremy Bentham, the panopticon (Foucault 1984, 217–18). Several floors of cells are laid out in a circular building; the cells open onto a central, circular courtyard, so that each cell is visible from the guard tower that stands at the center of the courtyard. The design maximizes the efficiency of surveillance and control since a single guard can oversee each cell; the tower need not even be occupied continuously if prisoners cannot see into it. Prisoners are at each moment located and individuated in this "antinomadic" regime of hypervisibility.

Most diagrammatically, the panopticon works by intensifying and problematizing the interiority of the watchtower to the cells of the prison, since watching can otherwise take place only from "outside" or "above"; that is, embeddedness is otherwise inimical to the perspective required for watching. Thus one answer to Blake's Zen-like question—"Does the Eagle know what is in the pit? / Or wilt thou go ask the Mole...?" (3)—is Enlightenment in the form of the panopticon, a kind of Eagle/Mole or yin-yang machine that distinguishes inside and outside only by imbricating them, a motor that deploys a force field between these poles. In other words, inside and outside are produced not only by being divided but by continuous interpenetration and reversal, by being problematized. To problematize is taken too often as the aim of critique when problematization is often also the mode of that which is to be critiqued. But there is no way back, no way, no *no*, that could bring us to unproblematized relations (where inside is inside and outside outside).

The panopticon stands in for a range of other "antinomadic" techniques that will be enacted concurrently and over the next half-century in England by such measures as systematic numbering of houses, establishment of a police force, a burgeoning network of controlled-access turnpike roads, decennial censuses, the spread of clinical medicine and medical networks, other expanding information-gathering and surveillance networks, and specifically antinomadic strategies such as restrictions on casual labor, poor laws, other institutionalizations, and so on.

Just as the panopticon locates bodies and scrutinizes behavior, so too do its participants come to police themselves and others. This is not primarily a matter of subjective "internalization" of discipline but, as Foucault insists, an effect of the extension of techniques that constitute the physics of disciplinary power (see Foucault 1984, 213). For example, the more English local governments were mandated to send an increasing range of data to the Home Office, the more they could themselves be policed according to the amount and quality of information they sent (Eastwood 1989, 291). But surveillance is not a perfectly self-amplifying system: networking (often by post) was also a primary strategy of radical groups such as the London Corresponding Society, although yet again such groups were also thereby subject to increased surveillance.

It is on the basis of its similarity or resonance with the multiple other forms of discipline that the panopticon can be claimed as paradigmatic, but the panopticon produces and marks nomadism not only in binary contradistinction to its own centrality and fixity but in a more problematic relation to the thickness of the metastasizing sprawl of disciplinary networks in which it participates. Every network is already a network of networks (grafted onto others, like a spiderweb strung among tree branchings or a text among texts); by achieving a certain density of saturation it reveals each of its elements as networks as well. Disciplinarity is a *plaid*, a pattern of patterns that works not by being radiated from a center but by generating correspondences among nodes in multiple networks; Lacan called them "points of caption," upholstery buttons that fixate the social fabric. The local, spiderweb-like structure of gazes in the panopticon is made in relation to the web of webs formed by its distribution in the landscape. Far from separating inside from outside, a disciplinary landscape ensures that nobody can ever be simply inside or outside a prison or an asylum: how could we ever be simply inside or outside what is everywhere among us?

But a prison or even a prison system can only operate as a metaphor (e.g., of a "carceral" society) insofar as it is also a *different* kind of structure than others in which discipline operates, since metaphor demands a similarity between *different* realms: "love is a rose" is a metaphor, while "a rose is a rose" is not (at least, not immediately). Once identified, explicitly panoptic structures can be found all over the place, for instance in Romantic poems. Coleridge's poem "To William Wordsworth," for example, traces a scenario whereby a wild hope kindled by the French Revolution is "summoned homeward, thenceforth calm and sure," to her station in "the dread watch-tower of man's absolute self." Poems such as Wordsworth's "I Wandered Lonely..." or Keats's "Much Have I Traveled..." trace similar scenarios of nomadic wandering giving way to transcendent watching and self-watching. The title of Coleridge's short-lived journal, *The Watchman*, signifies for Jon Klancher a similar panopticization enacted in its relation to earlier journals such as the *Idler* and the *Rambler* (Klancher 1987, 38). Because in these instances the spatial relations of the panopticon become part of a temporal structure, the panopticon exemplifies Jameson's description of an "ideologeme" ("smallest intelligible unit of the essentially antagonistic collective discourses of social classes") as capable of being either narrativized or spatialized (Jameson 1981, 76, 87). The poems reenact as ontogeny (as "personal development") a long-term phylogenetic or collective panopticization of culture, the key point here being that panopticization becomes a masternarrative insofar as it orchestrates these resonances across scale. The figurative ecology "within" a poem works only in concert with the poem's distribution across space and time: readers of the poem, by recognizing a certain kind of poeticity in it or by recognizing themselves or each other through it, are themselves recognized, individuated, and culturally located by the poem in its distribution—an identification partially enacted even in the designation "readers of the poem." The logic of the Romantic poem as a *portable panopticon* (what Matthew Arnold would call a "touchstone") will be the subject of a later section.

The metaphorical function of the panopticon, then, becomes nearly indistinguishable from the panoptic function of metaphor. A simple illustration of this function can be taken from the title of Luther's famous hymn, "A Mighty Fortress Is Our God." The title is a textbook metaphor to the extent that it posits a god who operates in the realm of spirit as a fortress operates in the realm of flesh. But it is important to note that the difference between realms is assumed as part of the metaphysical competence required to recognize it as a metaphor at all: to recognize it as a metaphor is to some extent to be *subject* to it. The literal-minded reader, who understands the assertion to mean that Protestantism asserts itself as a siege mentality—as the simple worship of actual battlements—is not simply mistaken. While analysis of metaphor requires such a strategic refusal of its terms, the refusal is insufficient in itself to account for the work of metaphor. Protestantism may not simply be the worship of warfare and impenetrable boundaries, but a complex set of mediations and interpenetrations *between* warfare and religion (legitimized by the metaphor) do form its foci; it is at the points where the metaphor meets the non-metaphorical that it achieves both its effectivity and vulnerability (that is to say, its meaning), where it is both generalized and specified. By the same token, to learn that actual surveillance towers built along English coasts to watch for the "importation of revolution" from France must be among the primary referents of Coleridge's "watch-tower" does not resolve the metaphor by grounding it in historical fact but opens up a series of related questions, such as how "national security" came to be worshipped in the name of such a stupid nonentity as "man's absolute self" (or vice versa), how nationhood itself is *really* a metaphor (a provisional but constitutive displacement and condensation of identity construction), and how all of the above have legitimized the ongoing horror story of English Literature threatened with an invasion by the "French" theory that helps to ask these questions (see Simpson 1993, 40–83).

More than functioning as a metaphor, then, the panopticon is a Romantic *symbol* in de Man's sense: "always part of the totality that it represents." De Man called the Romantic preference for symbol over allegory and irony a "defensive strategy" and "an act of ontological bad faith" insofar as the symbol, unlike allegory and irony, refuses to acknowledge the "radical difference" that separates language—and a "self" caught in its predicament—from the "world of empirical reality" (1983, 208, 211, 217). But if the difference between language and the world is not necessarily more or less radical or definitive than differences that inhabit each, then to make it so is to engage in a "defensive strategy" no less mystified than one that transcendentalizes unity and presence. Such a strategy attempts to reduce the purchase of difference on both language and the world by making it absolute; it seeks absolution. The way symbolic self-referentiality marks the *double* impossibility of either connecting to *or divorcing* itself from "the world" is shown by how easily de Man's theory of the dialectic between (symbolic) mystified participation and (ironic) demystified withdrawal seems to represent his attempt to efface and avoid—and to come to terms with—the relation between his past as a collaborationist intellectual in Nazi-occupied Belgium and his later American academic career. Far from closing the case with a "gotcha!" or a neatly conventional loop between "life" and "work," the identification of such referentiality and self-referentiality in de Man's theorizing only constructs de Man as a symbol in turn, implicating all his critics in a dialectic of participation and withdrawal in which no absolution of difference is possible. The symbol continuously both separates and binds by being incorporated into a self-referential knot; chasing its own tail is its gambit for making the world revolve around it. The symbol of de Man is an unclosable case.

If metaphor produces both similarity and difference, the symbol also conspires to produce the totality it represents. A detour through several related paradigms will show how the symbol also works through a strategic short-circuiting of totalization.

Lacan's "mirror stage," a paradigmatically panoptic instance, is exemplified by the infant's fascination by its mirror image: the frozen, discrete, and sovereign image that will forever exceed its own discombobulated nonself (Lacan's "hommelette") as an ideal or telos (Lacan 1977, 1–7). But it is not necessary for the infant actually to see its image in a mirror for this process to occur, since the mirror is "merely a metaphor" for a much more extensive and varied process whereby the infant is "mirrored" back to itself by the selective and repeated responses of its caregivers, their distribution of attentions and withdrawals, and so on. For example, "one-day-old infants show exact, prolonged segments of movement correlating precisely in time with the speech patterns and rhythm of adults talking to them" (Fausto-Sterling 1985, 75). Strangely, then, the metaphor of the mirror image (like the mirror image of the metaphor) is singular and discrete, while the extensive and varied range of events that are the metaphor's referents are multiple and discombobulated (like the infant's preself); in other words, the mirror drops out, leaving a *metaphor of metaphor.* By the same token, one could say that the panopticon *performs a disciplinary function by becoming a metaphor.*

Althusser translates Lacan's mirroring into an acoustic metaphor of "hailing" (interpellation) that characterizes the operation of ideology: a cop on the street calls out, "Hey, you there"; the hailed person turns around and "by this mere one-hundred-and-eighty-degree physical conversion, he becomes a *subject*" (1971, 174). The hail works just as well if the subject runs away; it only doesn't work if the subject (then no longer a subject) fails to respond at all.

Strangely, Althusser's "hailing" resembles the "sheriff's hand on my shoulder" by which Peirce illustrated "secondness," a category of phenomenological relation that underlies the "thirdness" of "the law" as Lacan's Imaginary duality underlies the Oedipal triangulation of the Symbolic. For Peirce, though, secondness is characterized by impact, friction; the resistance of one object against another; the in itself meaningless violence or "brutality" of fact around which meaning accretes: "A court may issue *injunctions* and *judgments* against me and I care not a snap of my fingers for them. I may think them idle vapour. But when I feel the sheriff's hand on my shoulder, I shall begin to have a sense of actuality" (1955, 75–76). Peirce's metaphor depends on the friction of physical contact, while Lacan's and Althusser's metaphors of sight and hearing seem to allow refusal-without-consequences, or rather, they overstate the difference or distance between coercive and hegemonic or ideological power (between "the empirical world" and "language"), when either only operates where it interfaces with the other. A more apt metaphor (elaborated in chapter 4) might characterize the hail or gaze as the throwing of a ball: one has a "choice" of catching it or dodging it or letting it strike; what one does not have is a choice *not* to come into relation to it.

Foucault's physics of ideological and disciplinary power work by adjusting an economy of choices, by ensuring that the costs for resisting power are high enough and ubiquitous enough to be effective, but not so high as to induce too much of the resistance they are made to subvert. Lazare Carnot, a Revolutionary French physicist and government minister, developed two ideal conditions for "maximum generation of power" in mill wheels that describe disciplinary logic just as well: "that the water, or other motive agent, should enter the machine without shock and leave it without appreciable velocity" (Cardwell 1971, 182). Power optimization will also drive the steam engine, in the repressive 1790s, to adapt and develop feedback devices—basically types of disciplinary "self-consciousness"—in the forms of *governors* such as the "Whirling Regulator," which opens a valve when pressure causes weighted arms to rotate too quickly, and *indicators*, which monitor the rise and fall of pressure inside the engine (see Hills 1989, 85–94). To recognize that technology and politics are being construed in terms of power optimization or to identify the technological mandate as the "metaphor" of a political one (or vice versa) may still be to miss everything, unless the mill wheel and steam engine can also count as working metaphors, shaping in their terms a differential (an asymmetry) as an occasion for the generation of power over which they and their proprietors will be privileged mediators.

Before leaving this series of paradigms, Althusser's development of a visual analogue for "hailing" is worth exploring at greater length, for it takes us back to some of the primary contradictions among these models. Althusser describes the "Absolute Subject" as an ideological center that—like the panopticon's watchtower—acts as guarantor of the intelligibility of the positions it constructs through its hailings, meaning

that all ideology is centred, *that the Absolute Subject occupies the unique place of the Centre, and interpellates around it the infinity of individuals into subjects in a double mirror-connexion such that it* subjects *them to the Subject, while giving them in the Subject in which each subject can contemplate its own image (present and future) the* guarantee *that this really concerns them and Him. (1971, 180)*

For Althusser, then, the field of subjectivity is organized *anamorphoscopically.* The
anamorphoscope is a device in which a
cylindrical mirror is placed at the empty
center of a picture that has been systematically distorted so that its image in the
curved mirror looks "right." To distort
the image properly, the painter must
watch the image's image in the convex
mirror as his hand traces it on the flat
surface; in other words, for the painter
it operates as a kind of external brain,
recoordinating the translation device
between eye and hand. The image must
be constructed—as it will be viewed—

Anamorphoscope

with reference to the mirror. Although the painted image refers first to its mirror
image rather than its "real" referent (like pi and the circle, the two images were
"made for each other"), it is more germane that the representation is represented
and that the function of this apparently closed loop that empties itself of content is
to rearticulate its subject.

The anamorphoscopic mirror acts as that which "is what it is"
(like Althusser's God who proclaims "I am that I am") and at once merely the image
of all others constructed by their distance and distortion from it. This guarantor of
the intelligibility of subject positions is what Lacan called the "phallus."

Imagine, instead of the central mirror of Althusser's anamorphoscope, a set of voluptuous mirrors arranged, like a school of fish, so that each re-
flects and distorts the others, where nothing is reflected (no "content") but the positions of the mirrors with respect to each other. Players function in the system to
the extent that they reflect and distort, by virtue of their differential position, the
other mirrors, but no one mirror is positioned to present a totalized and undis-
torted picture; one looks to others to find an image of oneself amid images of images of others. This figure, a school of mirrors, is more suited to the mobile and
multiple interrelations that characterize postmodern power and knowledge.

The mirror dropped from Lacan's metaphor returns as the choreography of its dancing fragments. The subject constituted in the school of mirrors
does not look up to an image that will exceed it by virtue of superior discretion but
because it is also more fragmented and multiple than the subject can hope to be.

Flocks, Herds, and Schools. Mirroring—visual or otherwise—has long been recognized as the mechanism whereby flocks, herds, and schools are sustained. Many fish, for example, use their eyes to orient themselves to each other as well as using their "lateral line," a kind of head-to-tail "ear" that is "sensitive particularly to 'near field' motion of water produced by propagated sound waves" (Shaw 1962, 134); in other words, they are attuned to the most *local* information. Schooling fish achieve such "a remarkably constant geometric orientation to their fellows" that "they create the illusion of a huge single animal moving in a sinuous path"—a fish of fish (metafish) whose shape and behavior make it a different creature than its members: "from above they may appear rectangular or elliptical or amorphous and changeable" (Shaw 1962, 128). Only the horizon of an ideology of unified subjectivity could

produce the surprising "discovery" that such finely tuned coordination could be accomplished without a "central control system"; the absolute constitutiveness of multiplicity continues to elude the biologist who, in order to study "the emergence of their schooling behavior," attempts to raise fish in isolation from their fellows and even from their own reflections (although the impossibility of isolating the fish from water and food render unattainable the "total vacuum of experience" necessary for a "perfect" experiment) and then wonders why so few fish survive early isolation (Shaw 1962, 128, 133). In 1962 a biologist could write of "the emergence of . . . behavior" without quite acknowledging the itself-emergent paradigm of "emergence." More recently, computer animation has demonstrated that flocks, herds, and schools can be modeled as "emergent behaviors" in a *distributed* network: "the aggregate motion of the simulated flock is the result of the dense interaction of the relatively simple behaviors of the individual simulated bird" (known as a "birdoid" or "boid"), "each acting solely on the basis of its own local perception of the world" (Reynolds 1987, 25). Three simple mandates are necessary to produce a robust flock: avoid collisions with nearby flockmates, match their velocity, and stay close to them. Here, the ongoing Western dream of perfect knowledge still enables the surprise that giving "each simulated boid perfect and complete information about the world . . . leads to obvious *failures* of the model" (my emphasis), necessitating the conclusion "that the aggregate motion that we intuitively recognize as 'flocking' (or schooling or herding) *depends* upon a limited, localized view of the world" (Reynolds 1987, 29–30). Significantly, it is again a kind of mirroring (intuitive recognition) that suggests that the computer model's principles must be roughly "true to nature"; a more radical reading is that the logic of mirroring at work *between* the model and its referent ("actual" bird flocks) may mirror that at work *within* the referent or the model, or even that, in some important sense, birds *are* kinds of mirrors, for a start. The distinction between nonorganic and organic systems is both threatened and recuperated: flock simulations are

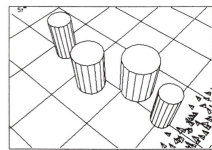

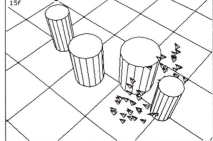

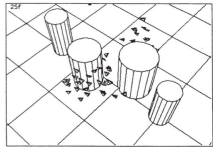

Frames from Animated Sequence of Flock of Primitive Boids Flying through Obstacle Course

"closely related to *particle systems*," which constitute "dynamic 'fuzzy objects' having irregular and complex shapes" (e.g., "fire, smoke, clouds"), although "the present boid behavior model might be about one or two orders of magnitude more complex than typical particle behavior. However this is a difference of degree, not of kind" (Reynolds 1987, 26). Birds, in turn, may be more complex than boids, but there is no way of knowing whether living creatures are in any absolute sense "more complex" than nonliving things, or whether one might posit some universal *threshold of complexity* beneath which no thing could exist at all.

These two excesses are poles of Lacan's subject-machine, by which Imaginary fixation is made to be deconstructed (or retroactively to have been deconstructed) by Symbolic circulation.

   If the resonance of the circle and its capacity to create a ripple effect (echoing across various dimensions of human life) describes a metaphorical fixation of discipline, the ever-varying meander of pi describes its metonymic

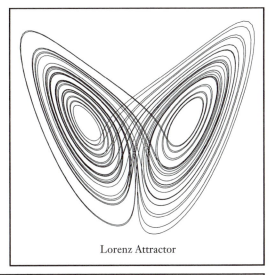

Lorenz Attractor

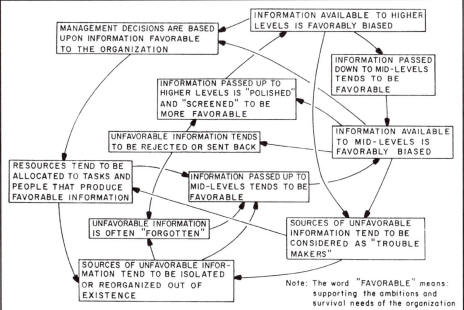

Note: The word "FAVORABLE" means: supporting the ambitions and survival needs of the organization

A School of Mirrors. In his study "Organizations and Systematic Distortion of Information," David Bella (1987) diagrams an institution as a kind of disinformational "strange attractor." Instead of suggesting the damage-control remedy of better self-policing, Bella's recognition that "tendencies to distort information are systemic properties of . . . organizational systems themselves" (360) may suggest another, more radical conclusion: that the truth or falsity of information is secondary to its performative and/or counterperformative potential, and that distortion is not merely endemic but the primary modus operandi of any "organization" or "system" (insofar as it exists at all only as it cuts across, engages, and distorts other ways of "carving up" the world).

sprawl. Circle and infinite meander meet in the figure of the spiral, whose center and circumference are continually deferred toward the infinitely large and infinitesimally small. The "strange attractor," a constrained but ever-variable orbit around emptiness, describes a definitively postmodern generation of disciplinary paradigms.

T W O

Horrors of Order and Disorder

Capital is a process and not a thing ... it is a dynamic and revolutionary mode of social organization, restlessly and ceaselessly

Clarence D. Thorpe, in analyzing all of Keats's relevant scattered pronouncements, concludes: "Such is the power of the creative imagination, a seeing, reconciling, combining force that seizes the old, penetrates beneath its surface, disengages the truth slumbering there, and, building afresh, bodies forth anew a reconstructed universe in fair forms of artistic power and beauty." This could be a summary of the theories of

imagination of all the romantic poets.
—René Wellek, "The Concept of Romanticism in Literary History"

transforming the society within which it is embedded. The process masks and fetishizes,

achieves growth through creative destruction, creates new wants and needs, exploits the

capacity for human labor and desire, transforms spaces, and speeds up the pace of life.
— David Harvey, *The Condition of Postmodernity*

Reversal, Turning Inside Out, Horizontalization

For Marx, the conversion of commodities into money and then back into commodities again — notated in the formula "*c-m-c*" — marks a precapitalist mode of production based on the use value of commodities (Marx 1972, 329–36). The inauguration of a capitalist mode of production and of the regime of exchange value turns the means and ends of the formula *inside out*: the revised formula "*m-c-m*" indicates that commodities have become aspects of the "code" or "channel" of an exchange whose end points are now monetary. The advantage as well as the problem with these terse formulas is that they make a single, linear structure out of a repeated and multidimensional process: every product and process comes to be implicated in a web of repeated cycles from money into commodity and back again. What justifies calling this web a "cash nexus" rather than a "commodity nexus" is that money is, in Wordsworth's phrase, "far more deeply interfused"; it is the repetition and multidimensionality of the cycles in which each object or process is implicated that confer value to it. By mandating the multiplication of these cycles, the spread of this nexus represents a seeming decrease in the fractal dimension of significant relations: "all that is solid melts into air."

      Such a change does not affect all relations evenly, but its pervasiveness is such that all relations must come into relation to it; this includes especially other kinds of values and relations that come to be identified in opposition to it. A succinct example: the primary meaning of the word "friend" in the Renaissance was someone who could provide material assistance, while by the nineteenth century the primary meaning had shifted to someone whose value is opposed to (although it may overlap with) that of a useful "connection" or a political ally. Since a change of this kind is probabilistic or connotative, affecting the difference of the word from itself as well as from other words — and thus only vaguely discernible even in a historical dictionary such as the *OED* — there is some difficulty in establishing, except on its own terms, that it has taken place at all, since all the language that could describe it is implicated. The minute reversal in a connotative hierarchy is the index of a polar shift in the logic of meaning that leaves no single word — nor any sets of relations among discourses—unaffected. What Kuhn called "the invisibility of revolutions" (1970, 136–43) is not only a matter of who writes histories (i.e., the "winners") but of what is allowed to constitute history and how it can be written. While the emergent hegemony of capitalist discipline in the late eighteenth century had painfully evident and dramatic effects on the lives of every human, animal, and plant within its reach, micro- and macroscopic language effects are among the most self-effacing. Derrida describes a similar process in "ordinary language, into whose deepest recesses the *episteme* plunges in order to gather them up and to make them part of itself in a metaphorical displacement" (Derrida 1978, 278). These recesses are "deepest" not because they are somehow far from individual or collective life but because they are so intimately and minutely woven into its fabric; this is a depth of scale rather than of space, a process that occurs not just in language (narrowly considered) but in the way the logic of capital infiltrates the landscape through rhizomic ("grassroots") extension.

     If the steady-state dynamic equilibrium of Newtonian mechanics, grounded in discrete and eternal particles, helped to shape a universe in the image of a commodity-based economy, the nineteenth-century rise of thermodynamics, with its "subtle fluids" and temporally (as well as categorically) dynamic universe, was tailor made for the regime of exchange. Michel Serres's account stresses the change from "mechanical systems . . . based on a fixity or an equilibrium" (a clockwork universe) to a world of *motors* that "produce circulation by means of reservoirs and differences in temperature"—a change in which the perfectly reversible processes that oriented prethermodynamic temporality are displaced by a glacially irreversible "arrow of time" (Serres 1982, 71): thermodynamics relativizes and dynamicizes only at the cost of introducing this implacable directionality, just as the "absolute invariance" of the speed of light will come to anchor Einsteinian relativity.

     When Watt started using "horsepower" to measure the output of his steam engines, it was in order to be able to claim from his clients a fixed percentage of the "savings" they would gain by switching from horses to steam (Cardwell 1971, 33, 72); that is, profit drove the steam engine as well as working to define and measure its difference from and interchangeability with the horse. The eventual form of the second law of thermodynamics, mandating a one-way flow of heat from hot to cold, represents a generalization of what had already been the principle of the steam engine, and before it, the waterwheel, which also extracts an energy profit from the "falling market" of a flow from higher to lower energy potential.

Carnot's "ideal engine" schematizes the parasitical perpendicularity of culture to a polarized nature. As the water-wheel gives way to the coal-driven steam engine and eventually to engines driven by gasoline, even the fuels themselves seem to become progressively more mediated by processing and refinery. The contemporary form of "recycling" differs from forms that have been going on for millenia in that the cycles themselves, driven by the profit potential that each mediation represents, begin to assume an ontological priority that further demotes the eternal ideal object in favor of an infinitely mutable one.

It is easy to cast these changes as progressive movements from fixity (where, for example, identities are based in fixture to immovable property) to a dynamism anchored only in patterns of flux (the sharkish swim-or-die logic of capital), although even the more "primitive" logic of the "gift" also produces values, identities, differentials, and relationships via its circulation. "All that is solid melts into air": Marx's masternarrative of capital, recycled as a characterization of modernity (Marx 1972, 476; Berman 1982), represents an attempt to historicize capitalism's thermodynamic logic as belonging to a particular phase of economy (and is second only to Yeats's "things fall apart" as a terse approximation of the second law). For the thermodynamicists who were Marx's contemporaries, such as Kelvin, this masternarrative was the whole story of the universe, human history being merely an ambiguous subplot (Cardwell 1971, 257). But when one can say, for example, that for a postmodern investor, a "hot" piece of land can be more "liquid" than a "choppy" currency, it is not so much that a dissipative process has taken place, but that the model of solidity and liquidity or commodity and currency (and the thermodynamics that underwrite the model) have become inadequate even in "ordinary language."

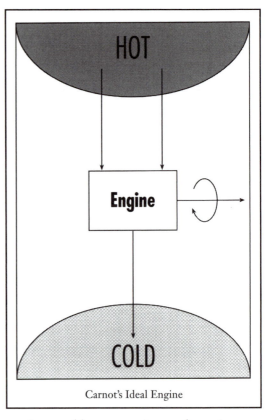

Carnot's Ideal Engine

A case could be made that a postmodern "information economy" relativizes the status of both money and commodities by the potentially even more volatile (and thereby even more tightly controlled) commodity or currency of information and images (producing what could be called an "*m-i-m-i-c*" economy), although insofar as maps of the circulation of information, money, and commodities could even be made or imagined, they would, no doubt, seem to overlap to a great extent. It remains to be seen, that is, whether the semiautonomous agency of information (as origin and/or end) establishes or legitimizes a different form of value.

Corollary to the "betweenness" of *things* (*m-c-m*) in the new Romantic regime of exchange is a redoubled internal differentiation mandated by the economic realization that domestic consumption rather than export is the primary engine of economic growth. Along with early industrial capitalism's mandate to work laborers to the limit and to pay them as little as possible arises the contradictory but corollary strategy of maximizing efficiency, allowing more time off and paying a wage that enables some disposable income and more consumption. Both labor and leisure had to be disciplined, to be continually separated and woven together. The mandate to maximize the difference between an exporting and an importing nation, or a working/producing class and a leisure/consuming class, also demotes the polarity in favor of an ideal "middle" class that maximizes production and consumption. The engine of economic growth is powered by a flow of products not only up and out (to one's betters and for export) but recursively back. Capitalism and the steam engine (a "difference engine") move by the same logic: by producing, managing, and exploiting relativistic differentials (as between hot and cold in the engine).

Catherine Gallagher finds resistance to the emergent regime of exchange value in Malthus's 1798 *Essay on the Principles of Population*. Against a marketplace increasingly situated as the engine of production, Malthus characterizes exchange as a necessary but minimizable parasitism that siphons energy away from the production of useful commodities:

the longer the circuit of exchange leading from the laboring body in the form of a commodity and back to it again in the form of food, whether that circuit be a certain number of exchanges or a certain amount of literal space traversed, the more inflated is the cost of food and the less productive is the labor. (Gallagher 1987, 96)

Malthus objects, that is, to elongation or deferral of the body's relation to itself too far beyond the circuit of hand-to-mouth. "However," Gallagher continues, "the short circuit of biological exchange favored by Malthus also seems to be the product of a circular logic," whereby

food and the body, commodity and labor, thus constantly indicate each other as the source and gauge
of their value. And outside this tight circle of production and consumption, a circle representing
the most restrictive economy imaginable, is a network of exchanges that seems
only to draw value away from its true site in order to dissipate it. (96)

Outside the circle, then, is a disorder and leveling of value that must be constantly guarded against. Wordsworth finds an emblem for this danger in London's Bartholomew street fair, where the disorderly circulation of people and commodities forms a "vast mill" and monstrous body of undisciplined egresses and ingresses,

> vomiting, receiving on all sides,
> . . . .
> . . . amid the same perpetual whirl
> of trivial objects, melted and reduced
> To one identity, by differences
> That have no law, no meaning, and no end.
> (1979, 546)

It is clear to Malthus that some exchange is necessary, but that "the problem could be diminished by making the production of productive bodies the telos of exchange, by shrinking economic circuits and centering them on biological needs" (Gallagher, 103). However, the body at the center of the inner circle carries the seed of an equally drastic disorder, since the very vigor of the productive body also becomes in Malthus's essay the sign of a drastic enfeeblement, through the overpopulation of the social body that this vigor will produce. Another mainstay of the "Great Chain of Being," the time-honored and static homology or *metaphor* between the individual and the social body, thus becomes a "temporally dynamic" *irony* whereby the strong body comes to represent its opposite: "the strong body entails a present and a future social condition: first a society of innocence and health and then one of vice and misery" (Gallagher, 84).

The dynamo that Malthus constructs is thus driven by matching repulsions from the body at its center and from the circumference of exchanges that detach themselves from it. In an important sense, then, Malthus's logic is precisely *not* circular, since it forbids both center (the ironic ideal of order) and circumference (the monster of disorder).

Barbara Duden offers another take on Romantic circulation and the body it constructs in *The Woman beneath the Skin* (1991). Duden examines the conflict between women and their doctors, and between conflicting paradigms of the body, in eighteenth-century Germany. She contrasts the emergent medical monopoly over the body with an earlier plurality of bodily paradigms and practitioners. This plurality had found its own image in a body whose fluids are themselves fluid in their relations with each other; that is, capable of metamorphosing into each other or being expressed in various forms through various orifices. Increasingly, then, a singular and autonomous medical discipline (articulated categorically from other disciplines) articulated categorical distinctions between irreconcilable kinds of bodies and their systems of circulation where multiple disciplines had found continuous (i.e., unarticulated) transformations.

The prediscipinary paradigm sketched by Duden suggests how *stress* comes to be postmodernity's "privileged pathology" (Haraway 1991, 212), since stress represents a conflict between multiple systems, is expressed fluidly in "biopsychosocial" effects, and mandates an interdisciplinary response. Although the pathologization of stress tends to fetishize conflict-free consensus, stress is inevitably an interdisciplinary crisis representing the return of a repressed prediscipinary paradigm (what Kuhn might have called preparadigm disciplinarity).

Duden's historical trajectory characterizes knowledge's present (disciplinarity) as monolithically and oppressively unified, while both prediscipinarity and an implicit postdisciplinary knowledge are plural and fluid. Although this construction differs schematically from the more familiar Romantic construction of the present as oppressively fragmented and the past and desired future as unified and whole, it does not escape the linear/cyclical form of Romantic memory and desire.

The opposition between medical-scientific and aesthetic discourse (precondition for their collusive monopoly on representing the body) is one of the constitutive structures of Romantic discipline formation. A greatly simplified version of this change is indexed in another story of reversal: Foucault's account of the shift of the "author function" from science to the arts in eighteenth-century Europe (Foucault 1984, 109). The shift is not, of course, a discrete one but an only retroactively observable qualitative shift in a dispersed and uneven quantitative process; it may be retroactively observable only insofar as it has begun to shift again. Prior to the shift, in any event, literary authority and value had been based on generic consistency and repeatability, while science was grounded in a set of canonical Great Authors. Increasingly, scientific authority came to rest in the repeatability of experiments and the irrelevance of the author, while literary value came to reside in the unrepeatably original authority of the artist. This chiasmic *crossing* of the author function is implicated in the new hegemony of an anonymous discipline and power-knowledge that individualizes its subjects (authors) and objects (e.g., patients) in order to control the circulation of meaning.

This inaugural discursive split reverberates across discursive space-time; *space* because it is echoed within the disciplines it configures (for example, the science/literature split can be said to be echoed in literature by the split between literary criticism and literature), and *time* because it enables disciplinary change to be configured as an exchange of features. Looking back to the literary anti-Newtonianism of the Romantics leads to a scenario whereby quantum physics (as a marker of modernity) and later chaos or complexity theory (as a postmodern marker) can then be taken as science's incorporation of (or liberation by) its disciplinary Others, at least insofar as these movements legitimize anti-Newtonianism from within science rather than without. The fact that these developments are widely hailed as liberatory and denounced as dangerous new interventions into as yet uncolonized realms of nature/culture represents an unresolvable ambivalence. In its very unresolubility it marks the changing terms of discursive struggle: the crisscross or double diagonality is always transverse to the direction in which the historical snake is moving. These disciplinary developments do not of themselves subvert the constitutive epistemological bases of discipline. For example, chaos and complexity theory do not of themselves enact an antiscientific science, but are also driven by the old disciplinary masternarrative that demands that we "imagine a unified science that weaves together all domains of human understanding into a coherent, fully satisfying whole," as Langdon Winner puts it in a review of two books on chaos (Winner 1993). The reviewer cannot help but gesture toward the self-referential quality of this unity: "The books, as it turns out, display remarkable unity themselves."

It would be very neat if "resistance to discipline in the name of predisciplinary power-knowledge" could be added to Sayre and Löwy's definition of Romanticism, but even or especially when considering Romanticism's emphasis on the wholeness and unity of knowledge, it is clear that this emphasis is not a predisciplinary stance but a retroactive one; unity is most often situated alternately as an origin or aim. For example, Keats's cheery assertion that "every department of knowledge we see excellent and calculated towards a great whole" is only the flip side of his lament over present fragmentation when set against the magisterial sweep of the past: "Each of the moderns like an Elector of Hanover governs his petty state" while "the antients were Emperors of vast Provinces" (Keats 1970, 92, 61). The derogation of fragmentation is (as usual) a ploy to inflate the derogator's own market share at the expense of his competitors. Unification and fragmentation ("leveling") are deployed simultaneously to produce a "temporally dynamic" history.

Carole Pateman's account of early modernity in England emphasizes a limited pluralization or horizontalization in the shift from traditional patriarchy (rule of the father) to fratriarchy (rule of the brothers) as the foundational myth of liberal democracy—and eventually, of Oedipalized psychic development as well (Pateman 1989). Pateman retells the story of pluralization along with the story of another reversal of polarity or turning inside out that implicates the status of public and private spheres, or rather (as in the case of the chiasmic crossing of the "author function"), produces their polarity through a reversal. Privacy, which had classically referred to "privation" (prohibitive exclusion from the public sphere) shifted to the Victorian concept of privacy as a privileged refuge from the "jungle" of "getting and spending."

Pateman's account of pluralization aligns the liberal ideology of the state with the Foucauldian story of the pluralization of knowledge and power in professionalism and the emergence of disciplines, and resembles T. E. Hulme's famous characterization (in 1936) of Romanticism as "spilt religion," the replacement of the singular social cement of paternalistic religion with the multiple forms of cultural and disciplinary unanimity (in Gleckner and Ensoe 1975, 58). Thomas Laqueur's account of the late-eighteenth-century shift in scientific paradigms of sexual anatomy shows how a related horizontalization was enacted on the human body, in the shift from a vertical sexual heirarchy in which female genitalia are conceived as homologous but inferior to male, to a horizontal incommensurability between (still binarized) sexes (Laqueur 1987, 35). Like Pateman's account of the state, Laqueur's story of the making of the modern body cannot simply be characterized as liberatory.

The rise of discipline, then, is simultaneous with its descent; power and knowledge are *brought down*, in all senses of the phrase: toppled, appropriated from above, but also *brought down to bear*. The Romantic valorization of the Promethean myth, with its account of the bringing down of power and knowledge, takes on a new and problematic resonance. The panoptic ubiquity of discipline, the invisible hand of capitalist control, and the "spontaneous" compliance that marks hegemonic power can be said to displace the coherence of religious dogma, the iron hand of the ancien régime, and the conspicuous displays of submission required by coercive power, but this displacement should not thereby be characterized as liberatory or oppressive. Instead it changes the terms by which political struggle can be articulated. If, to extrapolate into postmodernity, the old party line continuously mutates into a partyline, dogma into a floating multiple conversation, couplings into switchboards, we look forward to an operatorless networking that is both and neither perfect freedom and the perfect police state (which, as William Burroughs reminds us, has no need of police).

Mixture and Fixture: Political Thermodynamics in Burke and Paine

Edmund Burke, in his 1790 *Reflections on the Revolution in France*, offers various catastrophic social-hybridization scenarios, as in his lament that the "levellers" will so "pervert the natural order of things" that "the next generation of the nobility will resemble the artificers and clowns, and money-jobbers, usurers, and Jews" (1973, 61). While "artificers and clowns" represent traditional laboring classes (i.e., artisans and peasants), Burke's "money-jobbers, usurers, and Jews" represent a traditionally demonized "middle" class in the special sense that, while trade and money had been situated as parasitisms on production (however necessary as the "middle" or mediator in the *c-m-c* transaction), money-lending *mediates mediation*: it is a parasite's parasite; it is "between between," the metaphor and echoic truth of mediation.

In his reply to Burke, Thomas Paine draws on a populist tradition that gothicized the aristocracy as a parasitical class:

Aristocracy has a tendency to degenerate the human species. By the universal economy of nature it is known, and by the instance of the Jews it is proved, that the human species has a tendency to degenerate, in any small number of persons, when separated from the general stock of society, and intermarrying constantly with each other. (1973, 322)

Paine, in other words, demonized closure and too-thoroughgoing differentiation, just as Burke had demonized the collapse of hierarchical difference in a frighteningly "open" system.

Burke and Paine argue the contested issue of class difference and hierarchy in terms of a shared anti-Semitism, which is in turn justified by appeals to "natural" science (e.g., "natural order"), which in turn rely on an economic metaphor ("universal economy of nature"). This discursive collusion achieves epistemic currency—cops the ring of truth—around the fixation of race. That these two opposed positions should appeal to anti-Semitism is not surprising, the Jewish Other being a mainstay of English national identity since the Middle Ages.

Paine and Burke cite two contradictory features of the paradigm that will continue to define anti-Semitism into our day: Paine attributes degeneracy to the Jews' proverbial foreclosure of mixing (their endogamy or "marrying in," their maintenance of difference), while Burke finds degeneracy in Jewish mixing or "miscegenation" (exogamy or "marrying out"), predicated on the Jew's ability to "pass."

Apparently Mary Wollstonecraft refers to a similar "universal economy" when she asserts that the aristocracy "only live to amuse themselves, and by the same law which in nature invariably produces certain effects, they soon afford only barren amusement" (1989, 75). It may be that Wollstonecraft splits the difference between Paine and Burke: having just asserted that the "seeds of false refinement...shed by the great...spread corruption through the whole mass of society," Wollstonecraft seems to associate this hybridization-by-emulation with the merely decorative hybridization of flowers that produces "barrenness" in second-generation hybrids. The passage also seems to hint at a catastrophic masturbatory scenario (self-amusement leading to barrenness) that shortens the endogamous circuit to auto-eroticism, anticipating the Victorian typology of deviance that pathologizes nonreproductive sexuality.

It is easy to say that scientific, socioeconomic, and political "truths" are being constructed in each other's image even as these discourses are being differentiated from each other. But what kind of metaeconomy or ecology of statements does such a statement propose?

Burke's "natural order" is an ongoing stable plurality (and hierarchy) of kinds in a *homeorrhetic* system (that is, one in which a pattern is maintained although its content changes). Politics are differentiated from nature precisely to produce and valorize a "correspondence" between them:

Our political system is placed in a just correspondence and symmetry with the order of the world, and with the mode of existence decreed to a permanent body composed of transitory parts; wherein, by the disposition of a stupendous wisdom, moulding together the great mysterious incorporation of the human race, the whole, at one time, is never old, or middle-aged, or young, but in a condition of unchangeable constancy, moves on through the varied tenour of perpetual decay, fall, renovation, and progression. Thus, by preserving the method of nature in the conduct of the state, in what we improve we are never wholly new; in what we retain we are never wholly obsolete. (Burke 1973, 45–46)

Geologist James Hutton seems to write Burke's state into stone in his 1795 *Theory of the Earth.* Hutton, who as a medical student had written on blood circulation, characterizes geologic, astronomical, and physiological processes as types of a generalized circulation, finding an exemplary "circulation in the manner of this globe, as a system of beautiful oeconomy in the works of nature. The earth, like the body of an animal, is wasted at the same time that it is repaired";

Hutton's cosmos, like Burke's state, is an "exquisite mechanism" in which all things are perpetually "decaying from their natural perfection, and renovating their existence in a succession of similar beings to which we see no end" (cited in Gould 1987, 83).

Part of the similarity in these accounts dervives from how they deploy the dominant paradigm of "circulation" in the form of a closed and self-organizing system of eternally returning and perfectly reversible cycles, a form whose contradictions will become apparent in Malthus—and will implode into the turbulent and irreversible time of nineteenth-century thermodynamics.

"Circulation," in Barbara Duden's account, had "established itself around 1750 not only in physiology, but also in economics, the natural sciences, and journalism"; the "equivalence of very disconnected spheres of reality...was created through the exchange of metaphors, the flow of 'key terms' that occurred between the scientific, social, and political languages" (Duden 1991, 27). Instead of a scientific referent at the bottom of the discourses of circulation, then, one finds between them an intra- and interdiscursive "flow" that constitutes the truth-effect of an apparent "circulation of circulation." Duden's account is inflected to tell the story of modernity as the deterioration of a discursive plurality into an oppressive and collusively unified hegemony; what Duden leaves out of the account is that differences—no less than "equivalences" or "correspondences"—must be continually forged.

Politicothermodynamic contradictions between closed and open systems are also rife in questions of the persistence of differences in kind, for example in the theory and practice of inbreeding and crossbreeding to which Burke, Paine, and Wollstonecraft seem to allude. "By the beginning of the nineteenth century, practical attempts to improve the different breeds of cattle led to extensive inbreeding...to add up and concentrate desirable qualities," coupled with crossbreeding "to prevent degeneration" (Zirkle 1952, 6–7). Eighteenth-century European botanists had tended to valorize crossbreeding: Linnaeus had promoted research into hybridization, and as early as 1766, the German botanist J. G. Koelreuter described "hybrid vigor in interspecific crosses" and "assumed in consequence that nature had designed plants to benefit from crossbreeding"; by 1799, the Englishman Thomas Andrew Knight had generalized these assumptions and observations into a "principle of anti-inbreeding" (Zirkle 1952, 7). But typically, Koelreuter (anticipating Dr. Frankenstein's dilemma) took comfort from his experiments insofar as the sterility of his hybrids "banished the evil spectre of self-perpetuating hybrids at least temporarily" and confirmed Linnaeus's distinction between God-created species and mere garden varieties, which, "being monstrosities, can boast of but a brief life" (Koelreuter, quoted in Olby 1966, 49). Thus the relativization and dynamicization of "difference within" species can shore up the absoluteness of "difference between" only until its recursive effects are felt. A similar process had characterized the eighteenth-century debate over *sexual* difference within and between species: preformationists had split over whether whole subsequent generations in descending scale were contained in the sperm or in the egg; Linnaeus, while denying that sexual difference distinguished animals from plants, split the all-or-nothing distinction between "spermists" and "ovists" with the proposition that the male contributes the outer form to its offspring while the interior is contributed by the female; Koelreuter in turn exploded Linnaeus's distinction by showing that sexual generation produces in the offspring a kind of *statistical* averaging of the contributions of each parent. It is not quite enough to characterize these sequences as part of a general distinction between and triumph of *degree* over *kind* (quantitative over qualitative difference) in the hegemony of scientific knowledge, nor to tell how a stable plurality (in which difference between species is an original and ongoing condition) will eventually give way to a masternarrative of monogenesis (original unity) and subsequent differentiation. This latter masternarrative is well known as modernity's favorite bedtime story: the story of how the disciplines arose from an original unity of knowledge — discursive monogenesis — and expanded toward greater incommensurability (while maintaining, as the other pole of the engine, the promise of a "unified field theory" just ahead). The postmodern claim of incommensurability between narrative and nonnarrative (scientific) knowledge, by allowing the eternal "return of the narrative in the nonnarrative" without compromising the difference, may merely prime the engine: "All we can do is gaze in wonder at the diversity of discursive species" (Lyotard 1984, 26).

When the story of a stable plurality and that of proliferating difference implode, they produce a different kind of story in turn; a hybrid story in which plurality is conserved only insofar as its members *change* and in which differences are not subject to absolutizing, only to economizing where they are on the verge of becoming different sets of differences.

When in 1819 Keats uses homeorrhetic circulation to explain subtle but thorough *alterations* in personality over time, it is clear that Burke's and Hutton's stable thermodynamics inevitably give way, subtly but thoroughly, to an uneasy Malthusian dynamism. It begins calmly enough: the fact that "our bodies every seven years are completely fresh-material'd" means that "we are like the relict garments of a Saint: the same and not the same: for the careful Monks patch it and patch it" (Keats 1970, 322). But inevitably these speculations lead to volatile cycles driven by contradictions among reproduction, consumption, and production; cycles in which the possibility of a thermodynamic equilibrium continually recedes into the future: the possibility that the poet has "lost that poetic ardour and fire 'tis said I once had" leads him to hope that he may "substitute a more thoughtful and quiet power," but as yet he has only been able to achieve a relative calm troubled with intermittent turbulence ("I am more frequently, now, contented to read and think— but now & then, haunted with ambitious thoughts"), problematically unproductive insofar as he is "scarcely content to write the best verses for the fever they leave behind," and thus generating the hope that he may "someday" be able "to compose without this fever" (Keats 1970, 322).

Although the "universal economy of nature" to which Paine and Wollstonecraft appeal against Burke's "Great Chain of Being" would not be codified until 1860 as the second law of thermodynamics—the assertion that entropy inevitably increases in any closed system—its cultural currency is already evident, as are the beginnings of its derivative masternarrative, the ever popular Big Bang, which sets the beginning of the universe at a singularity of pure potential and the end in a "leveling" of heat death, a uniform dispersal of random kinetic energy. These two moments already structure Malthus's prohibited center (the virile body of explosive potential) and circumference (the vitiating and "feminized" kinesis of pure exchange).

Freud, in *Beyond the Pleasure Principle*, will schematize a related set of psychological principles grounded in late Victorian thermodynamics, for which "stasis" has come to occupy the position of origin and prohibited center. The "death drive" or "repetition compulsion" is identified as the instinct that would compel the infant (when left alone) to return to the "inorganic stasis" from which it came. Here (in Lacan's version), because of the biological prematurity of the infant at birth, culture intervenes to foreclose this recursion—or is it that the discursive ecology intervenes both to propose and to prohibit the reduction of psychology to thermodynamics?

Freud grounds his ontogenetic narrative in phylogeny:

For a long time, perhaps, living substance was thus being constantly created afresh and easily dying, till decisive external influences altered in such a way as to oblige the still surviving substance to diverge ever more widely from its original course of life and to make ever more complicated detours *before reaching its aim of death. (1961, 32–33)*

So while complication and decentering is the trajectory of life itself for Freud, the "death on its own terms" sought by the organism driven by this scenario comes as a "decentering of decentering," a kind of Copernican revolution necessitated (this time by "internal necessity") by the "ever more complicated" epicycles that the Ptolemeic paradigm had generated.

Freud's "pleasure principle" (p.p.) represents an evolution (an "out-spiraling") of the death drive (d.d.) along a longer curve of arousal (dynamic tension) and release (provisional equilibrium): p.p. is just another rotation of d.d., while the "reality principle" performs another turn, deferring gratification further in favor of the relative security of a still higher bottom line. Freud is adamant that these principles do not simply produce a spiral of transcendence but a contradictory or turbulent "vacillating rhythm" in the play of sameness and difference between d.d. and p.p.:

It is the difference in amount between the pleasure of satisfaction which is demanded *and that which is actually* acheived *that provides the driving factor which will permit of no halting at any position attained.... The backward path that leads to complete satisfaction is as a rule obstructed by the resistances which maintain the repressions. (36)*

The orientation of Freud's recursive "backward path" depends on an equation of "satis" and "stasis" and on a distinction between inorganic and living matter, producing a vacillation between them that, instead of being allowed to characterize things in general, enables Freud to dignify against the "death drive" an imperialistically expansionist Eros that operates "to combine organic substances into ever larger unities" (37).

Freud's thermopsychodynamics could be said to update various sets of prohibitions that define earlier "fluid economies" (e.g., that semen must pass from one appropriate bodily interior to another, that certain fluids emitted by the body may not reenter it, and so on). Incest prohibitions that orient a "traffic in women" around the Name of the Father (the grain around which the pearl of patriarchy is cultured) thus come through Freud to be grafted back onto the laws of thermodynamics.

Likewise, the increasingly strident advocacy, through the middle to late eighteenth century, of the breast-feeding of infants by their own mothers (see Perry 1991) had defined the interiority of the middle-class nuclear family in a "real" fluid economy against the mother who wet-nurses another woman's child and the mother whose child is wet-nursed by another, both marked as "alienating" their resources from their own children. The mandate for mothers to breast-feed their own infants thus has the function of "erasing class differences among women" (Perry 1991, 234) by universalizing a middle-class construction of "naturalness" that enforces a nostalgic economy of "unmediated" relations between mother and infant. That is, in effect, the mixture of the circulatory systems of money and breast milk is prohibited in order to secure the fixture of the family and the female body (as well as distinguishing and opposing maternity to female sexuality) in a general "reconfiguration of class and gender within English society and the colonization of the female body for domestic life" (Perry 1991, 234).

If incest taboos define a prohibited interior (a kind of closeness or consanguinity in which sex is prohibited), "miscegenation" taboos construct an exterior beyond which sex is prohibited, a limit of exogamy. As in Malthus's scheme, though, a prohibited interior and exterior do not add up to a fixed and unproblematic structure. Again, an instability or unresolvable contradiction is established between difference within and difference between, since one is both prohibited from and mandated to engage in sex with someone who is different; one is both prohibited from and mandated to engage in sex with someone who is the same. Around this contradiction or double bind are constructed identity or status categories of race, class, gender, sexuality, and age, problematizing the interface between internal and external others.

The Hegemony of Hegemony: Wordsworth's Fractal Distinction

The long-term homeorrhesis of Romantic ideologemes is obvious in the contemporary resonance of Wordsworth's famous warning, in the "Preface" to *Lyrical Ballads*, against what would become "mass culture." Wordsworth sets the singular named individuals of "our elder writers,...Shakespeare and Milton," in noble opposition to the generic plurals of "frantic novels, sickly and stupid German tragedies, and deluges of idle and extravagant stories in Verse" (1969, 735). Not long after being spoken by a French king, "Après nous, le déluge" becomes available as the motto of every middle-class Englishman.

Wordsworth's choice of Milton and Shakespeare as "our elder writers" was at least radical in his day insofar as it assumes an English national literature as standard, leaving aside without comment the institutionally enforced standard of aristocratic cultural literacy, the Greek and Latin classics. Now after more than a century of institutionalized English Literature, it has become possible to acknowledge both the democratizing gestures of Wordsworth's "Preface" as well as the complex set of exclusions and pathologizations that legitimize them: Wordsworth hystericizes "women's" genres (e.g., "frantic novels") against a male poetic tradition, simultaneously marks and devalues working-class and aristocratic culture as "idle," characterizes German literature as an effeminizing foreign import, and so on. These intersecting exclusions in gender, class, and nation encode a normative standard for Romantic cultural power that endows only a contractual and fraternal subject with positive political agency (see Pateman 1989). The "Preface" participates in the epistemic change Foucault describes as "a privileged moment of *individualization*" and, in the rise of disciplinarity itself, as a new kind of power that works to "characterize, classify, specialize"; to "distribute along a scale, around a norm, hierarchize individuals in relation to one another and, if necessary, disqualify and invalidate" (Foucault 1984, 101, 212).

Wordsworth's opposition of generic plurals to singular authors is consistent with an ideology that sets specters of "the masses" against the bourgeois individual. In the preceding sentences of the "Preface," for example, the historicized and plural collectivity of "a multitude of causes . . . acting with a combined force" (charged further by the now obsolete reference of "combination" to labor organizing) is demonized in opposition to the naturalized, internalized, and universalized "discriminating powers of the mind." Rather than just opposing individual to mass, Wordsworth uses the opposition to produce another more dynamic counterpoint: many-uniting-as-one is set against one-differentiating-among-many. The "savage torpor" that the forces threaten to produce is coded as working-class or aristocratic through its opposition to the bourgeois "voluntary exertion" it undermines. The new aesthetic discourse feathers its nest with the ideological plumage of English nationalism, middle-classism, and masculinism. These cross-legitimizing ideologies inform each adjective; the objectivism of medical discourse gives the "Preface" its pathologizing force. Thus Wordsworth's manifesto derives its currency from a *collusion* among aesthetics, politics, and science, at the very moment their *autonomy* is being asserted, buttressed by bi-univocal oppositions (assertions of nonrelation) between art, politics, and science — oppositions that come to structure the discursive Imaginary of modern humanism. The microscopic ubiquity of discipline codes every word and sentence as the very principle of its production.

A Wordsworth sonnet and his commentary on it (in a letter to his patron, Lady Beaumont) illustrate how the paradigm of individuation works through poetry and through an evaluative literary criticism that further operationalizes it:

> With Ships the sea was sprinkled far and nigh,
> Like stars in heaven, and joyously it showed;
> Some lying fast at anchor in the road,
> Some veering up and down, one knew not why.

A goodly vessel did I then espy
Come like a giant from a haven broad;
And lustily along the bay she strode,
Her tackling rich, and of apparel high.
This Ship was nought to me, nor I to her,
Yet I pursued her with a Lover's look;
This Ship to all the rest did I prefer:
When will she turn, and whither? She will brook
No tarrying; where She comes the winds must stir:
On went She, and due north her journey took.
(1969, 205)

In his 1807 letter (Wordsworth and Wordsworth 1969, 145–51), Wordsworth compares the sonnet to a passage from *Paradise Lost* in which Hesperus—the evening star—is identified as a poetical object because of its natural preeminence over other stars (i.e., it is brighter). Wordsworth's ship, on the other hand, is "still more appropriate" as a poetical object precisely because it is "barely sufficiently distinguished" from its fellows and the difference has to be *made* by the poet. The literary "improvement" Wordsworth posits between Milton and himself is from aesthetic differences fixed by convention—like prices and social differences—toward a kind of "free market" in which difference "floats," allowing Wordsworth to invest his poetic capital to generate a profit. The ships are compared to randomly sprinkled stars in the first two lines; in the last line the single ship must head "due north" for the comparison with the North Star, which is not brighter but centered by scientific knowledge and human perspective to fixate the whole starry sphere.

The octave of Wordsworth's sonnet stresses the natural preeminence of the ship in aristocratic terms ("tackling rich" and "apparel high") and in sensual and mythic or prehuman terms ("like a giant . . . lustily"). In the sestet, it is instead the *lack* of inherent difference that is stressed ("this Ship was nought to me"): difference is produced by the poet's "free choice" in conjunction with the individual "free" agency of the ship, not out of mythic lust but humanist love "free" to choose—and to "make over"—its feminized object. That is, a version of what Clifford Siskin calls "the lyric turn" (15–20), performed self-referentially insofar as it aligns signifier (poetic form) and signified (itself an alignment between ship and narrator) in the act of "turning," is used to validate as a masternarrative and to mystify as a free aesthetic decision the transfer of power from a quasi-feudal aristocracy to a bourgeois hegemony that depends on the production of difference. The bourgeois "self-made" individual is distinguished not only from aristocratic distinction but also from "the masses," who are represented as either too firmly anchored or veering too randomly about. One chooses and one is chosen not because of inherent nobility (fixity of position) but because of one's directedness (fixity of motion); the poem's trick is to make the choice seem both entirely free and entirely inevitable; one is entirely self-directed as long as one blows with the wind. "Hitch your wagon to a star" becomes the motto for the "manifest destiny" of the poet and his critic. The poem directs you to distinguish yourself and your own tastes; aesthetic pleasure in this poem is the reward for exercising your judgmental, selective, normalizing power in preferring poetry and this poem "to all the rest"; the poem is not merely *about* individuation; normative individuation is its would-be-performative cultural function.

      Wordsworth's letter operationalizes the principle of aesthetic selectivity by making it a fractal principle. After implicitly chiding Mrs. Fermor, a friend of Lady Beaumont's who had criticized the poem, Wordsworth sugarcoats the pill: "I cannot but add a word or two upon my satisfaction in finding that my mind has so much in common with hers, and that we participate [in] so many of each other's pleasures. I collect this from her having singled out the two little Poems, the Daffodils, and the Rock crowned with snowdrops" (Wordsworth and Wordsworth 1969, 149). In other words, Mrs. Fermor qualifies as a member of the select and exclusive few because she selects—and excludes—a few poems, and within these poems, individual lines: "The line, 'Come, blessed barrier, etc.,' in the sonnet upon Sleep, which Mrs. F. points out, had before been mentioned to me by Coleridge, and indeed by almost everybody who had heard it, as eminently beautiful" (Wordsworth and Wordsworth 1969, 150). The truth of selectivity is produced by fractal self-similarity, operating across several "scales" to hierarchize poetry over other genres, individual poems over others, and individual lines within these poems; it informs the poetricentric Romantic/modernist fetish for precisely the right *word*.

      The author goes on to distinguish himself from the masses and the critics as a resolute and statuesque individual against an ephemeral swarm, and asserts with Coleridge "that every great and original writer, in proportion as he is great or original, must himself create the taste by which he is to be relished"; that is, intellectual and professional labor are valued for producing and directing desire. Desire, not labor, will power the developmental engine: "The mind being once fixed and roused, all the rest comes of itself."

      Just as Josiah Wedgwood had begun to produce expensive limited editions of pottery for the wealthy—the better to sell mass-produced sets of the same designs to the new middle class—so Wordsworth distributed limited editions of his poetry to "persons of eminence" in order to "quicken the sale of the work" (1967, 310) via emulative consumption and trickle-down aesthetics (see Siskin 1988, 159). Wordsworth and Coleridge will not merely follow but direct, distinguish, and validate Mrs. Fermor's and Lady Beaumont's tastes, and between them form the middle class in their image. The poem and the letter to Lady Beaumont are intelligible only as they participate in the marketplace even as they define themselves against it. It is no coincidence that Wordsworth, and Romantic poetry generally, has been used ever since to authorize a selective and exclusive cultural literacy at home, and abroad as a poet of choice for use in colonial schools.

> **Poem as Panopticon.** The identity-policing function of poetry is illustrated in Jamaica Kincaid's 1990 novel *Lucy* when the title character, a Caribbean woman working as a maid in the United States, remembers Wordsworth's "I Wandered Lonely" from her colonial schooling:
>
> > I remembered an old poem I had been made to memorize when I was ten years old and a pupil at Queen Victoria Girls' School. I had been made to memorize it, verse after verse, and then had recited the whole poem to an auditorium full of parents, teachers, and my fellow pupils. After I was done, everybody stood up and applauded with an enthusiasm that surprised me, and later they told me how nicely I had pronounced every word, how I had placed just the right amount of special emphasis in places where that was needed, and how proud the poet, now long dead, would have been to hear his words ringing out of my mouth. (Kincaid 1990a, 17–18)
>
> Mortified by her opportunistic assimilationism, Lucy made a "vow to erase from my mind, line by line, every word of that poem," but found the poem's work difficult to undo: she dreamed that night "that I was being chased down a narrow cobbled street by bunches and bunches of those same daffodils that I had vowed to forget, and when finally I fell down from exhaustion they all piled on top of me, until I was buried underneath them and was never seen again" (18). In an interview, Kincaid acknowledges that, like her narrator (named for Lucifer from *Paradise Lost*) and like "every colonial child," she had indeed been made to memorize Wordsworth, "a two-edged thing because I wouldn't have known how to write and how to think if I hadn't read those things" (1990b, 507).

Yet the aesthetic of selectivity can only work if it effaces its own politics as it seems to empty itself of content into a tautological and self-validating "sharing" of tastes. Thus Wordsworth asserts that the purposefulness of his poetry represents not a politically and professionally interested program but a "general principle or law of thought of our intellectual constitution"; namely,

that the mind can have no rest among a multitude of objects, of which it either cannot make one whole, or from which it cannot single out one individual, whereupon may be concentrated the attention divided among or distracted by a multitude[.] After a certain time we must either select one image or object, which must put out of view the rest wholly, or must subordinate them to itself. (Wordsworth and Wordsworth 1969, 148)

Wordsworth borrows the authority of constitutional law to socialize and naturalize the aesthetic problem of making wholes and singling out individuals.

It is, then, against a Romantic aesthetic that must seek singly directed individuals and wholes, and which responds to poems as individuals and wholes, that contemporary work in cultural studies takes as its problems collective categories such as class, race, nation, gender, and culture—categories not freely and exclusively defined but internally divided and ongoingly contested and implicated in power.

Junkyard. In 1988, someone smashed the door of my 1970 Chevy. A friend and I drove from Minneapolis to a junkyard in rural Minnesota, looking for a door. Windy Hill Salvage was a sublimely impressive site: forty acres of junked cars spread out over rolling hills under a big gray sky. I remembered what Eliot remembered that Dante had said to Virgil: "I didn't know death had undone so many." A huge man with a bushy beard and mud-splattered overalls—a former Hell's Angel named Tom, who worked at the junkyard—drove us around the forty acres in his pickup, looking for the right door. Tom sullenly resisted my attempts to make conversation, only cursing his job, his bosses, his truck, the weather. After about half an hour he had found several '70 Chevies that turned out, on closer inspection, to be too rusty or too damaged. Then, suddenly, his sneer softened into an almost beatific Mona Lisa smile, and he turned and met my eyes for the first time and said in a bemused tone, "Funny how those '70 Chevies jump out at you." When I asked what features enabled him to identify them (sometimes from blocks away and in various stages of decay), he just replied, "I don't know, they just jump out at you." It was as if he had said, "Beauty is Truth, Truth Beauty; that is all ye know on earth, and all ye need to know." The point was, though, that they jumped out at *him*, not us—that was why he was being paid. The distinction between him and us was his ability to make distinctions that we could not. Nor was his knowledge reducible to technicality (e.g., an ability to recognize certain discrete features), but it had that feature of professional knowledge called "indetermination": it depended on his acculturation as a reader of that forty-acre text and its historical and generic categories and particularities; it was not something he could simply tell us. His apparently aesthetic pleasure was not separable from the power relations between us. Not that professionalism or aesthetics can make a Mona Lisa out of a Hell's Angel but that both resistances and acquiescences to power are found in what gets situated as aesthetic pleasure; no less the case in that big salvage yard called Western Culture.

Mixing Mixture and Fixture: "The Clod and the Pebble"

> Love seeketh not Itself to please,
> Nor for itself hath any care;
> But for another gives its ease,
> And builds a Heaven in Hells despair.

So sang a little Clod of Clay,
Trodden with the cattles feet:
But a Pebble of the brook,
Warbled out these metres meet.

Love seeketh only Self to please,
To bind another to Its delight:
Joys in anothers loss of ease,
And builds a Hell in Heavens despite.
—William Blake

Blake's "The Clod and the Pebble" aligns the opposition of individual and collective with the related ideologeme of purity and mixing. The clod of clay, already a mixture of two elements, earth and water, is "trodden with the cattles feet"—mixed and dispersed still further—while the "pebble of the brook" retains the purity of its identity defensively as a single particle of dry earth holding its own against the flux of the water. The self-sacrificingness of the clod, "trodden with the cattles feet," works intertextually to transvalue Burke's "leveling" scenario of "learning . . . cast into the mire, and trodden down under the hoofs of a swinish multitude" (92), seeming to pathologize instead the sadistic masculinist and classist purity, binarity, and individualism of the pebble, although probably at the cost of sentimentalizing a kind of feminized masochism. Merely to note the political difference between Blake and Burke, though, is to miss how a generic differentiation and controlled mixing of poetry and politics defines both texts. Mixing *as* purity, the poem's code, backfires to define the category of literature *against* the discursive field it might have sought to infiltrate: is the clod of the pebble's party without knowing it? In this sense, the poem, in spite of itself, resembles the old joke that "there are two kinds of people: those who divide the world into two kinds and those who don't" or Leonard Cohen's assertion that "there is a war between the ones who say 'there is a war' and the ones who say 'there isn't'" (1993, 202). But, then again, it is also because it is a recursive machine—because it cannot help signifying "in spite of itself"—that it continues to sustain self-difference and counterperformativity as enabling contradictions as well as antagonisms.

Counterperformativity and Self-Difference: Elisabeth Hands

Elisabeth Hands, a servant and working-class wife as well as a poet, offers a different permutation of the individuation paradigm that alters its status in defining order and disorder, in her 1789 poem, "Written, originally extempore, on seeing a Mad Heifer run through the Village where the Author lives":

> When summer smiled, and birds on every spray
> In joyous warblings tuned their vocal lay,
> Nature on all sides showed a lovely scene,
> And people's minds were, like the air, serene;
> Sudden from th' herd we saw an heifer stray,
> And to our peaceful village bend her way.
> She spurns the ground with madness as she flies,
> And clouds of dust, like autumn mists, arise;
> Then bellows loud: the villagers, alarmed,
> Come rushing forth, with various weapons armed;
> Some run with pieces of old, broken rakes,
> And some from hedges pluck the rotten stakes;
> Here one in haste, with hand-staff of his flail,
> And there another comes with half a rail;
> Whips, without lashes, sturdy ploughboys bring,
> While clods of dirt and pebbles others fling.
> Voices tumultuous rend the listening ear:
> "Stop her," one cries; another, "Turn her there":
> But furiously she rushes past them all,
> And some huzza, and some to cursing fall.
> A mother snatched her infant off the road,
> Close to the spot of ground where next she trod;
> Camilla, walking, trembled and turned pale:
> See o'er her gentle heart what fears prevail!
> At last the beast, unable to withstand
> Such force united, leaped into a pond:
> The water quickly cooled her maddened rage;
> No more she'll fright our village, I presage.
> (Lonsdale 1990, 424–25)

To "identify" this poem by its genre or period, or by the gender or class of its author, may risk domesticating both differences and similarities between Hands's poem and the hegemonic Romantic standard that renders its identities problematic. The poem could be called a *satire* of the restrictive conformism of rural life and as such, opposed generically to Wordsworth's idealizations of the rural poor. The poem is arguably "pre-Romantic," as marked by its couplets, by its use of the discrete occasion as allegory (the female author as mad heifer) rather than weaving of poem and incident into Romantic "symbol," by its stress on conformity, and so on. The poem is arguably an example of "women's writing" and the socioeconomically enforced anxiety and self-deprecation of feminine authorship: if the commanding subject position that characterizes the narrator of Wordsworth's sonnet marks his privilege, Hands marks her own socioeconomic destiny to be received as a curiosity. The important point here is not so much that the poem originates in a subject position (an observation that tends to reify class and gender) but that (as in the Wordsworth sonnet) it considers how the act of writing may be allowed to rebound upon a subject manufactured in its wake. Like Wordsworth's sonnet, then, Hands's poem elaborates the social facts of its own writing and reception.

In any case, the differences and similarities between Hands's scenario and Wordsworth's are manifold. The fractal resonance or overdetermination of master narratives in the Wordsworth texts, the overcoding that cements their monumentality, the extent to which they still "resonate" in the near ubiquity of disciplinary micropower—all these can be opposed to the flat underdetermination of the key turns in Hands's narrative.

The mad heifer distinguishes herself from both the herd and the crowd, and from individuals who are not individuated but merely recognizable "types" of women (the concerned mother and the rural maid). The paradigmatic opposition of one to many is operative in the poem, but it is not *aligned* with other oppositions: collectives are both animal and human, the individual is animal and female; order and disorder are not divided between the individual and the group, and the scenario is not a unidirectional tale of deterioration or progress, nor even quite the Romantic spiral back to "the same but different." Wordsworth's ship establishes its singularity as the narrator looks on from above, while Hands's heifer ends up leaping into a pond: the trajectory of the poem is toward reembeddedness rather than transcendence. The situating of individuation as madness, as animal, as female, and as temporary can be read as a negative example corroborating a Romantic individualism that is sane, human, masculine, and eternally progressive. But Hands's heifer is no Byronic hero; the primary distinction is that neither her escape nor her recapture are heroic or tragic (charging the individuation scenario with power and danger) but, at least according to the Romantic norm, curiously matter-of-fact. The flat facticity of the swerves in the narrative can be read as a hermeneutic challenge (too easily "solved" by calling it ironic) but can only be activated as a theoretical difference: the poem analyzes power not as an internalization scenario but as a set of social techniques, a "literal" gauntlet of what Foucault calls the "tiny, everyday, physical mechanisms" that constitute disciplinary "systems of micropower" (1984, 211).

There is something else besides the difference between confidence and anxiety (and the social positions that inform them) in the contrast between Wordsworth's assertion, in the letter to Lady Beaumont, of his "invincible confidence that my writings (and among them these little poems) will co-operate with the benign tendencies in human nature" and Hands's very different prophecy of her reception: "some huzza and some to cursing fall." Rather than imagining the progress of her text in a moral economy, Hands offers only a flat and undercoded but nonhierarchizable opposition between "some" and "some."

Two other Hands poems imagine their reception in explicit detail: "A Poem, On the Supposition of an Advertisement appearing in a Morning Paper, of the Publication of a Volume of Poems, by a Servant-Maid" and "A Poem, On the Supposition of the Book having been Published and Read" (Lonsdale 1990, 425–29). These poems commit the Romantic generic sin of exploring how their reception will be constrained by a system of gender and class that implicates both readers and author. Rather than mystifying and internalizing the social conditions of production and reception, these poems make the productively impossible demand that they be read *counterperformatively*: they can be validated as poetry only by denying them the dismissive reception that they imagine for themselves.

To say that Hands's poems merely elaborate her self-description as one "born in obscurity, and never emerging beyond the lower stations of life" (Lonsdale 1990, 422), may be to underwrite the masternarrative of individuation and professionalization. Hands writes, and even writes about writing, *without becoming a writer*. This mark of exclusion is, even as it is being marked, also claimed as a mark of resistance: she writes *in order not to become a writer*. It is here that an aporia can be established between Sayre and Löwy's characterization of Romanticism as a problematically retroactive "opposition to capitalism in the name of pre-capitalist values" and what might be called resistance to Romanticism in the name of post-capitalist values. Hands's "failure" to become a writer is in this sense articulable with Marx's dream that one could, in a postcapitalist society, "hunt in the morning, fish in the afternoon, rear cattle in the evening, criticize after dinner…, without ever becoming hunter, fisherman, shepherd or critic" (Marx 1972, 160).

In the Wake of the Book: "The Mask of Anarchy"

The significance of Hands's resistance to making the pacification of the "mad heifer" into a moral masternarrative appears more starkly when the poem is set alongside Percy Shelley's "Mask of Anarchy," where the transformation of a female figure from hysteria to serenity is made to signify the progressivist victory of a chaoticized and aestheticized hegemonic power over coercion and oppression.

Shelley wrote "The Mask of Anarchy" in 1819, in Italy, upon hearing that mounted English troops had charged a crowd of protesters gathered in Manchester to rally for parliamentary reform (ten were killed, many more wounded). Mary Shelley copied out the poem, and they sent it to Leigh Hunt for publication in *The Examiner*. Hunt, afraid of prosecution for sedition, did not publish the poem until 1832; that is, not until after many of the reforms that the rally and poem had been intended to further had already been passed (see Shelley 1977, 301n).

Shelley carefully styled his poem to the cultural class of the audience he imagined. Like Hands's "Mad Heifer," "The Mask of Anarchy" is an "occasional" piece fixed to an event ("Written on the Occasion of the Massacre at Manchester"), intended for a middlebrow, journal-reading audience. It employs traditional features such as its familiar tetrameter couplets and the rather passé or déclassé figures of personification and allegory around which it is structured. Most important, it violates the bourgeois opposition between poetry and politics by its explicitly propagandistic message of nonviolent resistance.

Shelley's *Prometheus Unbound*, on the other hand, differs diametrically in every respect. Written (as Shelley asserts in his preface to the poem) "to familiarize the highly refined imagination of the more select classes of poetical readers with beautiful idealisms of moral excellence" (135), it was published as the title piece of an authorial volume, and it is keyed to the highbrow cultural literacy of its audience, elaborating classical mythology rather than current events in epic unrhymed blank verse in which complex "lyrical insertions" are interwoven (i.e., an "organic form" rather than a conventionally regular pattern). Eschewing, in *Prometheus Unbound*, the déclassé figures of allegory and personification, Shelley weaves the complex relations between characters into an ambiguous and multireferential symbology. Far from forwarding an explicit political program, Shelley here strategically announces in his preface that "didactic poetry is my abhorrence" (135).

Shelley's schematic polarity between high- and lowbrow poetry functions not as a static structure but as the pretext for a carefully engineered mixing.

"The Mask of Anarchy" problematizes the relation of order and disorder from the outset. It may be, at first, surprising that the poem associates Anarchy not with the absence of government but with its too thoroughgoing tyranny, but the poem supports this association by showing how government establishes and maintains its own order at the ongoing expense of disorganizing and anarchizing the masses. "Trampling to a mire of blood / The adoring multitude," Anarchy and his troops shake the ground, "tearing up, and trampling down" everything in sight (302, 305), anticipating the fascistic fantasy of the heroic and phallic soldier slogging through the slimy and disarticulated bodies of the masses (see Theweleit 1987, 244–49, 385–435).

The identification of order gained at the expense of the disorder that it produces explains Anarchy as a description not of what government *is* but what it *does*, the polarity between the two suggesting another ironic contradiction in the perfect metaphorical self-similarities of the Great Chain of Being. The problematization of order and disorder between individual and mass and between governors and governed (or the dialectic between them) enables the scenario that follows: a new kind of order will have to be produced in order to resolve the contradiction.

The appearance of Hope, the first personification associated with the crowd, indicates that a solution is imminent. But she is a "maniac maid" who looks "more like Despair"; she runs obliquely by the crowd and lies down, waiting to be trampled,

> When between her and her foes
> A mist, a light, an image rose,
> Small at first, and weak, and frail
> Like the vapour of a vale:
>
> Till as clouds grow on the blast,
> Like tower-crowned giants striding fast
> And glare with lightnings as they fly,
> And speak in thunder to the sky,
>
> It grew — a Shape arrayed in mail
> Brighter than the Viper's scale
> And upborne on wings whose grain
> Was as the light of sunny rain.
>
> On its helm, seen far away,
> A planet, like the Morning's, lay;
> And those plumes its light rained through
> Like a shower of crimson dew.

With step as soft as wind it past
O'er the heads of men—so fast
That they knew the presence there,
And looked,—but all was empty air.

As flowers beneath May's footstep waken
As stars from Night's loose hair are shaken
As waves arise when loud winds call
Thoughts sprung where'er that step did fall.

And the prostrate multitude
Looked—and ankle-deep in blood,
Hope that maiden most serene
Was walking with a quiet mien;

And Anarchy, the ghastly birth,
Lay dead earth upon the earth.
(304–5)

Unlike the named personifications that have preceded it, the ambiguous "Shape" is described by Shelley's elaborate stylistic signature: the stringing of simile upon simile like a strange attractor around the "empty air" of its never-specified identity. It is at this turning point, then, that Shelley shifts to "high" gear, from allegory to Romantic symbology. The "Mask" began with personifications fixed not only to allegorical qualities but also to named contemporary historical figures (e.g., "I met Murder on the way— / He had a mask like Castlereagh"). The double fixture of sign and referent is characteristic of the masque, a courtly dramatic performance in which allegorical figures were often designed to flatter the royal family and courtiers who were to play the parts. Here, though, the poem works to sophisticate the common reader, to wean him from referentiality and "familiarize" him with the operation of the symbol. Rather than doubly anchoring itself to single referents, it produces its new strategic truth as a form of circulation among multiple similes that are themselves images of multiplicity (e.g., clouds, lightnings, flowers, stars, and waves) and ongoing transformation. The death of Anarchy and conversion of Hope from hysterical "maniac maid" to "maiden most serene" (a latter-day psychopharmacologist's dream) is to be *performatively* accomplished through the writerly discipline by which Shelley would transform his audience.

It is also at this point, then, that the poem turns back onto itself, seeking to rebind to itself the energies it calls forth: the Shape "is" the poem's intersection with itself. The telltale self-referential moment imagines the poem's own distribution in real space-time (as it participates in the dissemination or circulation of knowledge via print culture) as a series of footsteps that cause thoughts to spring up (that is, at each subsequent time and place where the poem is read). The curious absent presence of the object is explicable insofar as the poem does not really inhere in any given copy but is rather defined by the community of readers organized by its distribution (especially insofar as it was to circulate in the relatively ephemeral form of the journal). Unlike the Anarchy it vanquishes, the text exerts power not by distinguishing itself from its objects but by organizing them in its own image, in its wake. The sudden microscopic detail of the grain of wing feathers and flashy "Viper's scale"—webs of branchings and interlocked articulations—introduce fractal networks across which play the more subtle or liquid energies of light, water, and color. Postmodern versions of this apotheosis of print culture recycle Shelley's vision into networks of fiber-optic cable alive with laser-light information, a virtual world arrayed in e-mail.

The intervention of the "Shape" operates differently from the hierarchized binary of governor and governed (in which local order is maintained through its production of global disorder). Textual organization is a dissipative process, a *common disturbance* that, like Wordsworth's "something" that "rolls through all things," aligns and subsumes the dimensions through which it operates. Shelley's metastasizing flowers, falling stars, and rising waves are, in turn, merely types of the dynamic turbulence represented as the wake of the circulation of the book through cultural space-time, of thoughts through things.

Predictably, Shelley's new order is attained at the cost of exclusion. Until the poem's turn, Shelley's crowds resembled the actual crowd that gathered at Saint Peter's Fields in Manchester—which (like most mass protests of the day) included men, women, and children—while Shelley's allegorical figures had been male. After the intervention of the Shape, though, a single female allegorical figure, Mother Earth, addresses an imagined all-male mass audience ("sons of England") to act on her behalf, fitting insofar as "universal male suffrage" was the reformist goal. The new dissipative order is thus produced on behalf of a fraternal political subject predicated on its exclusion of "the disorder of women."

The Roughness of the Beast: "The Second Coming"

Turning and turning in the widening gyre
The falcon cannot hear the falconer;
Things fall apart; the center cannot hold;

Mere anarchy is loosed upon the world,
The blood-dimmed tide is loosed, and everywhere
The ceremony of innocence is drowned;
The best lack all conviction, while the worst
Are full of passionate intensity.
Surely some revelation is at hand;
Surely the Second Coming is at hand.

The Second Coming! Hardly are those words out
When a vast image out of *Spiritus Mundi*
Troubles my sight: somewhere in sands of the desert
A shape with lion body and the head of a man,
A gaze blank and pitiless as the sun,
Is moving its slow thighs, while all about it
Reel shadows of the indignant desert birds.
The darkness drops again, but now I know
That twenty centuries of stony sleep
Were vexed to nightmare by a rocking cradle,
And what rough beast, its hour come round at last,
Slouches toward Bethlehem to be born?
—William Butler Yeats

Yeats's "Second Coming" describes the phenomenon of increasing entropy quite explicitly in the hydrodynamically specific figures of the widening spiral (a pattern of turbulence and fingerprint of nonlinear dynamical systems) and the rising flood tide (a normally local, orderly, and periodic event amplified into a global dissolution). Single words echo and intensify these more fully developed entropic figures: "anarchy" (nearly synonymous, here, with entropy), "loosed" (let go, melted), "troubles" and "vexed" (denoting turbulence), and "vast" (denoting not only immensity but the waste of countless undifferentiable particles like the "sands of the desert," a nice figure for the universal entropic state called "heat death").

As it turns out, the poem does not merely propose a unidirectional movement toward entropic heat death, but a reorganization, a phase transition. The widening gyre is, after all, only half of the picture of interpenetrating spirals that made up Yeats's figure of cyclical history: the Yeatsian universe does not simply explode outward toward heat death from an originary big bang but is "a great egg that turns inside-out perpetually without ever breaking its shell" (Yeats 1966, 33).

As its title suggests, the poem also looks back to the advent of Christ, which it represents as an earlier world-historical phase transition (although the whole poem works to throw into question what comes as a savior and what as a destroyer and whether these arrive simultaneously or in succession). Just as the next one will, the earlier transition has arisen out of an apparently innocuous and periodic event, "a rocking cradle" (metonym for the infant Christ). In fact, an accelerating rocking motion can be represented in what is called "phase space" as a spiraling. This rocking is apparently to be understood as another kind of oscillation that—propagating and amplifying itself like a seismic wave and inducing a sympathetic vibration, a transdimensional resonance—has shaken even the monolithic order of "stony sleep" into the entropic "sands" from which the nightmarish "shape" (presumably a sandstone sphinx) of the new order pulls itself together. The new order is represented as a more virulent return of that which had been superseded by the old (hence the return of the sphinx of premonotheistic Egypt).

If it is clear that phase transition can generally be described as a shifting reconfiguration of stony order and sandy disorder in the space of culture, it is also clear that something in or out of the poem escapes this generality—an indignant noise kicked upstairs to the higher dimension of time, where, by the author's sleight of hand, it seems to disappear without a trace (or does it?) into the pure and perfectly periodic eternal ticktock of cycles that Yeats maintains at the expense of lower-dimensional (spatial) flux.

It is apparent, at any rate, that Yeats envisions the entropic scenario as involving violations of hierarchical difference of some enormity, not only in the falling apart of things, but in their (subsequent and/or simultaneous) falling together. Like the classical image of the charioteer losing control of his horses, Yeats's falcon escaping the falconer's control works as an allegory of the disjunction of mind and body, human and animal, spirit and matter, and so on—as well as an allegory of allegory, of the loss of referentiality in the disjunction of signifier and signified. But the image of the conjunction of categories in the "rough beast" is no less frightening. The next phase seems to be emblematized by a conflation of animal rapacity, human cunning, and the relentless inevitability of a mechanism. The possibility of resistance or of differing, meanwhile, has been reduced to a mere reeling shadow—not even a possibility at all but an indignant fading memory of the previous phase, an ineffectual two-dimensional scribble (like a poem) on the entropic, shifting sands at the feet of the new higher-dimensional order.

One might attempt at length to differentiate between the narrative voice of the poem and Yeats's own (that is, to determine where the poem might be called ironic in a classical sense) and between the nuances of these voices—between Yeats's or the narrator's fear and excitement and disappointment and shock and acceptance—or between what is asserted as knowledge about the past ("now I know") and what is posed as a question about the future ("And what...?") and between these voices and positions and one's own. Each of these issues is indeterminate enough so that each reader will decide (or may *feel* without seeming to decide) for her- or himself, and open enough even so that one reader may feel or decide differently at different times, making the poem not a crystal ball in which the future of the world can be seen but a mood ring, a dime-store oracle, infallible in its ambiguity: you make of it what you wish, what you fear; you read only yourself there, and in the reading reconfigure or reconfirm your own desires and fears. Here again, then, Yeats achieves his famous wish to become a machine, a mechanical bird singing "of what is past, or passing, or to come" (1956, 192).

Nonetheless something escapes the mutual construction of poem and reader; for one thing, something sticks to you when you walk through the poem—in spite of irony and indeterminacy, and especially in spite of the most careful deliberations. Yeats's final question, for example, appears to be an open-ended one: you can decide for yourself what or who the "rough beast" might be (that is, the question of its referentiality is addressed to you), but in so doing—in accepting the terms of the poem—you may have lost sight of your right to assert that the beast is really smooth, not a beast, and no slouch, either. Yeats asks a sneaky and manipulative question; as if one were to ask a child, "What kind of squash do you want for dinner?" Very few children but many sophisticated readers of poems fall for this trick.

At the most vulgar level of response, then, there seems to be in the poem no question that the future looks pretty rough. It's a horror show, and the monster has won, or is winning, or will win, if only for a millenium or so. But one finds that one can even accept the terms of the poem and still assert what one wants, as if a child were to respond, "I want ice-cream squash." Sticky questions deserve sticky answers.

In Benoit Mandelbrot's *Fractal Geometry of Nature*, the theoretician proclaims his own arrival and the advent of his theory as the monstrous offspring of violated discursive boundaries, especially as the study of fractals and chaos represents a serious miscegenation of "pure mathematics" and dirty, inexact, and applied sciences like climatology (in which important chaotic paradigms were developed). The study of fractals seems to reverse the traditional hierarchy between the abstract formalism of theory and the practice of computer technologies. Even the behavior of an equation must be studied as it is iterated, played out on a computer graphics screen, as if one had discovered a creature with a new kind of agency, determined yet unpredictable, and had discovered that one must study it in the field, like an anthropologist—even as if one were only looking through the wrong end of a telescope at one's own culture.

Among the central exhibits of chaos theory are geometrical figures first suggested in mathematics by Poincaré late last century but largely ignored or stigmatized by mainstream mathematicians as a "Gallery of Monsters," an epithet Mandelbrot proudly reclaims as a badge of honor, but then recuperates as a "museum of Science" (1982, 9). Poincaré had made only a few remarkably uninteresting sketches; the irreducible role of the computer in visualizing *persuasively* these beastly figures has made it impossible even for a scientist to ignore the nonlinear interdependence of knowledge, rhetoric, figurality, technology, history—well, almost impossible. Even so, fractals have begun to leave strange footprints through assorted academic fields.

Like Yeats's beast, fractals are characterized by their "roughness." Each gear-tooth serration of a nondifferentiable curve such as the Koch curve is serrated by smaller teeth and so on *ad infinitesimum*. A normal gear edge is rough to human hands but smooth to a dust mite crawling along it and rough again (because of tiny irregularities) to a microorganism; the Koch curve is irreducibly rough, rough *mise en abîme*. In fact, the designation "fractal" (as in "fracture") refers to roughness; fractal dimension is, very roughly, a measure of roughness across scale.

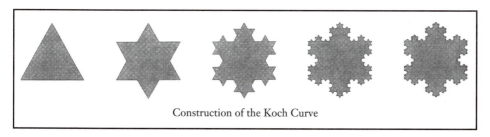

Construction of the Koch Curve

Yeats's beast is also rough—in the sense of "unfinished"—because it has not yet been born (presumably this is also why it "slouches," having no coherent agency but the inevitability of accident and gravity). So too the irreducibility of fractal roughness ensures that such figures (like the retroactive fictional configuration called Romanticism or the proleptic fictional configuration called chaos theory) cannot quite be born, cannot quite become fully incarnate in the world, since their infinitesimal detail can never be fully represented on computer screens, whose resolution is necessarily limited to a certain number of pixels per square inch (as matter generally may be limited by its particularity). And yet they are born, impossibly, somehow, and yet technologies are elaborated around them and vice versa; they do things in the "real world"; the hare does overtake the tortoise or they mate and their monstrous offspring finish the race together. To recognize the provisionality of every discursive configuration is to acknowledge that the slouchy agency of the not-yet-quite-born may be the only agency there is or ever has been.

Yeats rehearses the arrival of a regime whose story is that it is always "past, or passing, or to come." To prophesy that a discursive earthquake and a monstrous new age are arriving is also, after all, only to affirm what may always be the case: the discursive body is always falling apart and together, always rough and slouching. For this reason, that which announces itself as a rough beast may be more trustworthy than that which asserts its smoothness and humanity: the only radical text is that in which the monster wins without ceasing to be a monster and where the victory is cause for rejoicing.

Serrations. Just south of San Francisco, alongside Interstate 280 (which the signs remind us is the "World's Most Beautiful Freeway"), is a small lake nestled in the San Andreas Fault. When I used to travel that road, I would sometimes see birds floating upward in a slow spiral column in the air currents above that lake and remember those famous lines ("Turning and turning..."). The freeway is officially named for Father Junipero Serra, a missionary recently beatified (hence the unofficial designation as "The World's Most Beatified Freeway")— beatified in spite of Serra's participation in both the blatant and subtle practices of genocide against the Native American peoples who once lived there. For some peoples, the arrival Yeats seems to foretell in "The Second Coming," the arrival of what he calls in *A Vision* "the most implacable authority the world has ever known," has taken place long ago. What comes in the name of Christ or "the human" also has its teeth.

T H R E E

Fractal Logics of Romanticism:
Concentricity and Eccentricity

Wheel within Wheel: Blake's Recursive Physics

... the Twelve Sons of Albion

Enrooted into every Nation: a mighty Polypus growing

From Albion over the whole Earth: such is my awful Vision.

. . . .

I see the Past, Present & Future, existing all at once

Before me; O Divine Spirit sustain me on thy wings!

That I may awake Albion from his long & cold repose.

For Bacon & Newton sheathd in dismal steel, their terrors hang

Like iron scourges over Albion, Reasonings like vast Serpents

Infold around my limbs, bruising my minute articulations

> I turn my eyes to the Schools & Universities of Europe
>
> And there behold the Loom of Locke whose Woof rages dire
>
> Washd by the Water-wheels of Newton. black the cloth
>
> In heavy wreathes folds over every Nation; cruel works
>
> Of many Wheels I view, wheel without wheel, with cogs tyrannic
>
> Moving by compulsion each other: not as those in Eden: which
>
> Wheel within Wheel in freedom revolve in harmony & peace
> —William Blake

Blake's opposition of the "wheel without wheel" (i.e., the chain of cogs) that character-izes mechanist physics to the "freedom . . . harmony & peace" of "wheel within wheel" offers an obvious place to investigate the interface between the two faces (bad cop and good cop) of Romantic disciplinarity.

   The passage from *Jerusalem* maximizes both difference and sim-ilarity between images to suggest the thoroughness of disciplinary saturation and im-perial expansionism across various realms. The assembled figures represent vegetable, mineral, and animal nature as well as military, industrial, mercantile, and educational culture; crucial features are divided between various groupings of the multiple images.

   If the cogs and waterwheels (like Blake's more famous "dark Sa-tanic Mills") represent the crude, rotary articulations of machinery, related images such as the "polypus" (that is, either an octopus or branching tumor), "scourges," and "serpents" are characterized by seamlessly nonarticulated, flexible, plural, and linear extension; while the coat of mail or plated armor ("sheathd in dismal steel") and woven "cloth in heavy wreathes" characterize a power that operates as a rigor-ously interlinked planar collusion of forces. The concatenation of images seems to be governed by a logic that works to exhaust reconfigurations of the same set of fea-tures; thus, for example, the coat of mail and oxymoronic "iron scourges" conspicu-ously yoke hardness with flexibility, while flexibility is conjoined with softness in the figures of cloth and polypus. The proverbial ability of the polypus to grow a new head and tail when cut in half makes it (like *Terminator 2*'s liquid-metal man — or like that sublime object of eugenics, the human genome) a nicely gothic figure for disciplinary reproduction and indestructibility.

Blake's strategy for representing disciplinarity, then, mimics the disciplinary strategy itself, offering multiple images, each characterized by constellations of multiple features, subject in turn to multiple groupings that maximize both similarity and difference to cover the figurative field with their recombinations. But against this strategy of coverage and overdetermination, Blake sets the seductively underdetermined excess of the "wheel within wheel" of Edenic physics.

The configurations of features assembled in Blake's disciplinary figures very closely resemble the problematics of eighteenth-century atomic theory, which seems to be primary among the objects of Blake's caricature. The inherited distinction between metaphysics and physics continued, through the eighteenth century, to contribute to conserving the apparent contradiction between the rotary movement that seemed to dominate in heavenly orbits and the straight-line inertial motion that had been written into law for at least the sublunary world. These distinctions also participated in conserving serious disjunctions between the laws of astronomy and chemistry. Furthermore, debate about the nature of matter revolved around questions of atomic discretion or extension, hardness or softness, elasticity or brittleness; that is, versions of the same features distributed among Blake's images. The widely accepted (but by no means uncontested) Newtonian "hard" atom had come into contradiction with another widely held tenet, that of the conservation of vital force (*vis viva*), since force inevitably must be lost when absolutely hard particles collide, leading to the unacceptable conclusion that the universe is "running down." Newton's solution to this dilemma had been to propose a God who continually intervenes to "wind up" the universal clock, while Descartes and others sought to integrate compensatory explanations and mechanisms without appealing to divine intervention; that is, to make science and its universe eternally self-sufficient. But neither the drive toward disciplinary self-sufficiency nor the deus ex machina solution (which depends upon an originary bracketing off of religion from science so that it can return as needed) could keep logical contradiction out of the charmed circle of what would later be called "physics." Not until 1931, when Goedel's famous theorem was proven, could the impossibility of self-sufficient logical systems be demonstrated in scientific terms.

Newton compared the force lost on impact between inelastic particles to "motion communicated by means of stirring to such liquids as molten pitch, oil, and water," which "is quickly lost" (Scott 1970, 4). Although Descartes's atom could bounce, it didn't get a chance to, since Cartesian space was absolutely full of matter, consisting of particles (unlike Newton's) both divisible and brittle, in which forces are communicated by the rotating and grinding of particle against particle (avoiding the problem of action at a distance); this grinding produces fine matter that fills up all the interstices between the particles. Blake's "cogs tyrannic" and "dark Satanic Mills" are particularly geared to caricature the grinding of this Cartesian plenum. So while the otherwise bouncy fullness of the plenum always threatened to petrify into a brittle china shop, Newtonian hard atoms in their void paradoxically threatened to produce a universal quagmire of viscosity. No perfect distribution of features could eliminate these dangerous tendencies. Accordingly, contradictions within the disciplinary hegemony of Newton's empty, static space (in which matter is embedded and moves), in conjunction with contradictions between it and other arrangements (such as the plenum, a fullness of moving matter), will eventually produce the synthesis of matter and space that characterizes modernist physics (together with its canonized paradox of particle and wave), as well as determining its discursive unconscious in the form of what Lacan would call a "pattern of the gaps in play": embedded emptinesses moving through matter in a seductive reversal of the Newtonian model. Theories of chaos may hold out, in turn, a provisional synthesis or conflation of the Newtonian model with its Other that displaces the disciplinary fault lines among them.

In the meantime, the "conflict between atomism and conservation theory," along with related sets of contradictions I have begun to suggest here, generated various explanations through the eighteenth and nineteenth centuries: that absolute hardness is a limit case only approached in nature by "infinitesmally soft" atoms, that attraction and collision between hard atoms are buffered by repulsive forces at short distances, that hard atoms reside in elastic molecules or in clouds of "caloric" or in an (almost) perfectly elastic "ether," and so on. The productive viability of these contradictions continued until what Wilson Scott calls "the change from a hard cosmos to an elastic cosmos circa 1860" (1970, 296). The new elastic universe was made to order for both the ideological and technical requirements of a socioeconomic system organizing itself around the flux and transformability of commodities and currency.

Blake's short poem "Mock On" offers a more explicit and schematic critique of atomism, and points toward the crux of the contradiction at its heart:

> Mock on Mock on Voltaire Rousseau
> Mock on Mock on tis all in vain!
> You throw the sand against the wind
> And the wind blows it back again

And every sand becomes a Gem
Reflected in the beams divine
Blown back they blind the mocking Eye
But still in Israels paths they shine

The Atoms of Democritus
And Newtons Particles of light
Are sands upon the Red sea shore
Where Israels tents do shine so bright
(477–78)

The poem counterposes the extended and continuous wave form of wind (related to the "beams" of light) to the punctual discretion of Newtonian or Democritan atoms (represented as grains of sand), seeming to favor the former. But the concluding image marks the binary division (i.e., recursive wave and punctual particle), in turn, as strategic rather than essential by problematizing the act of division itself: it remains a pointedly open question whether the "Red sea shore" refers to a given and carceral boundary between categorically different entities (Egypt and Zion, land and water) or a liberatory path through, a constitutive "parting" or "departure" that performs difference on what was otherwise the same (water divided from water).

But more important, the act of positing the atom is depicted as producing a recursive backlash that rebounds upon the positer. The figure of recursion opposes and exceeds both the mechanistic separation of Newtonian subjects and objects bound by one-way causal chains and the self-canceling symmetry of the equal-and-opposite (reactionary) universe.

Blake's 1807 letter to the *Monthly Magazine* develops the model of recursion. Blake writes to register his indignation at the police arrest and imprisonment of an astrologer: "The Man who can Read the Stars. often is opressed by their influence, no less than the Newtonian who reads Not & cannot Read is opressed by his own Reasonings & Experiments. We are all subject to Error" (1982, 769). The upshot is not only that disciplines (e.g., astrology and Newtonian science) produce and are subject to the worlds in which they operate (i.e., "live by the sword, die by the sword"), but that this production necessarily is flawed with ironies that cannot be foreclosed: no prophecy can be self-fulfilling without also becoming self-thwarting as well.

This principle continues to be underrepresented in contemporary accounts of discursive construction: Edward Said's parable of how discourse subsumes the world is a telling example. Said describes how books on the fierceness of lions (regardless of what lions' "actual" character may be) privilege observations of fierceness in readers' firsthand experiences of lions. These observations are buttressed by other books that propose origins of the fierceness and ways of handling it, further tending to reduce the lion to the quality of "fierceness." Finally, "reality" begins to yield to its representation when "the ways by which it is recommended that a lion's fierceness be handled will actually *increase* its fierceness, force it to be fierce" (1978, 93–94). Said's vignette, besides being inflected by the Romantic false hope or nostalgia for unmediated encounter with "reality," may also underwrite his too thoroughgoing attribution of creative agency to Western Orientalist discourse in producing its Other—as if the West were not also vulnerable, via something like its own "countertransference," to construction in the same encounter. Even so, this kind of truth production (that is, production in and against one's own image) might deserve to define a political will to power, leaving the curiously distracted, inertial, or unthinking resistance to such production to be situated not as cultural integrity or pure particularity or opposing material interests but as a Will to Play or a Perversity Principle.

In any case, Blake's point differs from Said's (at least in emphasis) in that neither discursive recursion in the form of self-amplification nor self-canceling can be perfectly "true" (that is, it cannot either simply reproduce or negate itself), hence the inescapable subjection to "error." Ironically, and in a strange but characteristic validation of Blake's point about how assertions rebound, the journal's editor returned Blake's letter to him, unpublished. Blake continually staked his career (in a very material sense that will be the subject of a later section) on the dubious security that that which cannot be said or which can be said repeatedly but not heard or understood—that is, what a given discursive configuration excludes as its foundational act—is at once its origin and center, its truth and its eventual vanquisher. If the Romantic polarization of poetry and politics enabled Shelley to claim poets as "unacknowledged legislators of the world," Blake could be confident—although or even *because* he was even less read in his day than Shelley—that he was "more famed *in heaven* than I could well conceive" (710, my emphasis), member of a "shadow canon" that would come to have its fifteen minutes of fame sometime in the future. Related Blakean constructions depend on this neat topological trick:

It indeed appear'd to Reason as if Desire was cast out. but the Devils account is, that the Messiah fell. & formed a heaven of what he stole from the Abyss. (34–35)

the Giants who formed this world into its sensual existence and now seem to live in it in chains; are in truth. the causes of its life & the sources of all activity. (40)

This is a crucial trick (since it traces a way of questioning the power and hegemony of hegemonic power), but it also tends to slide toward the antipode of Said's success-breeds-success model of discursive expansionism, becoming its silent partner; that is, toward the neutralizingly ironic or avant-gardist logic that can become stuck on success-as-failure and failure-as-success.

The two juxtapositions of Blakean recursion with Newtonian physics are especially pointed in that it is precisely this recursion that the mechanist physics of Blake's era leaves out of the account. This exclusion produces a kind of truth in turn, since it is what allows recursion *to recur*; the coming-back-to-haunt (return of the discursively repressed) is what comes back to haunt; the recursion of recursion constitutes its "truth." Although the eventual product and model of this process will be that darling of chaos theory, the "feedback loop," to assert that Blakean recursion anticipates theories that would not emerge until almost two hundred years later is neither a testament to Blake's prophetic genius nor to the liberatory or redemptive nature of chaos. It is rather a discursive or recursive effect of oppositions within and among literature, science, politics, and religion that were activated in Romanticism. Simply to describe such discursive effects in turn as subject to chaotic explanation is part of a chaotic will to power that must remain an ambivalent part of this project. In any case, to read Blake as "ahead of his time," anticipating various forms of anti-Newtonianism that would eventually find their way firmly back into physics, is also to forget that the coherence of the Newtonian position and the incoherence of antiatomism have always been provisional and often retroactive constructions of a range of conflicting positions.

Another form of recursion was suggested by Roman Jakobson (1960, 350–77), who identified the "poetic" function in language as that aspect of a message that refers to *itself.* No utterance, according to Jakobson, can perform a single function; rather, difference between utterances does not reside in their uniqueness of kind but in their different hierarchies of the same set of (six) functions. This classical structuralist relativism allows analysis of discursive interpenetration (against an essentialist fixation of discursive identities), but only by ossifying a supposedly transdiscursive structure in a way that prohibits certain questions. This articulation into functions and their various combinative hierarchies, which seem to exhaust or "cover" the linguistic field, characterizes disciplinarity itself.

The Romantic disciplinary split between politics and aesthetics, for example, meant that the reactionary political journal, *The Anti-Jacobin,* could publish radical poetry with the winking acknowledgment that "what We should call good Politics, are inconsistent with the spirit of true Poetry" (1797, 4), while Tom

Paine could damn Burke's *Reflections* by asserting that it "degenerates into a composition of art" (1973, 288), and Keats could echo the denunciations of Wordsworth's politically programmatic poetry by stating baldly that "we hate poetry that has a palpable design on us" (1970, 61). Similarly, the discursive split between the scientific and literary authorizes hybrids only as lower (or "sterile") forms: it became possible in early-nineteenth-century England to write a science fiction novel (Mary Shelley's *Frankenstein*) in which scientific and literary authority are thematized as a volatile mix, or to write an epic poem of botany (e.g., Erasmus Darwin's *Zoonomia*) in which scientific and poetic authority are not yet inimical, but only science fiction and not poetry science could remain intelligible in the emergent disciplinary hierarchy.

Jakobson's diagram of the linguistic exchange features the addresser and addressee as end points, mediated by a channel across which passes the message, which refers via a code to the context (i.e., the world) in which the transaction takes place. But what happens, for example, when the code or channel is being *addressed*, or when "the medium *is* the message"? What if we want not only to analyze a film or book as the "channel" or "code" whereby a message is sent from a writer to reader, but also to regard the writer and reader as aspects of a channel whereby films and books (or the codes, channels, and contexts they constitute) interact with each other? These questions constitute violations of the definitional "incest prohibition" at the heart of Jakobson's exemplary structuralism (e.g., only heterosex between an addresser and an addressee is permitted; code-to-code intercourse is prohibited) and bring us to the foundational mutations of poststructuralism already gnawing at it. These mutations are analagous to Marx's transformation of *c-m-c* into *m-c-m* (a "turning inside out" that cooperates with standing the Hegelian dialectic "on its head"), where money as the purely instrumental "code" by which commodities are exchanged becomes the telos or end point of the exchange. If it is meaning that we are after and not information or communication, it is where Jakobson's six functions become indistinct, or rather, the moving interfaces where they transform into each other (e.g., via "canalization" or "codification"), that we must follow.

In any case, Blake's antiatomism was not, in itself, an antiscientific position, but part of a debate that was and is ongoing both in and between science and literature. Although many or even most writers on the subject in Blake's day had accepted an ultimately particulate nature for matter, interpretations continued to differ radically. Arguments split between nations (e.g., pitting Britain's Newtonian void against France's Cartesian plenum) as well as between the adherents of various doctrines, between the nascent disciplines of chemistry and astronomy, between mechanics and what would become thermodynamics, and so on. We could say that it is the relative incoherence or recalcitrance of these divisions among themselves (the impossibility of reducing them to a single axis) that constitutes the semiautonomy of scientific discourse. Blake opposed the discretion of the Newtonian atom and the brittleness of the Cartesian atom, but he embraced a version of the participatory God that Newton's hard atoms required and a version of Cartesian vortices that were meant to obviate the need for Newton's God. The eventual victory of the atom is a hollow one for the legacy of Newton, since its defining features — hardness and indivisibility — have been shed along the way.

The argument implicit here runs against the notion that science is driven to achieve consensus, or driven by advancing from paradigm to paradigm, or even that contradictions between paradigms are irritants around which the pearls of new syntheses are eventually secreted — stories that follow the boring and inadequate curve of arousal and equilibrium, driven by a scientific death drive to locate, behind everything, the stasis of eternal and unchanging law: to give the universe a heart of stone instead of a trembling and restlessly chaotic flame. What if science also follows the movement of its contradictions, if contradictions have staying power or are conserved even as their content or location changes? This question also runs counter to a modernist ideology of science as primarily busy establishing facts (or in the recycled version, "constructing" them) — the firm ground of certainties and consensus on which to stand to reach higher and higher heights — while literature and the arts deal in ambiguities, defamiliarizations, and subversions. While this ideology has entailed serious and very real consequences, a descriptive critique cannot shoulder the responsibility of addressing them alone. Instead (for the moment, anyway), we move away from the vertical paradigm of building a building (a scientific Tower of Babel) and toward a transverse one — more like moving a heavy object on rollers, whereby one must always take the rollers left behind and reassemble them in front again. This paradigm shift from building to ongoing dismantling — indexed too in postmodern thermodynamics by a preference for homeorrhetic and far-from-equilibrium systems — is again not in itself liberatory but a model apparently tailor-made to the redoubled dynamism of postmodern capital and discipline. Dismantling is also (although not exclusively) one of the "master's tools."

It is also possible to write the story by placing Blake in a scientific backwater: behind his time, still fighting against an atom whose dynasty had already been established, engaged in "resistance to science in the name of prescientific values." But although the victory of an "elastic universe" over Newtonian hard atoms problematizes this scenario, and even though the indivisibility of the New-

tonian atom has been discarded along the way, many of the contributions of its adherents have been retained, just as thermodynamics was developed from the since-
discredited *anti*-Newtonian assumption that heat is an independent entity (a "subtle
fluid"). Radical and irreducible ambiguity in the genealogy of atomic theory is suggested by the fact that the modernist atom bears as much or as little resemblance to
either the Newtonian atom or Blake's vortex. To put it another way, the atom has
always been the locus of a vacillation between atom, antiatom, and nonatom. Similarly, the modern law of the conservation of energy is not (as it first appears) a simple outgrowth of the earlier principle of the conservation of *vis viva* but in fact the
eventual product of *opposition* to this principle. Conservation could only be conserved
through the proposition of a change in state (through conversion of lost force), although even so the inevitable remainder or excess could not be harmonized to produce a perpetual-motion universe. This conservation-through-change is also a typically Victorian "discovery" insofar as it tallies with new protocols for circulation
and exchange.

  The word "conservation," then, *is not conserved* in the former sense
of the word, except as it is converted in the process. But in tracing what happens to
the word, the chain of evidence is always compromised: we cannot say precisely
which of its features were lost, which reassigned to other words, which added from
other words in the probablistic flux of *parole*; no forensics (whether the word refers
to speech or to the traces of bodies) can extricate its own fingerprints from its chain
of evidence.

  Likewise, the word "atom" (historically) *is not atomic* in the former sense of the word; that is, it is not a discrete, hard, indivisible, unitary, and
eternal concept or particle. Clever sophistication and self-evident tautology meet in
these observations, marking the trajectory of a truth production whereby relations
within language and between words and things are made in each other's image.

  Accordingly, the "eme," or elementary unit (as in phoneme, sememe, episteme, ideologeme), could be considered a transdisciplinary analogue of the
atom, but the relatively recent proliferation of "emes" across disciplines does not
mark the hegemony of atomism or reductionism but rather their exhaustion. For example, a certain hand shape may be a "phoneme" in American Sign Language not
because it is simpler or less articulated than another but because it is positioned as
such by the language as a self-organizing system: ongoing use of the word "phoneme"
may efface the fact that the object in question is no longer either "phonic" or an
"eme." Likewise, Foucault's "episteme" is not an elementary unit of knowledge but
"the *total* set of relations that unite, at a given period, the discursive practices that

give rise to epistemological figures, sciences, and possible formalized systems of knowledge" (1976, 191; my emphasis). The spread of the regime of "micropower" that Foucault's account locates in the late eighteenth century describes a logic whereby the smallest and most dispersed unit is also that which most characterizes the totality, or as D. A. Miller characterizes it, "a social order whose totalizing power circulates all the more easily for being pulverized" (1988, xiii).

The force of Blake's often-repeated instructions on how to "see the World in a Grain of Sand" (1982, 490) is again to resist the reduction of the universe to individual particles or discrete singular units (the grain of sand again standing for the supposedly indivisible and internally undifferentiated atom). Blake proposes instead a "scaling" and plural universe of worlds within worlds. This model is less likely to slide into the warm-and-fuzzy pluralism in which it usually wallows if its resemblance to the Foucauldian episteme (as a correspondence between smallest and most "total" that marks the regime of micropower) is kept in the foreground. Like Blakean scaling space, the fractal time that can hold "Eternity in an hour" is not divisible into discrete and uniform units. The linked series of aphorisms that follow these instructions (in Blake's "Auguries of Innocence") depend mainly upon the logic of recursion, whereby a one-way "pecking order" or hierarchical "food chain" between global and local phenomena is made to backfire (e.g., "A dog starvd at his Masters Gate / Predicts the ruin of the State" [1982, 490]). Again, the final stanza of the poem proposes and problematizes a distinction between mechanist reason and humanist organicism; that is, between those who live in night and see God as "light" and those who live in day and see God as a human form. But again this logical dilemma, the problem of the binarity between binarity and nonbinarity, makes the contradiction an active one, and looks toward an antimechanist and antiorganicist strategy that has its avatar in postmodernism. Such a strategy, in turn, remains recognizable as such only as long as (or to the extent that) the mechanism/organism axis remains problematic.

Eden, for Blake (according to a tendency to spatialize temporal scenarios), need not just represent a Romantically lost or fallen world and/or possibly reattainable future goal but also an extant though partial world that threads through the present. Blake's figure of the *vortex* mediates between the Edenic concentricity of wheel-within-wheel and the hellish eccentricity of wheel-without-wheel. Against the comforting epistemological solid ground of the particle, Blake's epistemology sets the apparently vertiginous figure of the vortex: "The nature of infinity is this: That every thing has its / Own Vortex" (1982, 109). In other words, things are not like atomic building blocks or commodities in a homeostatic system, but rather the thingness of things is a homeorrhetic phenomenon contingent on the position of the thing in question at the resonant intersection of a series of cycles or transactions (whether economic, semiotic, or the like).

The vortical return-with-a-vengeance (although by Blake's time vortical atoms had been largely discredited) in modernism is not limited to vorticism in aesthetics. Peirce wrote, in 1903, that

a question at this moment under consideration by physicists is whether matter consists ultimately of minute solids, or whether it consists merely of vortices of an ultimate fluid. The third possibility, which there seems reason to suspect is the true one, that it may consist of vortices in a fluid which itself consists of far minuter solids, these, however, being themselves vortices of a fluid, itself consisting of ultimate solids, and so on in endless alternation, has hardly been broached. (1955, 68)

If the subsequent transformation of particles into quanta ("packets of energy" also described in cultural theory by Deleuze and Guattari's "articulated flows") obviates Peirce's "third possibility," Serres's slogan for the turbulent universe of chaos theory, a "global vortex of local vortices" (1982, 117), marks its reascendancy, seeming to understand Peirce's "endless alternation" of vortex and particle as itself a vortex. Foucault's "perpetual spirals of power and pleasure" (1984, 324) play out the same model; Baudrillard argues that its own spiraling makes Foucault's discourse "a mirror of the powers it describes" (1980, 87).

Blake's "wheel within wheel" image is taken directly from Ezekiel's vision of the chariot and its four "living creatures":

This was their appearance; they had the likeness of a man. And every one of them had four faces and four wings. . . . And they went every one straight forward: whither the spirit was to go, they went; they turned not when they went. As for the likeness of the living creatures, their appearance was like burning coals of fire . . . and their appearance and their work was as it were a wheel within a wheel. (Ezekiel 1:4–16)

It is easy to identify several features that overdetermine the image for Blake's antiphysics. First, because Cabalism traditionally forbade study of Ezekiel's chariot (the Merkabah) as a dangerous object of contemplation for any but the most adept, it stands nicely for "that which cannot be said or can be said repeatedly but not understood," a vacillation between supreme mystery and forbidden demystification that defines Blake's career as exemplary of the position of modernist artists and intellectuals. Furthermore, the image offers not a simple plurality (a plurality of units) but a scaling plurality: the scaling self-similarity of "wheel within wheel" is

"A Global Vortex of Local Vortices" (A Small Region of the Mandelbrot Set)

juxtaposed to the scaling *self-difference* of the four creatures, which are identified as lion, ox, eagle, and man, even though each has *all four* faces, seeming to make their identities contingent on their positions (that is, on which way they are facing). Blake marks the scaling plurality in naming the creatures "Zoas," that is, by taking the Greek plural, *zoa* ("creatures"), and pluralizing it again in English—a nice trick that commentators have too hastily dismissed as a mistake in Blake's self-taught Greek.

A contemporary version of this dynamic can be found in Dorion Sagan's construction of the human body as "metametazoa"; that is, as an excess produced out of multiple interactions between other sets of creatures, each of which may be metazoa in turn (Sagan 1992). Sagan contrasts his metametazoa to the Romantic environmentalism of "Gaia" (the name for the Earth as a single organism comprising multiple organisms), which takes unity rather than multiplicity as both its building block and its horizon (a position represented by Urizen in Blake's *Four Zoas*). It is unclear whether the whole concatenation of machine wheels, animals, and human bodies figured in the Merkabah can be described as human, except insofar as it is surmounted by the figure of a throned man. If the human, then, can be described as an interaction of self-difference and self-similarity, it remains unclear how it differs from any other identity except insofar as it appears "under the sign" of the human. Accordingly, the figure differs from another famous image of a scaling universe, the 1651 title page of Hobbes's *Leviathan*, which had represented the

commonwealth as a gigantic man made up of hundreds of men—a perfect self-similarity gained at the expense of positing a perfect binary difference between it and the landscape over which it towers, suggesting the domination of nature by culture.

The equivocal relation between singular and plural in the Merkabah is suggested further by the description of the sound that its/their motion produces as "a noise of tumult like the noise of an host" and simultaneously the singular "voice of the Almighty" or "voice of one that spake." The motion of the Merkabah is also paradoxical: the spirit of the figures is in the wheels, whose function would seem to be to turn, yet "they turned not when they went; they went every one straight forward," and

Various Chariots. Blake's 1805 watercolor of the Merkabah *(above)* depicts Ezekiel's "four living creatures" back to back, facing outward (an arrangement duplicated by the positions of each creature's four faces), while his 1827 illustration from *Job (right)* depicts his own "four zoas" as the four quadrants of the inner picture, reduplicated in the four chorus-line angels of the top quadrant. The framing wheel-within-wheel of yet they went "up and down" and "ran and returned." Accordingly, Blake sometimes depicted the never-definitively-visualizable Merkabah in back-to-back formation, sometimes as a "chorus line."

If the extension, externality, and grindingly brute force of friction operative in Blake's "wheel without wheel" has been understated in recent accounts of disciplinarity, the Edenic operation of "wheel within wheel" has been recognized as its corollary insofar as it works by creating spontaneous compliance or resemblance, by allowing gyroscopic "degrees of freedom," and without even laying a hand on its subject. The "action at a distance" that characterizes the kind of gravity that Blake (this time in agreement with Newton) preferred to Descartes's plenum (which required gearlike physical contact for the communication of motion) will come to define the operation of ideology in Althusser's "hailing" and Lacan's "mirroring."

Ezekiel's whirlwind (in the watercolor) is translated into the rounded frame of Leviathan coils, twisting worm, and braided clouds that surround the inner picture from *Job*. (*The Whirlwind: Ezekiel's Vision of the Cherubim and the Eyed Wheels.* Purchased 1890. Courtesy, Museum of Fine Arts, Boston)

The monstrous victory of the four zoas, dehierarchized and in their irreducible "fourness" or "someness," concludes Blake's epic by ending the "war of swords" and "dark Religions," thereby inaugurating the reign of "sweet science." Understanding that the friendly fascism of disciplinary power has also assumed its avatar in the guise of "sweet science" does not simply reveal a crypto-dystopia behind Blake's utopian annunciation, making Blake's epics simply misrecognized genealogies of modern power/knowledge. It does mark the passage—between kinds of power—not as a climax or singular historical event but as an ongoingly repeated and over-and-under-determined moment of possibility, and suggests that the persistent undercon-structedness of such moments will continue to be a definitive locus of struggle.

Irony: A Vortex amid Vortices

Thomas Carlyle's trick, in *Sartor Resartus*, was to produce a "polyphonic" text by imbricating two personae: a befuddled English editor-biographer and a Romantically obscure German philosopher-autobiographer. The echoic imbrication of these personae throughout the text is the principle of its construction; rather than concealing this mechanism, its endless permutations allow the editor to wonder aloud whether "these Autobiographical Documents are partly a mystification" since his subject's "intricate sardonic rogueries, wheel within wheel, defy all reckoning" (Carlyle 1937, 202), while for the philosopher "all Speculation is by nature endless, formless, a vortex amid vortices" (195), allowing Carlyle's fascistic certainty to emerge in reaction to this confusing flux.

Similarly split subjectivities are deployed by De Quincey (in *The Confessions of an English Opium Eater*) and Coleridge (in his preface to "Kubla Khan"), who act, in effect, as their own doctors (or talk-show hosts) by presenting their writings as "case studies" in opium addiction. Chatterton made a name for himself by pretending to be the discoverer of the Old English poems that he had forged; Coleridge accomplished another more or less duplicitous version of the same move by adding glosses and archaisms to "The Rime of the Ancient Mariner" to make it into the simulacrum of a repeatedly edited Renaissance text (see McGann 1985, 135–72); Wordsworth in the "Preface" to *Lyrical Ballads* plays the critic with respect to his poems that follow in order to ensure the continual interpenetration of criticism and poetry. Keats's "camelion Poet" goes further, claiming "no identity" except in its circulation among the identities that it inhabits, careful even in its assertion of identitilessness to cover its tracks: "But even now I am perhaps not speaking from myself; but from some character in whose soul I now live" (1970, 157–58).

In each of these cases, subjectivity is not split but rather produced as the excess of a splitting or self-difference that both necessitates and inadequates each of the positions that it produces in order to mandate circulation and continual displacement among them, locating the heart of Romantic subjectivity in an unresolvable dialectic of embeddedness and transcendence. Foucault tells us that it is in "scission"—in the well-known difference between author and narrator of a literary text—that the "author function" operates, ensuring that neither associating the author with narrator nor distinguishing between them will be sufficient to dislodge or recode the mechanism. By the late Victorian period, Stevenson's Dr. Jekyl and Mr. Hyde scenario and Freudian psychoanalysis would elaborate the viccissitudes of split subjectivity as a recursive self-experimentation that defines the dangerous boundary between scientific and literary knowledge production.

Like recursive self-reference, with which it is often associated, *irony* became a privileged marker of the literary (and an important subject of literary theory) in Romanticism, looking ahead to a time when ironic self-reference would explode to the horizon of Western culture to become a privileged marker of postmodernity itself. With the Romantic pluralization of power-knowledge comes the famous rise of Bakhtin's "heteroglossic" or "dialogistic" novel, in which all voices must appear in (explicit or implicit) ironic quotation marks (1981, 67–68). In the rush to acclaim Bakhtin's dialogism for a kind of happy pluralism it has been too often forgotten that the multiple voices woven into the novel also construct and are constructed by what Bakhtin called "a verbal-ideological center" (1981, 48), a center not unlike Althusser's anamorphoscopic "Subject" in its codependent relation to the "subjects" with which it colludes. The novel coheres and its trajectories take shape insofar as its voices are identifiable and differentiable by their distance and movement from or toward this center, all the more resilient because it is no succinct point but the axis of mutational density in a shifty "system of intersecting planes" (Bakhtin 1981, 48).

The prevailing academic (and essentially Romantic) position on irony has generally been to associate it with freedom from — or subversion of — ideological convention, "dialogizing it from within," to borrow Bakhtin's phrase (1981, 46). This tellingly partial position marks the uneasy status of the academic intellectual, still stuck where Blake and Wordsworth found themselves two centuries ago, between patronage and a marketplace, where survival must entail both implication in and disjunction from both. This double bind — or rather, enabling contradiction — is particularly acute or chronic but not particular to the artist or academic. In any case, plural and even mutually exclusive audiences and productive constraints produce "double consciousness," heteroglossia, irony.

An oppositional take on irony, then, might identify it with an ideological "damage control" function, a way to live or write or read at a distance from multiple and otherwise irreconcilable positions without directly engaging these positions. Walter Benjamin identified this "distracted" reception as a way in which the ideological purchase of any cultural production is limited (1969, 239–41); the prevalence of this kind of reception in modernity and postmodernity does not *in itself* carry a politics (except insofar as recognizing it acts as a corrective to the liberal ideal of the "informed citizen") but does alter the kinds of political strategies that are likely to be effective. Baudrillard inflated this distracted or ironic relation to culture into the insurmountable and inertial resistance of the "masses" to ideologization (1983, 1–2), while for Slavoj Žižek it is precisely distraction and irony ("not taking it seriously") that enables the hegemony of a dominant ideology: "In contemporary societies, democratic or totalitarian, that cynical distance, laughter, irony, are, so to speak, part of the game. The ruling ideology is not meant to be taken seriously or literally. Perhaps the real danger for totalitarianism is people who take its ideology literally" (1989, 28).

Recent accounts of *literary* irony have identified two terms and associated these with inter- or intrasubjective positions. D. C. Muecke aligns a "lower" and an "upper" term with an innocent "victim of irony" and an ironist or "ironic observer" (1969). Paul de Man's irony splits off a "fictional self" from an "empirical," "actual," or "world-bound self" (1983). Anne Mellor aligns "creative" and "de-creative" positions with Friedrich von Schlegel's "two opposing psychic drives: one [which] seeks order and coherence (to become being), while the other seeks chaos and freedom (to be becoming or to become nonbeing)" (1980, 8).

The attribution of subjective positions (often within a "split subject") to the terms of the figure points toward an association of all forms of irony with dramatic irony, as does de Man's remark that "the ironist invents a form of himself that is 'mad' but that does not know its own madness" (1983, 216). Clearly, dramatic irony specifies a case in which a lower (embedded or unselfconscious) term is occupied by a character in a play or other literary work, and an upper (transcendent or self-conscious) term by an audience or reader complicit with the author and sometimes with another ironic observer in the work itself. This special case clearly remains structured by the two terms but also contributes descriptively to the figure: irony inevitably posits an *other*, whose voice it encloses in explicit or implicit quotation marks. This term might be designated the o-term; in the word *irony* it occupies the heart, the interior, the center. The "upper" term could be called the i-term; it stands at the head of the word as an observing "eye," posits an "I" where only the "me" of metonymy and metaphor had been. The physicality of the letters could also be drawn into the formula; the o representing a w/hole, a horizon, or a circumference; the phallic i standing for a vertical axis of the transcending spiral, positing an ultimate point but breaking off before it can arrive there. The straight line and circle—i and o—are in fact the "limiting cases of the logarithmic spiral" (Wehl 1952, 70): such a spiral is a leading visualization of the figure of irony. The division and relation of the two terms performs a kind of ideological work that remains to be specified.

These terms need not be characterized as a hierarchized duality. The lower term can be seen as comprising two (for example, a thesis and an antithesis), while the next (whether called a second or third) synthesizes or transcends these (or in only slightly less Hegelian terms, as the Oedipal triangulation mediates the mother-child dyad). The figure can also be construed as a quadrature in which one term occupies the upper position, relegating the other three to the lower, as does time in its pre-Einsteinian relation to the three dimensions of space, or Los in Blake's *Four Zoas.* As long as they describe hierarchical dimensions, the proliferation of terms tends to keep collapsing back into two.

While moving the two-term model toward an *n*-dimensional figure, it will be helpful to see what happens when the modern two-term models of irony are stretched to rectify them with the still-popular classical definition of irony, which also opposes two terms: "saying one thing" and "meaning the opposite." This definition, at any rate, indicates how irony can be identified as the condition of language itself, insofar as saying or writing something implies the absence of its referent.

Opening Byron at random, I find a suitable test case immediately in *Don Juan* I:6, where Horace's mandate that epics begin in medias res is characterized as "the heroic turnpike road" (1986, 379). Irony is indicated insofar as turnpike roads are understood as anything but heroic. Nonetheless, the epic convention, associated by metaphor with the safer and straighter course and state-controlled access of the turnpike road, is identified as the heroic way. This identification, the "thing said," would align with the lower (naive or mystified) term of the ironic figure, while the higher term would be associated with the opposite "meaning"; that is, that the convention/turnpike is *not* heroic, or more trenchantly, that *unconventionality*—the wandering and difficult but "free" path of genius—is the heroic one. One of Blake's "Proverbs of Hell" renders the same idea: "Improvement makes strait roads, but the crooked roads without Improvement, are the roads of Genius" (38). It is easy (maybe only a little too easy) to recognize these as conventional formulas of bourgeois individualism.

Furthermore, though, it could be maintained that Byron's statement also works to ambiguate, exceed, or deconstruct the oppositions that it puts in play. The generic identity of Byron's text, for example, is here made to turn on the axis of epic (traditionally the highest or most privileged genre) versus anti- or nonepic, but this ambiguation does not thereby escape ironic hierarchy. Byron's *Don Juan* participates in a historical process whereby the right kind of generic ambiguity becomes a marker of literary value (a mark of unmarkedness): a famous example is the Romantic reevaluation of Shakespeare's ambiguous mixtures of comic and tragic forms as a mark of genius rather than a defect. In each case, an "upper" generic term is made to wander freely around "lower," fixed genres. Tzvetan Todorov's tautological "Typology of Detective Fiction" makes an excellent modern example of this definitional mystification:

> *As a rule, the literary masterpiece does not enter any genre save perhaps its own; but the masterpiece of popular literature is precisely the book which best fits its genre. Detective fiction has its norms; to "develop" them is also to disappoint them: to "improve upon" detective fiction is to write "literature," not detective fiction. (1977, 43)*

Edward Said identifies a very similar device at the heart of Orientalism, whereby the Orient is defined as eternally the same; it is allowed to change only as it becomes Westernized (1978).

Before leaving the Byron example, it is important to note that irony occurs in conjunction with both metaphor and metonymy: metaphor by which the epic convention (tenor) is associated with the turnpike road (vehicle), and metonymy whereby the term "heroic" is allowed to slide between product and process—between the heroic as that which is produced by a particular process (here a certain kind of narrative), and the process as itself heroic (i.e., "heroic poetry")—and perhaps toward a heroic *producer* as well. Metaphor, metonymy, and irony form a signifying field from which each is only ideally isolable. Thus, for example, the relative straightness of the turnpike road versus the windings of individual paths is one of the oppositions polarized in the metaphor by the presence of irony. In fact, it concretizes the figure of irony nicely, "straight" being virtually synonymous with "nonironic" (the lower term of the figure), while "crooked" or even "perverse" characterize the upper—ironic—term. Irony polarizes the terms of the metaphor along a temporal axis as well, pushing epic and the heroic to a past superseded by the present mundanity of the turnpike.

The apparently metonymic sequence between process and product is also axiologized by an irony that valorizes pure process as its upper term, a valorization reproduced in Mellor/Schlegel's identification of "product" and "process" terms of the ironic figure. Thus Byron's Horace "makes" the road, effectively denigrating the epic convention as a mere product and allowing Byron's own practice to stand in unspoken opposition, at least for the moment, as an unproduced process.

The Byron example serves at least to complicate the distinction between the terms of irony, as well as between irony and other rhetorical figures: multiple axiologizations are made to resonate and/or interfere without being reducible to a single polarity. A second approximation of the figure that begins to account for these complications can be derived by reexamining the three theorists of irony mentioned above.

Mellor is careful to distinguish the works of Romantic ironists from those Romantic works that conform to M. H. Abrams's model, as she characterizes it; that is, works that "present a confident movement from innocence to experience to a higher innocence, that circuitous journey which leads the protagonist spiraling upward to a more self-aware and therefore more meaningful communion with the divine" (1980, 6). She is similarly careful to distinguish Schlegel's conception of irony as "analysis of thesis and antithesis" from the Hegelian dialectic in that the latter is "progressive and transcendental," each thesis generating a new antithesis, which "leads to a broader synthesis in an upward and outward spiraling growth of human consciousness." Romantic irony, she argues, is "open-ended" and nonteleological, based on unresolvable contradiction that "allows for no genuine resolution or synthesis" (11). Nonetheless, Mellor evokes the same spiral figure to sneak the telos of consciousness-expansion back into her description of irony, which she associates with Schlegel's "self-becoming" as "a process of enlargement..., a dialectical movement between destruction and creation, creation and destruction, that produces an ever-expanding consciousness of life as becoming" (13–14). This little bit of cheating (not particular to Mellor) itself expands to produce the assertion that "Romantic irony, therefore, can potentially free individuals and even entire cultures from totalitarian modes of thought and behavior" and "bring us pleasure, psychic health, and intellectual freedom" (188). Mellor's recuperative scenario recalls how Freud's denial of vertical transcendence produced a horizontally expansionist Eros.

Like Mellor, de Man takes up with Schlegel in characterizing irony as "an endless process that leads to no synthesis," and like Mellor he reproduces the telos and the spiral figure in describing the operation of irony as "freedom, the unwillingness of the mind to accept any stage in its progression as definitive" (recalling the Freudian differential that will "permit of no halting at any position attained"; no closing of the circle), and as "the recurrence of a self-escalating act of consciousness" (1983, 220). In other words, ironic consciousness goes *up* a spiral staircase where *down* is "the narrowing spiral of a linguistic sign" (222) in which the ironist remains caught. Like a fox that chews off its own trapped foot, the ironist is produced out of a "splitting." The split that engenders irony is a "falling (or rising) from a state of mystified adjustment into the knowledge of . . . mystification" (214).

If Mellor has the good excuse of coming of age in an era of feminist "consciousness-raising," de Man had the bad conscience of having come of age as a collaborationist writer in Nazi-occupied Belgium, and thus had a historical reason for his denial of history, for asserting the disjunction between a "world-bound" and "fictional" self, for the rejection of "any stage" as definitive, and for the painful or cowardly recognition that "knowledge of mystification" is not the same as demystification.

Muecke seems also to propose a spiral figure for irony in his title, *The Compass of Irony* (1969), which can be made to explicate de Man's "falling (or rising)" as an *orbit* or "free fall" in which the continuous set of possible positions for the upper ("free") term constitute a spiral around the "fixed foot" of the compass, which would correspond to the lower term. The compass model—which could be characterized further as a kind of gyroscope, modernist atom, orrery, or other orbital system—represents a second approximation of the ironic figure.

Gyroscopophilia: Wordsworth's "Slumber"

De Man's test case for his figure of irony is Wordsworth's lyric, "A Slumber Did My Spirit Seal." The lyric's eight short lines may have generated more commentary than any comparably short work in the history of English poetry. While this may make further attention to it suspect, the poem's terseness and dissemination mark it as an exemplary episteme engine:

> A slumber did my spirit seal;
>   I had no human fears:
> She seemed a thing that could not feel
>   The touch of earthly years.
>
> No motion has she now, no force;
>   She neither hears nor sees;
> Rolled round in earth's diurnal course,
>   With rocks, and stones, and trees.
> (1969, 149)

De Man finds in the lyric "two stages of consciousness, one belonging to the past and mystified, the other to the now of the poem, the stage that has recovered from the mystification of a past now presented as error"; in the second, "an eternal insight into the rocky barrenness of the human condition prevails." The stages are separated by "the radical discontinuity of a death" and correspond roughly to the two stanzas of the poem, to the two terms of de Man's figure of irony (1983, 224–25) — as well as nicely characterizing de Man's professional movement from Belgian collaborationist journalist to American academic.

Clearly, though, the poem could also be made to fit Abrams's recuperative model if the first and second stanzas are read as Wordsworthian *Songs of Innocence and of Experience*: de Man's characterization of the narrator's apparent recognition of death's finality as an "eternal insight" works only if we ignore the many other poems in which Wordsworth proposes a third and "higher" state of "recompense" (roughly equivalent to Blake's "Organiz'd Innocence") in which the child's inability "to admit the notion of death" — after disillusionment at least as regards bodily immortality — is recuperated as a true "intimation of immortality" of the spirit. From this third perspective the materialist notion of death's finality, with which the poem seems to conclude, must be characterized not as "an eternal insight" but in its turn as error, slumber, mystification — just as Wordsworth repeatedly identified his own materialist phase as a depressive illness and an error from which he had recovered.

Wordsworth's early critics expressed puzzlement at the curiously flat or matter-of-fact quality of lyrics such as "A Slumber," conspicuously truncated before the "point" of the narrative is made: in regard to the related poem "Strange Fits of Passion," reviewer Francis Jeffrey thought it damning enough to print the final two lines and exclaim, "There the poem ends!" (cited in Perkins 1967, 366). Like other "Lucy" poems, "A Slumber" works not by making a "point" but by folding its truncation back into itself; it overdetermines a resolution, as if it played all but the last note of a melody. The blank space between stanzas, where feminine death and masculine awakening are made simultaneous, is only a particularly discrete instance of how the poem works by manipulating what is not said.

The poem opens by suggesting a series of phase-shifted readings. If the statement that "a slumber did my spirit seal" indicates a discrete event in the past, then the previous existence of an unsealed spirit is implied, making the line the narrator's description of his birth (as in the "Intimations" ode, where "our birth is but a sleep and a forgetting"), and rehearsing the traditional Christian equation of slumber with the physical body. Of course the sealing of a spirit need not be taken as a sudden discontinuity equated with the instant of birth, but may be understood as a gradual process, a becoming-sealed (again as in the "Intimations" ode, where "shades of the prison-house begin to close / On the growing Boy"). Or it may be that the anteriority of spirit to the bodily slumber that seals it is not establishable (that they mutually construct each other in a kind of "self-organizing system"). This coconstruction may be marked by the ambiguous Miltonic diction that allows both "A slumber sealed my spirit" and "My spirit sealed a slumber" as acceptable readings. Furthermore, if "seal" can mean "to affix a seal to," subject and object could be related as owner and possession, or even as form and substance (insofar as such a seal gives shape to an otherwise amorphous blob of wax).

The same kinds of ambiguities could be shown to hold for the relation between stanzas, between the two terms of the figure of irony, and between the other dualities the poem seems to coordinate with these. In addition to the already identified oppositions of body and spirit, slumber and awakening (unconsciousness and consciousness), past and present, and idealism and materialism, the lyric opposes genders aligned with the poem's subject and object and genres aligned by diction with the two stanzas: the sentimental (with its discourse of slumbers, fears, and feeling) and the scientific (which speaks of motion, force, and diurnality). The poem works ideologically by making these alignments or by allowing them to be made.

Primary among the ambiguities generated by the poem's first line, though, is that several models of change—developmental scenarios—seem to be proposed. One possible model describes a unidirectional gradualism from one term (or stage) to the next. Another (de Man's model) describes rupture or discontinuity between stages. A third constructs the relation as cyclical, an "endless alternation" between one term and the next. This last relation is so far only implicit; that is, insofar as the narrator is able to describe his having been sealed, he must have first been unsealed, sealed,

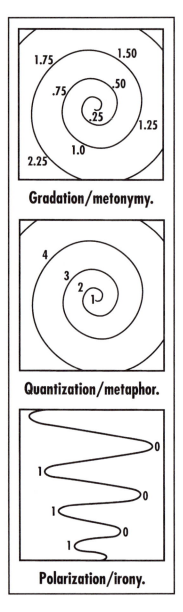

Gradation/metonymy.

Quantization/metaphor.

Polarization/irony.

and then unsealed, for the state of being sealed seems to be characterized by unconsciousness of itself.

Each of these scenarios can be modeled by the figure of the spiral: gradualism describes travel along its one-dimensional path; the view down the axis of the spiral (for which two dimensions are necessary) discovers discrete and discontinuous (quantized) levels, while the perpendicular (third-dimensional) view construes an ongoing oscillation between extremes.

These "views" can also be coordinated with rhetorical figures: metonymy travels a path of displacement along a continuous series of adjacent points; metaphor looks along the axis and finds homology (structural similarity) as well as "condensation and displacement" between levels; irony finds a cyclical *polarity*— the back-and-forth of an "unresolvable dialectic"—that had not been evident in one or two dimensions. Although each "observer" sees the *whole* figure (unlike the proverbial blind men and the elephant), their accounts differ radically.

The narrative position developed in the second stanza reiterates the concentric/eccentric figure. Here the poem's "she" has become pure, inert matter, while the narrator seems to have assumed the transcendental position (or non-position) of spirit, for his description of the corpse being "rolled round with earth's diurnal course" demands a perspective from above the earth's surface and at least some exemption from the full force of the earth's gravity—as if the narrator were a kind of satellite—in order that she be observed to *roll* relative to him. Wordsworth describes a similar relation in a scene from *The Prelude* in which the narrator remembers how stopping suddenly during ice-skating made him feel as if the landscape continued to spin by him, "as if the earth had rolled / With visible motion her diurnal round!" (1979, 53); again the point is the narrator's apparent exemption from the earth's rotation.

To read the narrative position as orbit is to push it toward the outer limit of its tendency: toward pure spirit, which cannot ultimately even be characterized as orbiting the first (material) term but must be equated with Newtonian space itself: a stationary, higher-dimensional field in which matter is embedded. A less extreme, more "naturalistic" reading is also possible, in which the corpse rolls with the earth, buried just beneath its surface, while the narrator, although he too must be rolled around with the earth, is at least able to move about on it: the corpse is *mobile* ("capable of being moved from place to place"), but the narrator is *motile* ("moving or having the power to move spontaneously"). Such a reading only begins to account for the observation that she *rolls* relative to the narrator, tending to emphasize instead the insignificance of his freedom to move relative to his being subject (along with the corpse) to the much larger forces of the earth's gravity and rotation.

A first approximation of the narrator's relation to Lucy, then, constitutes a kind of orbit, a gyroscope stabilized by the spin of an interior rotor (the corpse's course), a gendered motor. The narrator must observe and speak from an outer ring or sphere (a "gimbal"), although his precise degree of freedom is indeterminate: the more gimbals, the more degrees of freedom; that is, the less a perturbation of the outer ring will affect the rotor. The image allows the narrator's degree of freedom to range from a fraction (if we construe him as walking the earth above the corpse) to infinity (if he occupies a higher-dimensional matrix), producing a subject stretched between embeddedness and transcendence.

This model pictures an Imaginary Other reduced to a *fixation*, an axiologization of the wandering orbit or gimbal of the Symbolic. De Man's paradigm of irony (taken from Baudelaire) turns on the force of gravity as well: the philosopher stumbles and laughs at his own fall, splitting his subjectivity into a "world-bound self" (a body subject to gravity) and a "fictional self" (a mind or spirit that looks on, as if from above). It is worth noting that the orbital freedom of the I-term (touted by Mellor and de Man) is, according to the terms of the figure, a local freedom only: the subject in orbit can flail in all directions free from gravity, but can *only flail*, and cannot alter his determined orbit around the Other term on which he depends. He has unlimited knowledge (from his higher perspective) to see and speak but not the power to act or to be heard. Irony here is a kind of knowledge without power that construes (retroactively) a prior power without knowledge. To alter the model slightly, the swimmer caught in a whirlpool is not ironic unless he sees the branch he might have grasped, had he the knowledge, and now can only grasp intellectually, having no longer the power (a seemingly airtight alibi for quietism).

The possibilities for the narrative position in the poem constitute a spiral, then, approaching absolute identity at the apex or center and absolute difference at infinity. The narrative stance forecloses the central position (for it would not allow the observation that she is "rolled" relative to him) and, it would seem, the (Newtonian) higher-dimensional position as well, since higher dimensionality of this type is a category of nonrelation belied by the torque of identity and difference that operates throughout the lyric. Somehow his spirit, his vision, his voice still orbit what he construes as her body, her blindness, her silence. Masculine consciousness and insight over the dead body of the lost woman is a figure dear to the heart of disciplinary knowledge.

The narrator's position does not change from stanza to stanza: he describes his earlier state from the same higher-dimensional position as he describes Lucy in the second stanza. The poem, then, posits a *phase transition* that has turned the narrator inside out, although he speaks, after the fact, from the second phase throughout. This transition can be described as moving from inside (being sealed, spirit embedded in matter) to outside (orbiting, matter embedded in spirit): a transition to a higher dimension, or to a greater "degree of freedom."

Passage between discontinuous dimensions can only partially account for the transition posited in the poem. An example from physics—the passage between magnetism and nonmagnetism—pictures a continuous passage between *fractal dimensions* (see Peitgen and Richter 1986, 129–31). At absolute zero, the poles of a magnet are perfectly aligned at every scale, from its most punctual particle to its totality: it is perfectly *self-similar.* As the temperature rises, disorder (disalignment) appears first at a subatomic scale, implicating larger scales as it rises: perfect self-similarity is lost, since perfect alignment only appears at a coarse scale, but "lakes" of disorder appear at finer scales. At infinite temperature, a perfect self-similarity of nonaligned poles is observed at all scales, but this self-similarity is again lost with cooling, since "islands" of order begin to appear at a small scale as poles of individual particles become aligned, although only nonalignment is observable at a coarse enough scale. In passing from absolute zero to infinite temperature, the system moves from zero degrees of freedom (a kind of fascism in which each particle perfectly embodies the polarity of the entire system) to infinite anarchic freedom, from a fractal dimension of zero (a stationary network of zero-dimensional points) to three (since each point in random motion describes a scribble that eventually fills space). Like Wordsworth's narrator suspended between unoccupiable extremes, the system moves from lakes of disorder in a continent of order, to islands of order in a sea of disorder. Far from making a simple interiority, embeddedness can only be understood as "interfusion" across scale. At the transitional point between magnetism and nonmagnetism, a categorically different kind of self-similarity appears: in any given island of order are lakes of disorder—and vice versa—*ad infinitesimum* and *ad infinitum,* regardless of how fine or coarse the scale; this "swamp" is a mutual interpenetration of the other two states. Furthermore, though, the deterioration of order may be accompanied by the creation of dissipative structures as well (patterns of turbulence) as the system passes from one phase to the next (e.g., in the distribution of "lakes" and "islands"). Wordsworth's lyric and the picture of magnetic phase transition both describe transition to higher degrees of freedom or dimensionality as a kind of reversal of embeddedness around a seal, producing self-similarity and difference.

While I have understood the "she" of the second stanza to refer to Lucy's corpse, others have understood it to refer to her spirit, diffused into the landscape. This reading also posits a dissipative process but assigns it to the poem's object instead of its subject, although it would seem that a spirit could not be "rolled" except by the expedient explanation late-nineteenth-century physicists called an "ether drag hypothesis." The same problem arose in assigning an orbital position to the narrator as higher dimensional spirit: pure spirit and pure body are here limits that can only be approached; higher dimensionality cannot be simple nonrelation: instead, discontinuity and continuity between terms coexist in phase transition. Whether we read a tendency toward pure spirit or toward pure body is finally irrelevant, since the poem works by foreclosing both of the poles it defines (e.g., punctual fixation and diffuse matrix).

So what is ironic about the poem? The spiral schematization of irony suggests that irony might be intelligible as a perpendicular view that construes an oscillation. As such, it finds *polarities* (a back-and-forth between negative and positive limits) where metaphor and metonymy had not. Its polarization is both local and global: in addition to polarizing sequential points on the spiral, making an apogee and perigee, irony polarizes the whole spiral into a lower (origin) and higher (aim) as well, tending to forget the continuity between points that characterizes metonymy and the isomorphism that characterizes metaphor, although this forgetting is never really complete, since continuity and isomorphism remain visible even to a perpendicular view. Irony finds transition impossible: origin recedes perpetually behind and aim perpetually transcends; in the gulf between, one looks around and around to find oneself (in Arnold's famous Wordsworthian phrase) "wandering between two worlds, one dead, / The other powerless to be born."

Irony, that is, asserts the pastness of the past and the futurity of the future as an irreconcilable difference while acknowledging, simultaneously, a simultaneity—an irreducible interpenetration of terms in the swamp of the Real, the tangle of texts and bodies in which we live.

The ideological physics of the poem offer a schematic account of the poet's phase-shifted relations to his sister Dorothy and friend Coleridge, who called the lyric "a most sublime epitaph" and first speculated that in it, "most probably, in some gloomier moment he had fancied the moment in which his sister might die" (cited in Perkins 1967, 263). As in "A Slumber," William associated Dorothy with a superseded stage of his own development in "Tintern Abbey." He represents the passing of this stage as the passing of a light from the world in the "Intimations" ode. *Lucy* is also a *light* (from the Latin), and her passage is represented explicitly as the passage of a light from the world in the related poems "Lucy Gray" and "Strange Fits of Passion." In "Lucy Gray," the title character vanishes, along with the lantern she carries, into a blizzard, and her footprints are traced to a bridge where they abruptly end; she has become a voice in the wind. Here again, gradualism and discontinuity coexist in the passage from a bodily walk on the earth to an incorporeal voice whirling around it; the footsteps ending halfway across the bridge represent both phase transition and its impossibility, or rather, that a thwarted lateral transition leads to an enforced (vertical) transcendence: to being "kicked upstairs." In "Strange Fits of Passion," the narrator imagines the death of his beloved as the moon sets behind her cottage. Here again multiple narrative structures are put into play: *gradualism* (in the slow descent of the moon as, paralleling the narrator's own journey and the steps of his horse, it comes "near, and nearer still" to Lucy's cottage), *discontinuity* in the seemingly instantaneous moonset ("down behind the cottage roof, / At once, the bright moon dropped"), and the *cyclicality* of which the moon is a traditional emblem.

When considering explicitly, in *The Prelude*, his relation to Dorothy, Wordsworth again characterizes himself as a "moon," crediting Dorothy with having

> Maintained for me a saving intercourse
> With my true self; for, though bedimmed and changed
> Both as a clouded and a waning moon,
> She whispered still that brightness would return,
> She, in the midst of all, preserved me still
> A Poet, made me seek beneath that name,
> And that alone, my office upon earth....
> (1979, 409)

In 1829, when William explicitly faces the possibility of Dorothy's death from an illness, he employs the same imagery in a letter: "Were She to depart the Phasis of my Moon would be robbed of light to a degree that I have not courage to think of" (Wordsworth and Wordsworth 1979, 69). This last image, reproduced by William more than thirty years after the Lucy poems and precisely upon imagining "that his sister might die," is a particularly convincing illustration of the strength of the figurative web that binds Dorothy, Lucy, and William. William's ongoing dependence upon his sister is well known: from 1794 until around 1831 (when she became incapacitated), and both before and after William's marriage brought Mary Hutchinson into their household, Dorothy was employed at the continual menial labor that allowed William the leisure to be a poet; she provided the emotional support that sustained him as an intellectual and notated in her journal events that he wrought into poetic figures. At the same time, Dorothy's attendance on her brother rescued her—at a cost—from the fall in class that working as a governess had represented.

If William relegated Dorothy to the o-term of the ironic figure, to the always-already past of emotion and direct contact with nature, he associated his friend and colleague Coleridge with the never-yet-reached i-term (the "evermore about to be"), with abstruse intellect and the abstraction from nature into culture, and with the epic genre Coleridge's notes were to have supplied. For Wordsworth, these relationships seem to have functioned as phase-shifted dualities: Dorothy is to William as William is to Coleridge. Wordsworth imagines (in *The Prelude*) that if he could have caught Coleridge sooner, he could have performed precisely the saving role for Coleridge that he assigns Dorothy in relation to himself: his "temperature less willing to be moved" and "more steady voice" might have "soothed / Or chased away the airy wretchedness / That battened on thy youth (1979, 202). The thermodynamics stay the same: the cooler (less entropic) and earthy stability of the Imaginary is to balance the airy chaos of the Symbolic.

Irony tended to polarize the affective content of Wordsworth's relation to what he construed as beneath and above him. When he looked down — at the lost past of emotion and nature—he tended to cry with a tragic irony, and laughed with a mocking irony when he looked up at the productions of culture, reserving his most extensive mockery for pretension to learning. The final (canceled) verse of "Strange Fits of Passion" distinguishes the *directionality* of these ironies nicely. After his lover has died, the narrator recalls her reaction to his fears for her death:

> I told her this; her laughter light
> Is ringing in my ears;
> And when I think upon that night
> My eyes are dim with tears.
> (Norton 1986, 171n)

That is, innocence looks forward to her death with ignorant and dismissive laughter, while experience looks back at the death of innocence with impotent and nostalgic tears. This polarization tends to play out also as laughter for the pretensions of the upper classes of discourse (reason and philosophy, or as we now say, theory) and for the pretensions of the upper classes, and as sentimental tears for the lyric and the lyric poet dead to the world or to his poetic powers, for the underclasses of discourse, for the poor. Coleridge, too (in his 1807 poem "To William Wordsworth"), wept real crocodile tears over the grave of his poetic powers and praised Wordsworth's performance of such powers in *The Prelude*, as Wordsworth had wept over Lucy and praised Dorothy in "Tintern Abbey," addressing Wordsworth as "Friend! my comforter and guide!" and contrasting Wordsworth's steadiness with his own whirling "tumult" (1985, 127).

As is well known, Coleridge and Wordsworth from their first collaboration tended to align themselves in such a hierarchy, Coleridge providing supernatural subjects and ideas for *Lyrical Ballads* while Wordsworth supplied the natural subjects and the bulk of material. Somewhat later, the idea for a philosophical epic was Coleridge's; Wordsworth was to flesh it out. Wordsworth expresses his sense of his dependence on Coleridge's ideas for the main philosophical section of *The Recluse* in two 1804 letters to Coleridge: "I am very anxious to have your notes for the Recluse. I cannot say how much importance I attach to this, if it should please God that I survive you, I should reproach myself for ever in writing the work if I had neglected to procure this help" (1967, 452). Several weeks later he again reports having feared that Coleridge might die before sending along his notes, and "cannot help saying that I would gladly have given 3 fourths of my possessions for your letter on the Recluse at that time" (1967, 464). In December 1805, Dorothy reports to Lady Beaumont that William "is very anxious to get forward with The Recluse, and is reading for the nourishment of his mind, preparatory to beginning; but I do not think he will be able to do much more till we have heard of Coleridge" (1967, 664). In 1806, Wordsworth was still waiting for Coleridge's help when he reported to Sir George Beaumont that he had "returned to the Recluse" and that, "should Coleridge return, so that I might have some conversation with him upon the subject, I should go on swimmingly" (Wordsworth and Wordsworth 1969, 64). Coleridge never sent his notes (nor is it clear that he had written any), yet in his 1817 *Biographia Literaria*, he again dangles the carrot: "What Mr Wordsworth *will* produce, it is not for me to prophesy: but I could pronounce with the liveliest convictions what he is capable of producing. It is the first genuine philosophic poem" (1985, 414).

Not surprisingly, the philosophical epic that Wordsworth thought would be his professional credential as a poet, that which would retroactively justify the story of his life, remained "evermore about to be." *The Prelude* (like the "sheepfold" in his poem "Michael") is a structure he could never enclose but only leave to admonish future poets, the Imaginary circle that he set himself about completing before he could enter the Symbolic of his philosophical epic, but instead went around and around, back and forth on the spiral, never able to do so. The literal and the figural motion are one: Dorothy describes his habit of walking "backwards and forwards" while composing *The Prelude*, and "though the length of his walk be sometimes a quarter or half of a mile, he is as fast bound within the chosen limits as if by prison walls" (Wordsworth 1967, 437).

The Prelude, which was to have been an "ante-chapel" to the larger structure of *The Recluse*, became polarized into an "anti-chapel" (as it was printed in the 1814 preface to the *The Excursion*) as Wordsworth wrote to put off writing, labored to postpone labor, continuing both to approach and to defer his epic.

Subsequent critics have found a modern epic in *The Prelude*, more than enough to secure Wordsworth's place in Literature, but there is little evidence to suggest that Wordsworth ever regarded *The Prelude* as able to stand alone, as justifying itself or himself. First, there is no evidence that he abandoned his hope of writing the central philosophical portion of *The Recluse* until 1838, when he told a visitor that "he had undertaken something beyond his powers to accomplish" (cited in Wordsworth 1979, 522), but more important, he persevered in his original intent to publish *The Prelude* posthumously if he were unable to complete *The Recluse*. Only passage into a new phase could justify publication of *The Prelude*, and this new phase must be the professional poethood only *The Recluse* could confer—or death.

But Wordsworth experienced the labor of production, the "arduous labour" of the epic "which he had proposed to himself" (1969, 589)—and more often than not the act of writing itself—as labor indeed, often exhausting and painful, in spite of the traditional Marxist view that distinguishes textual production from the "real work of the assembly line" (Jameson 1981, 45). Many of Wordsworth's letters are prefaced with elaborate *preludes*, self-justifying apologies for procrastination that are themselves deferrals, metaprocrastinations. In the course of one such apology (which occupies nearly half of an 1803 letter to Sir George Beaumont), Wordsworth reports that he does "not know from what cause it is, but during the last three years I have never had a pen in my hand for five minutes, before my whole frame becomes one bundle of uneasiness, a perspiration starts out all over me, and my chest is oppressed in a manner which I cannot describe" (1967, 407). In an 1804 letter to De Quincey, Wordsworth again describes the "kind of derangement in my stomach and digestive organs which makes writing painful to me," adding that "this (I mean to say the unpleasant feelings which I have connected with the act of holding a Pen) has been the chief cause of my long silence" (1967, 452–53). In her journals, Dorothy often worries about her brother's labors: William has "fatigued himself with altering" (10/27/00); "William worked at *The Ruined Cottage* and made himself very ill" (12/22/01)"; "he fell to work at *The Leech Gatherer*; he wrote hard at it till dinner time, then he gave over, tired to death" (5/7/02); "William tired himself with hammering at a passage" (5/28/02). Dorothy could suffer from William's illnesses as well: "I was oppressed and sick at heart, for he wearied himself to death" (Wordsworth 1941, 145).

When he had to fix himself to a desk to write out verse, to edit or proofread or copy it—tasks he delegated to Dorothy or Mary when he could—he often found it excruciating. But if we can believe William's or Dorothy's representations of the poet, he seemed to have no trouble wandering at leisure or lying beneath a tree (in the manner of aristocratic portraiture of the period), composing verse in his head and speaking it aloud. Labor—the fixture to a desk—opposed itself to leisure—the wandering path; Wordsworth found himself more often than not in the gulf between, above a poet's labor yet still somehow "beneath that name." The force that opposes doing and being, that *ironizes* by polarizing poetry and philosophy—that pulls poetry to the o-term of the ironic figure and pulls philosophy (theory) to the i-term (or operates to polarize lyric and epic *within* the poetic genre), partially foreclosing their engagement in the Real (*neutral*izing them, as gears are allowed to spin)—is only one in which Wordsworth *participated*, even through his resistance to it, as did the reviewers who damned Wordsworth for "simplicity" and "difficulty" alike. The terms of irony, like fingers caught in a spiral puzzle-braid, are caught more tightly for their pulling.

The o-term is also constituted as a superseded mode of production that lives on as a lower stratum (a "survival"), a fixation of the symbolic field of the capitalist marketplace. High poetry and its practitioners in Wordsworth's time were particularly well situated to play out the contradiction between modes, suspended as they were between patronage and a bourgeois marketplace, neither of which could be relied on to pay the piper. Insofar as it remained fixed to patronage, poetry and poets can be described as "vestiges and survivals of older modes of production, now relegated to structurally dependent positions within the new" (Jameson 1981, 95), a new mode that increasingly defined freedom as the freedom to sell one's labor.

The evolution of modes of production seems to be an entropic process in which coercive relations of obligation (dependence) tend to be replaced by the spontaneous hegemony of the "free" market, but polarity is conserved in dissipation. If the upper pole had been occupied by the poet as amateur gentleman of leisure (circulating manuscripts among friends) and the lower by the itinerant balladeer a step above beggary, the turnpike between them rotates in recurrent Wordsworthian *wandering*, in which both the view-hunting tourist and the homeless itinerant are implicated, and which is nonetheless "fast bound within the chosen limits"—o and i—"as if by prison walls."

The narrator of "I wandered lonely," to choose an all-too-familiar example of the i-term, *does* very little. Like an aristocratic aesthete, he is occupied only in wandering, in gazing and gazing and lying on his couch; he looks down upon a collectivity ("a crowd, a host") above which he floats, and whom his aesthetic distance has reduced to so many identical daffodils. The thermodynamic reading of "A Slumber" reminds us that even the ethereal "lonely cloud," wander as it might or disperse to whatever fractal dimension, still orbits its fixation in the Imaginary Other on which it depends, as the individual orbits the collective. It is finally incorrect to state simply that one term orbits (or depends on) the other: rather, both orbit a mutual center of gravity that is, given a large inequality of mass, within the lower term. Without this correction it will seem as if the upper term were absolutely fixed in a helplessness that characterizes irony. The upper term is indeed skewered by its fixation, but eccentrically so; it is also skewed; it has an effectivity (an influence) that is tiny but not negligible. Still its power is not to escape but to engage, not to transcend but to descend.

The struggle that generated the classes of industrial capitalism was fought over *dependence*, each class asserting its own freedom and the dependence of the other or others upon itself. Apparently the battle was won by the bourgeoisie. Increasingly labor was seen to orbit leisure as well, when the home demand for "luxury" items was seen to be the engine of economic growth. Yet still the freedom to sell one's labor (ostensibly the "independence" of "Resolution and Independence") tended to take its place at the o-term of a hierarchized polarity in which the freedom *not* to sell one's labor still occupied the i-term: "I" the artist, the aristocrat, the private or domestic subject, the dutiful sister, lover and friend, is one who is not bought and sold.

If the aristocratic amateur and the itinerant balladeer of a fading era tend to give way to the poet for the marketplace, the polarity between dependence and independence continues to spin asymmetrically within each position or class no less than within the entire system. Wordsworth at once seeks and fears, identifies with and disavows, every class-based occupation. This interplay of identity and difference has been noted in Wordsworth's many accounts of encounters with beggars and the poor. In "Simon Lee," for example, the "Old Huntsman" works as an allegory of the poet left bereft with the fall of patronage: "No man like him the horn could sound, / And hill and valley rang with glee," but he has had to forgo his "blither tasks" and subsists "in liveried poverty," the "sole survivor" of his Master's death, "overtasked" to "unearth the root of an old tree" as he tries to enclose his small plot, "So vain was his endeavor, /... He might have worked for ever" (1969, 378–79). The poem's narrator appears to sever the root "with a single blow," thus seeming to assert an absolute difference between himself and the helpless old man. But *severing* is not *unearthing*. Forty years after he wrote "Simon Lee," Wordsworth had to admit that in *The Recluse*, at which he had labored so long, and which was to have enclosed his professional poetic plot (where he might live "in retirement") in the Symbolic field of the marketplace, he was "overtasked" indeed and "had undertaken something beyond his powers to accomplish." The "tangled root" was spread too deep in the Imaginary of a superseded mode of production for Wordsworth to unearth, and no new patron or public, no Coleridge could come along to help him do so. The nouveaux riches do not retire to enjoy their wealth any more than all the trappings of poetic legitimacy could secure Wordsworth as the "poet in retirement."

In the ironized relation of the poet to the marketplace we recognize the ambivalence that was to characterize an avant-gardism for which success (co-optation) is failure and failure (as uncompromised radicalism) is success. Like many writers of his time, Wordsworth couldn't seem to shake the association of publishing with hackwork, in which the freedom to sell one's labor is identified as a slavery (or prostitution) to the marketplace. Nonetheless the poet engaged in "*creating* the taste by which he is to be enjoyed*" (Wordsworth and Wordsworth 1969, 750) is a shrewd marketer indeed. In an 1800 letter to the publishers of the second *Lyrical Ballads*, for example, Wordsworth reports that "I had other poems by me of my own which would have been sufficient for our purpose but some of them being connected with political subjects I judged that they would be injurious to the sale of the Work" (1967, 309). Like politics, commerce could have no place in Literature: Wordsworth conveys his "particular request that no Books be advertized at the end of the volumes," the exclusion of the commercial (apparently as déclassé) taking its place here among a series of commercial decisions (1967, 309).

In spite of his careful marketing, Wordsworth seemed always able to detach ironically from his published works, if only because work and text seemed to exist in discontinuous realms. After Southey's bad review of the first *Lyrical Ballads*, for example, Wordsworth wrote to his publisher that Southey shouldn't have judged harshly since "he knew that I published those poems for money and money alone," adding defensively that "I care little for the praise of any other professional critic, but as it may help me to pudding" (Wordsworth and Wordsworth 1967, 267–68). Literature and its *text* seemed to float above the vulgar world of the *work*, of politics and the cash nexus of publishing and reviews.

Enclosure was not only a process that parceled out heath and commons, but a Urizenic web—a nexus—that chartered the streets of Blake's "London" and was to number the houses, that blocked out time (numbering the days and hours of labor and leisure) as well as space and colonized the field of the Symbolic, of disciplines and professions, in an ever-tightening grid. But the grid does not cover the plane uniformly, and continues to be curved by the old polarized hierarchies conserved in the new dissipative order, whether the process is disintegrative, progressive, or merely revolutionary.

When Marx imagined being able "to hunt in the morning, fish in the afternoon, rear cattle in the evening, criticise after dinner, just as I have a mind, without ever becoming hunter, fisherman, shepherd or critic" (1978, 160), he imagined not that the hierarchy of categories—of labor, in this case—would cease to exist (indeed, his ideal workday recapitulates a progressivist evolution of productive modes), but that it would cease to divide people: to say it plainly, that slots would continue to exist in people, but not people in slots. Irony is a disjunction between the slots you're in and the slots that are in you, an imperfection of self-similarity.

For us (and through us) as for Wordsworth, the rise of capitalism and the bourgeois revolution has always already been completed, is always in process, is always now complete. In Wordsworth's "evermore about to be" is the growth scenario of a capitalist technology that promises freedom from labor (or "retirement") or a psychoanalysis that promises health or a professionalism that promises authority just ahead. Irony ironizes the ironist and the ironized alike; the spider is spun by the web it spins. These double statements of causality—which seem to be short circuits ("closed causal loops")—are required by the nonlinear system of which they partake. They seem to reduce history to Althusser's "process without a *telos* or a subject" (cited in Jameson 1981, 29): an ironizing, a spinning. But just because the web only tightens when you pull, or because you only sink deeper into the quicksand of the abyss when you flail, does not mean there is nothing to be done.

Time in the School of Mirrors:
"Tintern Abbey" and "Frost at Midnight"

Wordsworth's "Tintern Abbey" and Coleridge's "Frost at Midnight" work to construct a "deep structure" of time around the simple concentric gimmick of flashback-within-flashback occurring near the center of each poem, troubling the narrative

. . . The picture of the mind revives again:
While here I stand, not only with the sense
Of present pleasure, but with pleasing thoughts
That in this moment there is life and food
For future years. And so I dare to hope,
Though changed, no doubt, from what I was when first
I came among these hills; when like a roe
I bounded o'er the mountains, by the sides
Of the deep rivers, and the lonely streams,
Wherever nature led: more like a man
Flying from something that he dreads than one
Who sought the thing he loved. For nature then
(The coarser pleasures of my boyish days,
And their glad animal movements all gone by)
To me was all in all.--I cannot paint
What then I was. The sounding cataract
Haunted me like a passion; the tall rock,
The mountain, and the deep and gloomy wood,
Their colours and their forms, were then to me
An appetite; a feeling and a love,
That had no need of a remoter charm,
By thought supplied, nor any interest
Unborrowed from the eye.
                               --That time is past,
And all its aching joys are now no more,
And all its dizzy raptures. Not for this
Faint I, nor mourn nor murmur; other gifts
Have followed; for such loss, I would believe,
Abundant recompense. . . .

. . . the idling Spirit
By its own moods interprets, every where
Echo or mirror seeking of itself,
And makes a toy of Thought.
                               But O! How oft,
How oft, at school, with most believing mind,
Presageful, have I gazed upon the bars,
To watch that fluttering stranger! and as oft
With unclosed lids, already had I dreamt
Of my sweet birth-place, and the old church-tower,
Whose bells, the poor man's only music, rang
From morn to evening, all the hot Fair-day,
So sweetly, that they stirred and haunted me
With a wild pleasure, falling on mine ear
Most like articulate sounds of things to come!
So gazed I, till the soothing things I dreamt
Lulled me to sleep, and sleep prolonged my dreams!
And so I brooded all the following morn,
Awed by the stern preceptor's face, mine eye
Fixed with mock study on my swimming book:
Save if the door half opened, and I snatched
A hasty glance, and still my heart leaped up,
For still I hoped to see the stranger's face,
Townsman, or aunt, or sister more beloved,
My play-mate when we both were clothed alike!

Dear Babe, that sleepest cradled by my side,
Whose gentle breathings, heard in this deep calm,
Fill up the interspersed vacancies
And momentary pauses . . .

Concentric Flashbacks: Wordsworth's "Tintern Abbey" (*left*) and Coleridge's "Frost at Midnight" (*right*)

flow of the poems like a whirlpool in a stream. But just as the circular form of the panopticon occurs with its extended and turbulent pi-form, these concentricities occur amid more imbricated temporal structures of flashforwards-within-flashbacks, flashbacks-within-flashforwards, and so on: Coleridge's narrator remembers his younger self dreaming of his still-younger self daydreaming "of things to come"; Wordsworth's narrator sees a version of his younger self in his sister, whom he imagines in the future remembering him in the present (now past). These imbrications produce an echo chamber whose interference patterns constitute the fabric of Romantic time; a meta-immediacy is produced as the excess of the multiple temporal mediations.

The developmental stages set up in "Tintern Abbey" have been rehearsed too many times by critics already; at issue here is how the machinery of the poem produces these concentrized stages in conjunction with, or even in reaction to, the interference pattern that is their matrix.

The "coarser pleasures" that the flashback-within-flashback situates at its center give a clue as to the continuum that the poem establishes along with its articulated stages. Typically Wordsworthian comparative adjectives (such as "coarser") are used sparingly, but with telltale consistency, throughout the poem: "Thoughts of *more deep* seclusion"; "my *purer* mind"; "another gift, of aspect *more sublime*"; "a *remoter* charm, by thought supplied"; "a sense sublime of something *far more deeply* interfused"; "anchor of my *purest* thoughts"; "my *dearest* Friend"; "*warmer* love—oh! with *far deeper* zeal / Of *holier* love"; "*more dear,* both for themselves and for thy sake." At their most schematic, the adjectives juxtapose a categorical (qualitative, articulated) and binary distinction between body and mind or spirit, along with a quantitative or continuous difference, both entirely conventional. Differences in kind and degree are both dissipative ones: the "purest thoughts" require the fixation of a material "anchor," while material depth and distance inevitably suggest infinite echoes of deeper depths and more sublime sublimities whose repetitively scaling self-similarity constitutes their truth-effect. This effect is grandiosely quantified in the final lines of *The Prelude*, which assert the function of poetry as a demonstration of "how the mind of man becomes / A thousand times more beautiful than the earth / On which he dwells."

A key phrase of "Tintern Abbey"—"something far more deeply interfused"—marks the point of saturation at which simple linear depths and their "deeper, dearer, warmer, holier, purer, sublimer" echoes give way to a qualitatively different and more valued kind of depth that exceeds a simple continuum. "Deeply interfused," as suggested earlier, refers to a depth of scale (a fractal depth) rather than a depth of space: that which is "far more deeply interfused" is not really even "depth" at all insofar as it does not require three dimensions; it is not farther away but more intimately ubiquitous, embedded, and epistemic. The most finely grained, filigreed, and filiated network is that which most defines the disciplinary body and mind in the likeness of the discipline that defines them, the fineness of its weave characterizing at once the dense opacity of bodily tissue, the intricate connectednesses of thought and imagery, the material extension of disciplinary systems. It is here, too, that Newtonian matter-embedded-in-space gives way to a universe in which space and matter, thought and thing are united by the unreifiable turbulence that agitates and subsumes each:

> ... a motion and a spirit, that impels
> All thinking things, all objects of all thought,
> And rolls through all things.
> (1969, 164)

The structured ambiguity of the typically Wordsworthian "something" allows it to stand in for the operation of an unreifiable constellation (money, god, nature, print culture, discipline) that has no discrete identity but produces identities in its wake via a homeorrhetic cycling that both differentiates and renders interchangeable the media through which it cycles.

The kind of sublimity or infinitude associated with this interfusion, like an infinitude of irrational numbers rather than the infinity of integers, is produced not by linear extension but by saturation and internal differentiation: it constitutes an infinite *between*. Difference is continually folded back onto itself: the poem is constructed as a switchboard, its circuitry elaborated by repeated cyclings back and forth between and among city and country; youth, adolescence, and adulthood; man and woman; interiority and landscape; and so on.

Each of these differentials — especially, here, temporal ones — are cast as economic opportunities, potential poetic capital. While the narrator of "I wandered lonely" had "gazed — and gazed — but little thought / What wealth the show to me had brought," the narrator of "Tintern Abbey" gazes upon the scene "not only with the sense / Of present pleasure, but with pleasing thoughts / That in this moment there is life and food / For future years"; loss brings "abundant recompense"; and so on. The ongoing differential between himself and his sister allows the narrator to posit that the features of the landscape will eventually pay a dividend to Dorothy because they had been "more dear" to him, "both for themselves and for thy sake." This complex projection-introjection and anticipation-nostalgia mechanism attempts to ensure that the structure of time will continually be under construction, and that the means of its production will be the poem. Through the Dorothy figure, feminine subjectivity is not relegated by its *essence* to an inferior status; after all, the narrator imagines his sister growing into a version of his own mature sobriety — after he has gone. But the rejection of essentialism means, as in Laqueur's sexual "horizontalization" scenario, only that the poem mandates that the asymmetry that situates Dorothy as a superseded stage be continually reproduced — *dynamically* — out of a repeated transaction, an ongoing alienation and reinvestment of surplus value whose engine is the poem.

Another version of the temporal machine deployed in "Tintern Abbey," Coleridge's "Frost at Midnight," operates as a virtual "heat engine" that sets the cold, quiet, solitary stasis of the present against the hot, loud, turbulent, crowded "Fair-day" of the deep past. This problematic is resolved in a future characterized as a chaotic ecology of intermittencies that succeed the relatively monolithic, but unstable, stages of the earlier sections of the poem. The surplus value of these temporal differentiations, in terms that structure Coleridge's career, takes the form of an infinite retroaction in which, for example, one can always write criticism when one can no longer write poems about why one can no longer write poems about why one could never have an authentic and unmediated experience.

The poem's opening stanza locates a present lack in the narrator's mode of engagement/alienation in the world. This lack is identified with an interpretive framework that orients the narrator via the narcissistic "echo or mirror" of himself that he finds in the so-called *stranger* (the film of soot that flutters over the dying fire). This lack leads nostalgically back to a previous interpretive mode — not philosophical metaphor but folklore — in which the "stranger" did not figure the self but prefigured the appearance of an other, albeit an other still to come from the narrator's past. The school scene that follows is situated at the transition point between hermeneutic modes, at the point where folklore is systematically replaced — disciplined — by philosophy. Still the narrator's lack or desire seeks the restoration of an earlier plenitude, referring nostalgically back again to his "birthplace" where the ringing bells had signaled pure futurity ("sounds of things to come"), again in a folkloric mode (by alluding to the story of Dick Whittington, to whom the ringing bells foretold his destiny to become Lord Mayor). The "stranger" is thus the site of a temporal backsliding through developmental stages that finds no ground, but, at bottom, the turbulence of pure futurity.

But still the unchanging stasis (figured in the opening stanzas by the "owlet's cry" that comes "loud, and hark again, loud as before" and by the film that "fluttered on the grate" and "still flutters there") persists in the persistence of desire:

> For still I hoped to see the *stranger's* face,
> Townsman, or aunt, or sister more beloved,
> My playmate when we both were clothed alike!
> (1985, 88)

The nostalgic slide toward more immediate closeness (reproduced succinctly in the series "Townsman, . . . aunt, . . . sister") continues to seek plenitude in the infinite regress to a past situated finally as prior to gender differentiation.

This impasse produces a rebound into a future characterized, in the final two stanzas, by maximal and fractal *differentiation*; a *virtual* future, according to N. Katherine Hayles's definition of virtuality as *"the perception that material structures are interpenetrated with informational patterns"* (Hayles 1995; emphasis in original). In its recursivity, this Coleridgean future exceeds the Judeo-Christian equation of World with Word: here, materiality is subsumed in a complex symbolic circuitry of cross-representation figured first by the coexistence of "lakes, and sandy shores" and "the crags / Of ancient mountain" with "clouds, / Which image in their bulk both lakes and shores / And mountain crags." This utopia is characterized not by simple fullness but by images of intermittency and interpenetration. The "red-breast"—traditionally (in English poetry, that is) the only bird that continues to sing throughout the winter—figures the interpenetrative persistence of song amid silence, and of color amid the black and white of bare branch and snow; the smoking chimney and thatch amid the otherwise uniform blanket of snow indicate the persistence of warmth amid cold and of difference (pattern) in sameness, while the association of song, color, and warmth as forms of turbulence place all of the images in a synesthetic continuum. This ideal future state is also a complex and interpenetrative ecology of regularities and irregularities: the transcended regularity of seasons (transcended since "all seasons will be sweet") does not yield stasis but maximally chaotic rhythms in which even uniformity (the monolithic "greenness" of the "general earth" in summer) is subsumed as simply one element in a chaotic series. Chaotic rhythms are specified in the interlocking images of turbulent storm-blasts, the baby's steadily regular but only intermittently heard breathing, the intermittent eave-drops, the "interspersed vacancies" of cognitive activity. The ecology of sounds, sights, and motions is one whose heterogeneities and intermittencies (especially in the spatial, temporal, and material patterns of flux and stasis, regularity and irregularity) achieve such a density as to constitute a kind of chaotic plenum, chaotic (and only a "kind of plenum") because it is only *more* full for being full of both fullnesses and "vacancies."

The fluttering film with its mobile and unpredictable patterns of excesses and gaps (its "puny flaps and freaks"), which had begun as an image of flux set against a monolithically and oppressively static world, has disappeared as a figure insofar as the whole world has now been made over into its image, into a version of what Kristeva would describe as the "semiotic chora" (1984, 25–30) or Foucault would anticipate as the "murmur" or "stirring of an indifference" in discourse (1984, 119–20).

The final representative of this chaotic ecology is the figure of icicles "quietly shining to the quiet moon," an image that displaces the static two-body mirroring between narrator and "stranger" with a complex circuit of reflections of reflections of borrowed light, further displacing the figure-ground or past-present relations between flux and stasis or warmth and cold with the dynamism of homeorrhetic form (i.e., a stasis of flux) maintained through continual melting and freezing.

"Frost at Midnight" is, as I suggested earlier, one of many versions of a Coleridgean heat engine or figurative combinatory. Like "Frost at Midnight," Coleridge's "Aeolian Harp" opens with the stasis of a desexualized domestic idyll whose hermeneutic structure is referentially fixed insofar as it is characterized by simple "emblems." This stasis gives way to a folkloric, orgasmic flux of fairies, sounds, swellings, and subsidings that finally subsume all phenomena into the philosophical pantheism of "joyance everywhere" before being fixated again by the dogmatic gaze of the wife's "more serious eye," Christianity being positioned (this time) as the resolving mediator between philosophy and folklore. Likewise in "Kubla Khan," a flat, enclosed, orderly and beautiful, productive, but essentially static landscape "slants" toward the violently sublime instability at its heart, a violent *jouissance* that always threatens to engulf all space and time. Each of these poems employs self-reference to situate the poems themselves as participants in the symbolic ecologies they describe. The strings of the aeolian harp, like the lines of the poem (and, subsequently, like all material bodies), are discretely differential units across which passes a continuous flux. The iambic pentameter in the central section of "Kubla Kahn" is figured neatly by the walled enclosure of "*twice five* miles of fertile ground" (pointedly altered from the "sixteene miles" described in Coleridge's source text), the tension of rhythm against meter landscaped into a Cartesian linearity that "slants" from the discretely metric—via "sinuous rills" and "meandering" river—toward the ultimately "measureless" (like a grid that warps into a singularity). In "Frost at Midnight," the fluttering film set against the bars of the fire grate restates the problematic of continuous difference (marked by sliding, slanting, sinuousity, and so on) set against regular and discretely articulated difference (rigidly parallel bars, poetic lines, and meter). In each case the effect of this problematic impasse or contradiction is to generate an ongoing combinatory of permutations that no narrative can finally resolve. While "The Aeolian Harp" settles dutifully for the triumph of the singular, fixative gaze of Christian dogma's "more serious eye" amid the randomly noisy flux of "Philosophy's aye-babbling spring," "Frost at Midnight" associates a similar panoptic gaze with philosophy, aligning the "stern preceptor's face" with the student's own eyes, "fixed with mock study on my swimming book" in what is only a radically unresolved midway point in the poem. Like "Frost at Midnight," "Kubla Kahn" concludes not with fixity but with a dream-within-dream and flux-within-flux of the thrice-woven circle of dancers whose center is not a stable ground but only the "flashing eyes" and "floating hair" of the prophet. An ongoing combinatory of flux and fixation and their permutations, both within and between individual poems, seeks provisional resolution in single images or single poems while guaranteeing that no such resolution will be possible, that the poem will continue to be written.

       In fact, Coleridge did continue to alter the final image of "Frost at Midnight," most notably by suppressing an early version in which the homeorrhetic "stasis of flux" so neatly enacted by the icicles is interrupted again by the infant's unresolvable desire to escape the constraint of his father's arms and "fly for very eagerness" toward the dynamic and glittering forms, an insubordinate desire that by definition seeks to violate its developmental, familial, and even species-specific positionedness. If Coleridge opted for a safer and more circular closure in the icicle figure, the economy of i-cycles already generated by the poem is set up to guarantee the priority of ongoing and chaotic vacillation between closure and openendedness over any resolution; thus the ambiguous "end" of the poem continuously freezes and melts, leaving a stalagmite of variant readings beneath it.

Nesting Doll Narrators: *Frankenstein*

Mary Shelley's 1817 novel, *Frankenstein*, is patterned in a rigorously concentric "Chinese box" structure. The monster's narrative (that is, text in which "I" is the monster) occupies the center of the novel; before and after it comes Frankenstein's narrative, which is in turn framed on either side by Walton's narrative. The author's preface to the 1818 edition (by Percy Shelley writing "as" Mary) stands "eccentrically" outside this structure by prefacing (but not following) the text. Shelley even took care to make both "cross-sections" of the two framing narratives nearly equal in length, so not so much as a bulge distorts the novel's concentricity.

This structure has been particularly durable in subsequent adaptations of the novel, for example in the framing tales and narrators that appear in many of the film versions. The structure grows a new layer in editor James Reiger's authoritative 1974 text of the novel: editor pushes author into the wheel-within-wheel of the narrative by placing the author's 1818 preface immediately before the body of the novel and her 1831 introduction immediately after it, allowing his own introduction to stand in

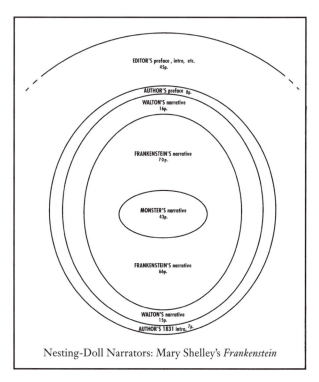

Nesting-Doll Narrators: Mary Shelley's *Frankenstein*

the transcendent, undoubled position at the "head" of the text, where Shelley had been. Reiger reperforms the eternal spiral of concentricity and eccentricity in the relation of editor to author and author to self established by the narrative structure of *Frankenstein*, fictionalized by Carlyle in *Sartor* or Coleridge in *The Rime of the Ancient Mariner*, and enacted by Chatterton.

The effect of this structure is to establish a field or gradient of intensities, and to mobilize or activate various problematics among its characters or narrative layers. Paradoxically, it is its instability, its tendency to collapse, that makes it so durable. If, like the novel, each man bears the monster within, eternal vigilance is necessary. This account of the novel may underwrite a Victorian feminism, but at the cost of gothicizing masculinity (charging it with seductive power and danger): more often than not, the vigilance produced goes toward the maintenance of masculinity. In other words, simply to laud the novel's critique of the masculinist dream of self-sufficiency by usurpation of female reproductive prerogatives may also be to underwrite the homophobic panic this damage control implies.

The play of similarity and difference between characters is marked in the book's reception: "Frankenstein" has been widely adopted as the nameless monster's name, Victor and Henry switch names in the 1931 film, and the "real" circumstances of the novel's writing (as noted in Mary Shelley's introduction) are woven into the "fictional" story in a number of subsequent adaptations (e.g., *The Bride of Frankenstein* and *Gothic*).

As has often been noted, the three narrators share troubled relationships with absent, negligent, or hostile fathers. Accordingly, all three are largely self-educated (at least in their early, "formative" years) and, in the absence of systematic education, make illegitimate connections between science and history, fiction, poetry, and mysticism. Intensity increases as the central narrative is approached. Where Walton's and Frankenstein's fathers had been absent or negligent but well-meaning, the monster is cruelly rejected by his. Where Walton and Frankenstein pursue first mysticism and poetry, and then science, in a kind of "serial monogamy," these are continually and dangerously conflated for the monster. If Walton is able to turn back from his ambitious mission rather than jeopardize his crew further, Frankenstein vacillates between ambition and moderation up to the moment of his death, while the monster pursues a single-minded ("pre-Oedipal") course in which his appeal to be saved or loved is continually and inextricably implicated in his destructive revenge and hatred.

Walton, the "framing narrator," complains that his "education was neglected": written accounts of ship voyages seeking the legendary Northwest

Passage occupied his youth, but "these visions faded" when he discovered poetry (11). The subsequent failure of his poetic ambitions led him back to seafaring and the search for a Northwest Passage, in spite of his father's deathbed injunction that he avoid the sea. But the sequence that begins with seafaring and leads to poetry and back again to seafaring turns out to be a chicken-and-egg scenario: "I have often attributed my attachment to, my passionate enthusiasm for, the dangerous mysteries of the ocean, to that production of the most imaginative of modern poets" (231), that is, to Coleridge's "Rime of the Ancient Mariner." The causal sequence of Walton's passions for poetry and seafaring may be shifty (especially in retrospect), but their braiding-together is clearly fraught with danger.

Frankenstein's seduction by reading begins with the alchemical texts he encounters as a young man, and his father's cursory disapproval is not enough to dissuade him. If his father had taken more time to explain *why* he should avoid alchemy, Frankenstein rationalizes in retrospect, he "should probably have applied myself to the more rational theory of chemistry which has resulted from modern discoveries. It is even possible, that the train of my ideas would never have received the fatal impulse that led to my ruin" (33). His father does eventually lead him on to empirical experiments with electricity, and to a formal course of study in natural philosophy, but this step—which might have been efficacious earlier—now can only contribute to the fatal series. Frankenstein's early reading has irrevocably induced a "contempt for the uses of modern natural philosophy," which require the exchange of "chimeras of boundless grandeur for realities of little worth" (41). So when the validity of alchemy is finally "exploded" for him and he applies himself to a modern course of study, Frankenstein is irresistibly driven by the dangerous mixed desire to integrate chimerical and grandiose ends with the empirical tools and methods that his studies provide.

While the two men are driven by the sequential fascination with and failure of disciplines and their subsequent braiding-together, the unity of discipline for the monster poses an even more dangerous threat. While many readings of the novel set scientific hubris and excess of ambitious desire against a humanist or domestic decorum, the monster reveals that the problematic is inextricably coextensive with language itself: his first consciousness of language impresses him that "this was indeed a godlike science, and I ardently desired to become acquainted with it" (107). The monster's first books are Volney's radical 1791 history, *Ruins of Empires*, and "*Paradise Lost*, a volume of *Plutarch's Lives*, and the *Sorrows of Werther*," a heady mix (within and among them) of politics and history, poetry and fiction, and religion. Of these, *Paradise Lost* is particularly formative: "I read it," the monster recalls, "as I had read the other volumes which had fallen into my hands, as a true history" (125). In an important sense, then, the monster's character—like the careers of Walton and Frankenstein—is produced by the inability to make appropriate disciplinary distinctions; that is, distinctions that tell us what we may and may not do with particular kinds of knowledge. While the monster's statement indicates that he must subsequently have learned the difference between "true history" and literature, his Miltonic rants make it clear that the monster's "genre trouble" has been formative.

In piecing together the "real-time" plot that underlies the narrative, the reader is made to resemble Walton, Frankenstein, and the monster as they reconstruct their own narratives with conspicuous and suspicious retroaction. At the ambiguous bottom of each plot, what the novel's reader finds are *problematic acts of reading* in which disciplinary division, recombination, and conflation—especially between science and literature—are all dangers. In this way, insofar as Shelley's novel is "science fiction," it continually thematizes and gothicizes its *own* constitutive disciplinary problematic. For the seductive dangers and anxieties of reading in general, and of disciplinary mixing in particular, the book is its own evidence. As for being pulled along fatally to a conclusion, readers have their own completion of the novel as evidence. The act of reading ceases to be subject to truth criteria by becoming a performative touchstone.

The 1931 film deftly translates this self-referentiality into cinematic terms. A "Master of Ceremonies" introduces the film by warning squeamish viewers to leave before the story begins, just as Frankenstein will warn his friends away from his laboratory, absolving himself from the consequences of their staying. The film viewer, like the novel reader, is made complicitous with the doctor by the morbidity of her or his own desire or curiosity, continually witnessed by the simple fact of continuing to watch the film. The climactic "creation" scene of the film features Dr. Frankenstein attending to his creature while his father, his friend Victor, and his fiancée Elizabeth sit and observe, modeling the appropriate gestures of horror for the film's real audience as the monster is animated. Like the film, the creature is spliced together from dead parts and animated by light and electricity; as such, it is appropriate that the film's monster is nearly mute, while the novel's garrulous monster had been thoroughly a creature of language. The monster reaches out, pathetically, toward the light that pierces the gloom, as if a filmic image should reach out in vain toward its projector. In the film's climax, Dr. Frankenstein and his creature are caught together in a burning mill whose multiple rotating wheels suggest the reels of the motion-picture apparatus.

The spatiotemporal (and narrative) linearity of film continues to be troubled by repetitive self-referential loops that set figures of linearity against figures of sprawl and cycle. Opening shot sequences are privileged self-referential occasions. In the title sequence of *Mystery Train*, for example, the almost-blurring-together windows of a speeding train suggest the relentless linearity of the passing frames of film, establishing a counterpoint to the thoroughgoing nonlinearity of the film's rhizomically connecting and disconnecting plots. The opening shot of *The Crying Game*—where a long, linear pan across a railroad bridge and river remains centered on the spinning wheels of carnival rides—establishes a visual combinatory of cyclicalities and linearities as an emblem for the vicissitudes of sex, gender, ethnicity, and nation that follow. Self-referential figures refer only instrumentally to the specificities of media in order to insert them, in turn, into a more generalized economy of self-reference.

Predictably, then, a little echo of the role played by literacy in advancing *Frankenstein*'s "fatal series" finds its way back into the film version, transformed into the danger of *illiteracy* to reflect the medium. When Frankenstein's lab assistant, Fritz, sneaks into an anatomy classroom to steal a brain for the monster, he bumps into a hanging skeleton that bobs up and down, causing him to jump back in fear. Seconds later, after snatching a jar containing a preserved brain, a noise frightens him and causes him to drop the jar, which shatters on the floor. He promptly grabs the other jar, containing an abnormal rather than normal brain, apparently unconcerned because *he cannot read* the labels that identify them. The apparently pure accident of the interrupting noise and the apparently pure arbitrariness of the illiterate choice come into play with the apparently pure determinism of the two brains. But because this scene immediately follows a scene of the anatomy class in progress, in which the students *giggle* at the bobbing skeleton, Fritz's frightened response is shown to depend on the context of his criminal act. Even though (or rather, because) the causal sequences are attenuated and multiple, the monster can be said to become a criminal because Fritz, acting on behalf of Frankenstein, is a criminal: the question of whether genetics, character, or actions are determinate is ambiguated into a school of red herrings whose choreography is a chaotic play of causality, a smoke screen for the authoritarian tautology that, finally, criminality simply breeds criminality. Similarly, the "pecking order" division of labor—beginning with Frankenstein's contemptuous mistreatment of Fritz (the doctor addresses the film's first words to Fritz: "Down, you fool, down!") and leading to Fritz's mistreatment of the monster—is also offered up as an additional causal explanation, but again the necessity of subordination is unquestioned; it simply must be managed with appropriate "mildness."

Self-reference in the novel has another dimension insofar as the disciplinary distinctions and conflations that structure the *plot* also structure the *narratives* in which the plot is embedded. The novel especially works a distinction between referential discourses, such as science and history, which are to be verified by their appeal to a "real world," and self-referential literary discourse, in which truth is supposed to be generated by "internal consistency."

Percy, writing as Mary, introduces the volume as the representative of a higher truth insofar as it must be distinguished both from a mere "series of supernatural terrors" and from physical fact: the story,

however impossible as a physical fact, affords a point of view to the imagination for the delineating of human passions more comprehensive and commanding than any which the ordinary relations of existing events can yield. I have thus endeavored to preserve the truth of the elementary principles of human nature, while I have not scrupled to innovate upon their combinations. (6)

These statements prefigure Frankenstein's introduction of his story to Walton (or rather, they echo them, having been written subsequently):

if you are inclined, listen to my tale. I believe that the strange incidents connected with it will afford a view of nature which may enlarge your faculties and understanding. You will hear of powers and occurrences, such as you have been accustomed to believe impossible; but I do not doubt that my tale conveys in its series internal evidence of the truth of the events of which it is composed. (24)

The monster, introducing his story to Frankenstein, offers an abbreviated echo of this introduction: "Hear my tale; it is long and strange" (96). Subsequently, Frankenstein attempts to elicit the aid of a magistrate in tracking down the monster, and again echoes the preceding introductions:

listen, therefore, to the deposition that I have to make. It is indeed a tale so strange, that I should fear you would not credit it, were there not something in truth which, however wonderful, forces conviction. The story is too connected to be mistaken for a dream. (196–97)

But now the magistrate's inability to rectify literary truth with action in the "official" world lets the monster's reign of terror continue, no less than conflation of the two had enabled his creation. The magistrate listens "with that half kind of belief that is given to a tale of spirits and supernatural events; but when he was called upon to act officially in consequence, the whole tide of his incredulity returned" (197).

For Walton, too, the sight of the "hard evidence" of actual letters referred to in Frankenstein's story "brought to me a greater conviction of the truth of his narrative than his asseverations, however earnest and connected" (207).

In this vacillation of truth criteria, Mary Shelley invests the legacy of her father and mother's generation. Mary's father, William Godwin, in his 1793 *Enquiry Concerning Political Justice*, had asserted that "every truth that is capable of being communicated, is capable of being brought home to the conviction of the mind" (Godwin 1946, 1: 93). It was in this vein that Godwin advised Joseph Gerrald, imprisoned in 1793 for his reformist activities as a member of the London Corresponding Society, on how to give his testimony, arguing that there is no one "upon whom truth, truth fully and adequately stated, will make no impression.... This is my theory, and I now come before *you* in practice" (Godwin 1988, 356). Gerrald was convicted and transported to Australia, where he soon died.

In an apparently stark reversal of his earlier, more sanguine position, Godwin's novel *Things as They Are; or, The Adventures of Caleb Williams* continually demonstrates the primacy, in the final instance, not only of ideology over factual evidence but, more generally, of material, political, and social interests over ontological or even rhetorical truth. Caleb is continually hounded by a panoptic power that frustrates his attempts to reveal his secret, his evidence (and self-evidence) that the new hegemony of mildness and reason (incarnate in his panoptic persecutor, Falkland) is founded upon violence and murder no less than the brutally coercive aristocratic power it has displaced. Likewise, Mary Shelley's mother, Mary Wollstonecraft, followed her progressivist tract, *A Vindication of the Rights of Women*, with the novel *Maria*, whose heroine remains alone and disbelieved in gothic imprisonment at the unfinished conclusion.

It is easy to attribute Godwin's and Wollstonecraft's apparent change of attitude to the waning of Enlightenment optimism as the government's counterrevolutionary repression was redoubled throughout the 1790s, and their change in genre to the Romantic "internalization" that accompanies these developments. If Godwin and Wollstonecraft were subject to such internalization, at least as it is enacted in their shifts to the more "private" form of the novel, the novels themselves thematize internalization as imprisonment and the failure to make oneself understood, even as the move from political philosophy to fiction is being dictated in large part by the coercive intersection of financial exigency and political expediency.

But, as in Coleridge's "Frost at Midnight," the end of the story is never the end. In Godwin's published version of his novel, Caleb is finally vindicated and liberated when Falkland is forced to admit "that the artless and manly story you have told has carried conviction to every hearer" (335). This version reverses the ending of Godwin's unpublished manuscript, in which Caleb remains imprisoned and his story disbelieved, Falkland having merely "acknowledged that it was told with great artifice and appearance of consistency" (341). The conventional distinction between "manly" artlessness and implicitly feminine artifice functions less as a generic fixation of the novel than as an ongoing contradiction ensuring that no adequate resolution can be attained. In any case, the upshot is about the same. Even when his story is believed, Caleb finds that he has "now no character that I wish to vindicate" and that his belated defeat of the haggard and self-loathing Falkland is cruelly redundant. Caleb's eleventh-hour justification for his memoir, that "the world may at least not hear a mangled and half-told tale" (337), is ironic insofar as it tells precisely half the story. In the other half (the first ending), Caleb languishes in prison, unheard, like "a GRAVE-STONE — an obelisk to tell you, HERE LIES WHAT WAS ONCE A MAN!" (346). Finally, then, the upshot of either ending or of any writing is the "death of the author" (his characterlessness beneath the gravestone of his text). The effect of this death is to install a two-stage fixation (character giving way to characterlessness, manliness to "once-a-man," truth to fiction, and so on) *within* a more comprehensive system in which the second stage has always already been in effect. In his *Enquiry* and advice to Gerrald, Godwin had imagined and attempted to speak from a place where truth and rhetorical persuasion merge into a praxis that would be performative; the self-referential (literary) dimension of this praxis is enacted insofar as *it is impossible to tell whether any of Godwin's statements about truth are themselves truth statements or strategic fictions.*

This same dynamic is enacted succinctly in Blake's final "Proverb of Hell," the Godwinian assertion that "truth can never be told so as to be understood. and not be believ'd." Blake's handwritten engraving (which makes it difficult to tell a period from a comma), coupled with his syntax and idiosyncratic punctuation (he sometimes seems to use a period in place of a comma to indicate a longer pause), configures in a single statement the two mutually exclusive propositions by which the careers of Godwin and Wollstonecraft have been (problematically) "periodized." The embedded and contradictory statement that "truth can never be told so as to be understood" begins to break the proverb into a series of fractally scaling echoes that define Romantic epistemology: Truth can never be told so as to be understood and not be believed . . . ; Truth can never be told so as to be understood . . . ; Truth can never be told . . . ; Truth can never be. . . . If the question of whether the series should be periodized as an erosion from big to little or an accretion from little to big is characteristic of the period, the proverb's fractal and echoic saturation by truth games is also simply its ongoing function.

This function, enacted in the interruptive and unresolvable dialectic of genre and truth, continues to engender *Frankenstein*, where its exhaustion continues to constitute both its victory and its defeat, and to gesture toward its displacement.

Postmodern Postscript: Concentric Collapse in *Twin Peaks*

David Lynch's 1989–90 television series, *Twin Peaks*, is noteworthy as one of the most developed instances of *auteurist* television, usually a contradiction in terms. As such, a self-conscious "depth" continually *curves* the surface of the text, otherwise a conspicuously flat, postmodern pastiche of recombinant generic features drawn from gothic and hard-boiled detective fiction, soap opera and retro-TV, and New Age spiritualism. The series's main character, a hyperprofessionally detached FBI man, is drawn into the underside of small-town white America as the question that drives the series and his investigation ("Who killed Laura Palmer?") expands into a network of questionable practices, and as narrative time-space keeps curving toward a discursive Big Bang or black hole where sex and violence merge in an ambiguous menagerie of dreams, demonic possession, incest, and murder.

This general curvature structures individual scenes as well. In one typical episode, the quilted flatness of picaresque and even slapstick scenes strung together with "and" and "and" and "and" slopes suddenly into a "depth" scene. In order to obtain her murdered friend Laura's diary, which may help unravel the sinister knot at the core of the plot, Donna is attempting to seduce Harold, a recluse who cultivates orchids and collects women's sexual case histories. Donna recounts an early sexual encounter in which she and Laura had gotten drunk and gone skinny-dipping with two boys; Harold sits writing down her story, centered in the background while Donna is foregrounded and off center, triangulating the viewer and Harold, his mirror image.

As Donna tells the story she becomes, or pretends to become, more and more self-involved. The speaking subject becomes the subject spoken as her voice becomes hypnotic, her hand becomes the boy's hand raised to her lips as they meet in the water. Harold drops his pen, and the camera is sucked into an extreme close-up of Donna, whose face and voice show the conventions of arousal. Donna concludes the story teasingly: there is no dark secret at the center (she and the boy merely kiss and part), nothing enunciated but merely the effect of enunciation.

The scene is structured concentrically: in the outermost ring, the viewer and Harold focus inward on Donna, who focuses inward in turn on her memory of the drunken, naked swimming. The implosion of the center staggers (un-balances) Harold by disturbing the way the story, its teller, its telling, and its listener are staggered (concentrized); it pulls him in and pushes him out along with the viewer he stands and falls for.

This concentricity is woven into a complex intertextual matrix. Harold's orchid cultivation associates him with a famous detective and an even more famous detective's client: Rex Stout's detective, Nero Wolfe, who solves crimes without leaving the apartment where he cultivates orchids, and General Sternwood of

Mall of America. The economic and ideological significance of stochastic flux is nowhere better incarnated and apotheosized than in the gigantic Mall of America, which opened in 1990 near the site where the first full-fledged shopping mall was born (like me) in Minneapolis in 1956. The circulation of pedestrian consumer traffic through the mall surrounds the circulation of amusement park rides (balloon rides, watercourses, merry-go-rounds) that fill the gigantic central courtyard; glimpses of these various carnivalesque orbits are offered continually to peripatetic shoppers through the various openings onto the courtyard. The mall is not oriented for its patrons by Cartesian perspectives or fixated by a singular grand entrance (rendered extraneous since the overwhelming majority of pedestrian traffic into the mall enters through undistinguished passages leading from the attached parking garage). Instead, seemingly fortuitous correspondences between fluxes function both to orient and disorient, producing a chaotic wheel-within-wheel in which Wordsworth's vulgar "perpetual whirl" of commodities and his sublime "something . . . that rolls through all things" perform the do-si-do in which Romanticism and postmodernity are historical partners.

Raymond Chandler's *The Big Sleep*, the dupe of his daughters and prisoner of his body and his doctors, which confine him and his orchids to a fragile, hothouse existence. Harold is the creature of a homosocial intertextuality that constitutes a subject in a dynamic of self-sufficiency and dependence (figured even more succinctly in the relation between hermaphroditic orchids and their human go-betweens and conservators), kept alive by the question of how knowledge can be attained by or on behalf of such a subject—or kept from him. All one can expect these problematics to generate is indeterminacy about whether this subject thrives on its own collapse, whether the revelation of the dark secret of female sexuality might be the nonrevelation of a nonsecret, and what might happen to patriarchy in its wake.

Permutations of concentric collapse structure other key moments in the series. In a late episode, a suburban family scene gives way to brutal incest and murder as the light jazz playing on the phonograph fades and intercut close-ups show the phonograph arm spiraling into the record's blank center, where it keeps skipping. The ambiguous end of the series resolves figures of spiraling and collapsing concentricity into a "strange attractor." The final scene sums it all up as a kind of circus tent in the woods—a house of mirrors or musical chairs or a shell game—where all characters (alive and dead, dreamed and real) repeatedly disappear and reappear as they duck into rooms and reemerge or not, encounter each other—or not.

F　　　O　　　U　　　R

Fractal Logics of Romanticism:
Binary Decomposition

Introduction: Paine's Headless Hydra

In fractal geometry, "binary decomposition" refers to a process whereby, through repeated iterations of a recursive mathematical function, a plane is divided and sub-divided into binary sections (e.g., black and white) in infinite regress of scale (see Peitgen and Richter 1986, 40–44). A mud puddle dries up, cracking into progressively smaller pieces, but somewhere between the phlegmatic wholeness of the mud puddle and the uniformly atomized dust (or *Between Crystal and Smoke*, in François Jacob's terms) is where everything (interesting) happens: with and against this one-directional deterioration emerge *patterns* of the distribution, shapes or sizes of the pieces. This "between" is not a simple compromise or equilibrium nor a static middle ground

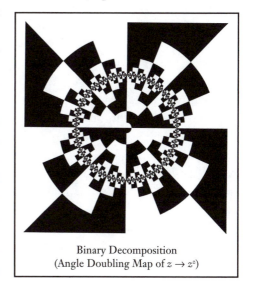

Binary Decomposition
(Angle Doubling Map of $z \rightarrow z^z$)

between order and disorder but an opportunistic movement in which a different kind of order emerges, a chaotic order (designated simply as *chaos* here) contingent on the continuous slide toward disorder with which it is opposed but also intimately aligned. An "arrow of chaos" would define this movement, rather than the movement from order to disorder usually identified as the ultimate sweep of the "arrow of time," as that which orients meaning in history. This reversal situates life itself not so much as a noble thermodynamic outlaw holding out against disorder, but more as a player in an ongoing intrigue.

The paradigm is useful here insofar as it offers a step or two beyond the focus on binarized difference to show how the spread (or saturation or explosion) of crucial differences across a historical field can coincide with both their apotheosis and downfall. Here I am concerned with how binary decomposition operates as a cultural logic, with how an ideological "gestalt" is made to cling upon an infinite brokenness, and vice versa.

The logic of binary decomposition informs Thomas Paine's critical account of the abdicated throne or vacant center of hegemonic power: "Every office and department has its despotism, founded upon custom and usage. Every place has its Bastille, and every Bastille its despot. The original hereditary despotism, resident in the person of a king, divides and subdivides itself into a thousand shapes and forms, till at last the whole of it is acted by deputation" (284). I have not been able to locate the botanical or zoological referent that seems to provide the central figure for this brilliant gothicization of the Great Chain of Being; it could be something like Blake's "polypus" or the related hydra—that is, either the mythological beast or its namesake, the small aquatic creature that scandalized eighteenth-century biology with its prodigious regenerative capacities and its ambiguous status as animal and plant (see Lenhoff and Lenhoff 1986). But it is of course precisely the absence of a "central figure" (the catachrestic logic of a metaphor without a clear referent) that operates the image. The diversification of a thousand shapes and forms, each of which still embody a power that is in some important sense "the same," characterizes the spread of disciplinarity as well as "deputizing" describes the workings of a panoptic and hegemonic power whose mode is the sprawl of diversification. The problem that Paine posits is that storming the Bastille or cutting off the head of a king can no longer address the working of the invisible hands of a headless despotism that has already reduced its "original" to a straw man or a figurehead. Finally only a *molecular* or *viral* politics can be effective in such a regime.

Gender in the School of Mirrors: *Frankenstein*

A crucial sequence in *Frankenstein* begins when the monster confronts his creator and demands "a creature of another sex" (Shelley 1974, 142). Frankenstein refuses absolutely at first, then relents, then begins to assemble a female monster, and then abruptly destroys it, enraging the monster and enabling the destructive cycle to continue. When discussing this vacillatory sequence in a literature class, a student asked why Dr. Frankenstein didn't simply create a *sterile* female monster. Then the monster would have had a mate, and the doctor needn't have worried about a potential "race of demons." Another student replied quickly that this was impossible because it would have short-circuited the plot and prematurely ended the book. This answer enacts the familiar convention that would situate fiction as a hothouse plant—a kind of house of cards or lesser, Newtonian universe whose author-god must keep stacking the deck in order to keep it up—but one that differs in this from the apparently sturdier and more flexible world outside books.

The doctor's either/or decision represents a potential fork in the road of the plot, a bifurcation where either decision—the decision to make *or* not to make a female monster, no less than the vacillation between them—may well reproduce the tragic series. The first student's blithely eugenic answer to the doctor's dilemma does indeed short-circuit examination of what else has been short-circuited by the way the either/or branching is constructed: as long as we're rewriting the novel, why couldn't the monster's partner be male? Is reproduction so tied in the novel's context to the definition of femaleness that the possibility of a sterile female would short-circuit the ideology of gender, threatening an even more catastrophic series by adding the option of making or not making a female/not-female? Can eugenics solve a dilemma it has created? But the second student's answer doubly short-circuits examination of the first question simply by calling it a short-circuiting, thereby working with it to contain what Foucault called "the great danger with which fiction threatens our world" (1984, 118). Here, the danger seems to involve the revelation of the flexibility and high-maintenance fragility—the *science-fictionality*—of the circuits through which gender is wired in and out of books. The joke is that the constructionist universe—by virtue of devices such as the double-question damage-control mechanism enacted by the two students—is perhaps *more* stably inertial than the self-organizing "nature" that ideology makes in its image.

The first student's question is "naive" by narrow literary-critical standards insofar as "the literary critic" is not supposed to rewrite the plot, but to account for what is *there*, whether historically, generically, or hermeneutically. But what happened in the class (as I argued) was that the book *continued to be written*, since the logic of short-circuiting and cross-circuiting is the ongoing work of the book. My purpose, in the classroom as well as here, is not to cure the disturbance—the gender trouble—that the plot enacts, but to prolong its life. That's my job: I'm a literary critic.

There are many branchings in the text where characters are confronted with choices, or where it seems things could go either way; this is no less true of the act of interpretation. If the logic of these branchings is the motor of the plot, it is not limited to the text. This chapter explores the fraying and braiding that weaves textual space-time into "real" space-time.

At what point does the tragic cycle begin, at what points might it have been averted or ended, and by what logic does it continue? Frankenstein suggests a self-amplifying "butterfly effect" that swells, "by insensible steps," from "ignoble and almost forgotten sources" into "the torrent which, in its course, has swept away all my hopes and joys" (32). I have suggested that the problematization of disciplinary division and recombination (e.g., between science and literature) situates reading itself as the ongoing source of the tragic (or gothic) series. There are, of course, numerous other crucial points in the plot: Frankenstein's creation or first rejection of the monster, the De Lacey family's rejection of the monster, Frankenstein's refusal to create a mate, his decision not to reveal the monster's existence, the magistrate's refusal to help, and so on. One can always argue, that is, that Frankenstein's mistake was not the creation of the monster but his rejection of it, not in rejecting it but in vacillating, not in vacillating but in keeping quiet, and so on. These relatively discrete sites are overdetermined in a nexus of structural factors in which the catastrophic series has somehow always already begun, is always beginning, always just ahead.

This causal or temporal shell game is precisely the form of gendering suggested by Lacan. Lacan's vignette of gender production is elaborated along with his revision of Saussure's model of the linguistic sign (Lacan 1977, 149–52), which features a signifier (e.g., the word "tree") fixed arbitrarily to a referent (e.g., a picture of a tree). Lacan's alternate model of the sign—two doors, marked "Ladies" and "Gentlemen"—refuses to allow a categorical distinction between word and thing (the bar dividing word from picture). Lacan also shifts the emphasis from a Big Bang mode of gender production (which looks back to an original primal scene or biological determinant always anterior to consciousness as its never-articulable condition of possibility) to a continuous-creation model that stresses the ongoing gaps-in-play by which Oedipal gender is sustained—ritually, as it were—only by an ongoing channeling or canalization. This model correlates, under the term *canalization*, practices that maintain the way that sexuality is supposed to be genitalized in the individual body (i.e., libido is supposed to "flow through" the genitals) with the "urinary segregation" that makes whole bodies flow through different doors. The "primary process" of metaphor, condensation, and displacement, whether it refers to the way erogenous zones or social traffic are configured, is precisely always in process, ensuring that the subject will always work both from and toward a fixation that will always exceed him-or-her.

This crux of gender is curiously enacted, in what could provisionally be called "real time," between Mary Shelley and her husband, Percy, in their collaboration on a passage in *Frankenstein* where Victor describes himself and his wife:

> *Although there was a great dissimilitude in our characters, there was an harmony in that very*
> *dissimilitude. I was more calm and philosophical than my companion; yet my temper was*
> *not so yielding. My application was of longer endurance; but it was not so severe whilst*
> *it endured. I delighted in investigating the facts relative to the actual world; she busied*
> *herself in following the aerial creations of the poets. The world to me was a secret,*
> *which I desired to discover; to her it was a vacancy, which she sought to people*
> *with imaginations of her own. (Shelley 1974, 30)*

Editor James Reiger notes that the final two sentences were added by Percy to Mary's manuscript, or as he puts it, "written by Shelley" (30n). He is careful to distinguish the contributions of each author; to Mary Shelley's statement (in her 1832 introduction) that she "certainly did not owe the suggestion of one incident, nor scarcely one train of feeling, to my husband, and yet but for his incitement, it would never have taken the form in which it was presented to the world," Reiger adds a catty footnote: "Shelley contributed more than his widow recalls here" (229). In his "Note on the Text," Reiger fusses over Percy's "status": "We know that he was more than an editor. Should we grant him the status of minor collaborator? Do we or do we not owe him a measure of 'final authority'? The problem in editorial philosophy is perhaps insoluble" (xliv).

Indeed, the passage cited above works both to provoke and to confound attribution: the editor, like Mary and Percy and Elizabeth and Victor before him, and like readers of his edition after him, are drawn into and out of an "insoluble" problem whose form is, finally, the double bind of gender itself, a primary irritant around which various pearls of writerly, editorial, and hermeneutic discourse must continue to be secreted.

The provocation and confounding of attribution takes the form of a series of questions of the passage: How are the character descriptions autobiographical, in content or at least in form (that is, insofar as they can be taken as stylistic "signatures" of each author), and to what extent do Mary and Percy write as representatives of their genders? How are the descriptions biographical, representing each author's portrait of the other — and of the other's portrait of themselves? But because Mary writes as Victor writing about himself and Elizabeth, while Percy writes as Mary writing as Victor (and so on), these are only the first steps into a house of mirrors in which distinctions between fictional and real characters are subject to a binary decomposition — or rather, revealed to be always-already shattered. Do Percy's additions represent mainly an attempt to imitate and build upon his wife's text (to "pass" as Mary), or to supplement with something categorically different what he must have felt was lacking in her text (to make Mary's text over in his image)? Or did Mary (as she claims) write the text as she did in order to please her husband or to fulfill a standard she had projected as his? Or did she write the novel (and especially the character of Victor) to expose and critique a masculinist Romanticism in which she understood her husband to be participating (as Mellor and others have argued)? Did Percy walk, knowingly or not, into the trap of self-caricature when his wife's text moved him to write as Victor? Or did both authors, after all, follow after their fashion the self-amplifying and self-thwarting logic dictated to them by textuality itself, having taken on another life of its own? This last question only throws us back onto the logic of the Frankenstein story itself.

These are, of course, more naive questions. We know the text to be both child and parent, and neither child nor parent, to its author; this causal loop (people are produced by their relationships or practices and vice versa) cannot help but suggest some third causal element (ideology, textuality, or the like), but rather than ground the indeterminacy in a third and firmer place, it only elaborates the strange attractor around which agency and causality circulate.

Shelley's work quietly thematizes questions of authorship as it goes. Walton makes notes on Frankenstein's spoken story, then Frankenstein "himself corrected and augmented them in many places" (207), just as Mary was to give her text to Percy with "carte blanche to make what alterations you please" (xliv). More significantly, Percy's description of Elizabeth (in the passage cited above) seems to form the model for Mary Shelley's description (in her 1832 introduction) of *her own* youth, spent "indulging in waking dreams" and "airy flights of my imagination" in which she "could people the hours with creations far more interesting to me at that age, than my own sensations" (222–23). To say that Mary's version of Mary here is styled after Percy's version of Mary's version of Victor's version of Elizabeth is probably an oversimplification.

A "close reading" of the passage in question only orchestrates the echo chamber more densely. Both descriptions use extended parallelism: Mary differentiates Victor and Elizabeth by *degree* ("more calm . . . not so yielding . . . longer . . . not so severe"), while Percy differentiates them as binarized *kinds* (e.g., discovering secrets versus peopling with imaginations). Being careful not simply to distinguish in kind between kind and degree, though, one must admit that Mary's distinctions are not by pure degree, since there are some differences in kind between the qualities that differ by degree: stability versus flexibility ("calm . . . yielding") and duration versus intensity ("longer . . . severe"). Yet again, these seemingly binarized kinds could, by "insensible steps" (i.e., by degrees), be transformed into one another (e.g., duration becomes intensity by being compressed). Percy's descriptions, on the other hand, reperform the division/mixing between science and fiction (masculine "facts" and discoveries versus feminine "aerial creations" and imaginative "peoplings") as a version of the problematic of gender.

The domestic "harmony in dissimilitude" that Victor romanticizes is a harmony never realized in the novel. The novel adumbrates neither a kind of simple complementarity (a joining together to make a whole) nor a zero-sum game (the division of a whole between the genders) but an ongoing failure to connect in which the "dissimilitude" between continuous (nonarticulated) difference in degree and discontinuous (articulated) difference in kind is both a branching and a braiding. Typically, Frankenstein discovers this "too late": while he had been able to control the discretely articulated features of his monster ("His limbs were in proportion, and I had selected his features as beautiful" [52]), the monster becomes horrific by the subtler—indiscrete—features that emerge only when he is animated: the strange color imbalance between hair, skin, and eyes; the convulsive expressions that play across the otherwise proportionate features. This dialectic reproduces the terms of a famous debate between the leading physiognomists of a previous generation: Johann Caspar Lavater grounded physiognomy in discrete and static features, while Georg Christoph Lichtenberg argued the primacy of expression over the features it orchestrates. The monster's horrific "aura" marks the failure of the body to coincide with its physically discrete location in a consensual, Euclidean space, or rather, it marks embodiment as embodiment *of this failure*; the way in which the body's recalcitrant self-difference constitutes it as a "material-semiotic actor" (Haraway 1991, 208).

The ongoing failure to coincide, in a spatiotemporal and discursive series, also serves as a rough account of the logic of the plot. I've noted how

Frankenstein's studies in modern science, which might have set him on the right course, contribute a vital ingredient to the fatal series only by being deferred. It is this same logic by which the monster is deprived of his mate at the last instant, and by which he takes it on himself to thwart the Frankensteins' consummation of their marriage at the last instant and then to keep the pursuing doctor just a step behind him, and finally, also the logic by which the monster appears just a moment too late to witness the death of his creator (or by which the novel ends a moment too soon for the reader to witness the death of the monster). As I also noted, the brain-stealing scene from the 1931 film meticulously applies the same interruptive logic.

This logic also structures the monster's fateful rejection by the De Laceys. The monster becomes "solely directed towards my plan of introducing myself into the cottage of my protectors" (128), and finally the moment arrives "which would decide my hopes, or realize my fears." Just as the noise interrupts Fritz in the film, so too the sounds of the returning family cause the monster to panic and throw himself at De Lacey's feet; the urgency of this action causes the family to interpret it as an attack. Driven violently away, the monster seeks out his maker with a redoubled resentment. Apparently, a certain urgency of desire—not simply a matter of degree but something irreducibly in the nature of desire—is self-thwarting to the extent that, if there is something on which everything depends, it must go wrong.

Muriel Spark described this logic—proleptically, as a kind of strange attractor—when she described the novel "as a sort of figure-of-eight *macabaresque*, executed by two partners moving with the virtuosity of skilled ice-skaters.... Both partners are moving in opposite directions, yet one follows the other. At the crossing of the figure-eight they all-but collide" (Shelley 1974, xxvii).

An interruptive logic also structures Shelley's account of the novel's conception in her 1832 introduction. Shelley first attributes the "present form" of the novel to her husband's insistence that she write for publication: "He was for ever inciting me to obtain literary reputation" (223). While this attribution may suggest an anxiety of authorship enforced for women, it was also still conventional to justify the audacious act of publication by appealing to some sense of duty. The same convention structures Shelley's justification of her introduction itself as a compliance with her publisher's request, since she would otherwise be "very averse to bringing myself forward in print" (222). In any case, it is not her husband's incitement but her resistance to it, in the form of the performance anxiety or "mortification" that she reports (on being repeatedly unable to "think of a story" in the ghost-story contest) that finally enables her subsequent production. In order for writing to take place at all, *it* must become a terror. Incitement—the mandate to produce—generates a turbulent cycle in which the subject's own resistance and blockage allows her to be "haunted," in their wake, by what Baudrillard-on-Marx called the "spectre of production." In any case, the novel's conception seems finally to be immaculate: Shelley has the monster appear to her in a reverie, followed by the "eureka" moment in which she sees the entrepreneurial opportunity to universalize herself ("What terrified me will terrify others") by making readers over in her image, just as Wordsworth had in *The Prelude* ("what we have loved / Others will love"). Shelley offers a mutually interruptive ensemble of accounts of the novel's genesis. This ensemble is characterizable by its "someness" or undecidability, which Shelley translates into an infinite regress:

Every thing must have a beginning, to speak in Sanchean phrase; and that beginning must be linked to something that went before. The Hindoos give the world an elephant to support it, but they make the elephant stand on a tortoise. Invention, it must be humbly admitted, does not consist in creating out of the void, but out of chaos. (226)

Shelley's use of the older term "invention" (a reorganization of already extant materials) against the new Romantic standard of "creating" (caricatured as pure origination "out of the void") jibes with the reading of the novel as a cautionary tale of production (associated with creation) usurping reproduction, but Shelley's gothicization of production cannot adequately be read as simple opprobrium, since it also invests its subject with seductive power and danger—and moreover, since Shelley's account paints her own production with the same brush.

It is at the interpenetrative border of production and reproduction that Shelley situates her account of the novel's genesis, making the novel in the image of Frankenstein's making of his monster. The novel queries the distinction between feminine reproductive labor and masculine productive labor and the derogation of the former by a productivist—"creationist"—ideology that sustains what Baudrillard called "an unbridled romanticism of productivity" (1975, 17). This query is sometimes instantiated in the turbulence of similarity and difference between parenting and writing, or in a still more homely sense, as the question of how it is possible to be either or both a mother and a writer, or the extent to which the two overlap or interrupt each other. This suggests that the focus should be displaced somewhat, away from the caricature of a male Frankenstein whose hubris is to usurp female reproduction and to hybridize it with production, and toward an inquiry into how their necessary hybridization becomes a problem in a regime based on distinguishing them. Marie-Hélène Huet reminds us that when Mary Shelley wrote the novel, she had already lost one child, had her second child with her, and became pregnant again in the course of writing the novel. Huet finds that Shelley's overassertion of her sole authorship and "erasure of the father" (i.e., Percy) comes out of "a tradition that closely associates monstrous births with the mother, stressing the principle of parental singularity" (1993, 61–62). Huet, then, implicitly revises Reiger's account of Mary Shelley as a cross-gender Frankenstein whose hubristic self-aggrandizement is to usurp her husband's role; the hubris of Huet's Mary Shelley is (paradoxically or not) one of self-*derogation*: she takes not the credit but the rap for her husband by claiming sole responsibility for the production of monsters. But Shelley presents this claim with as much glee as contrition or so-called self-hatred. It seems we must continue to read *Frankenstein* as an invalidation of the myth of masculinist self-sufficiency, in light of Carole Pateman's account of the foundational myth of liberal democracy as the brothers giving birth to the state. But it is also a validation of the myth's real effects, and a "reverse discourse" that exceeds itself. In other words, Shelley *takes on* (in the double sense of setting herself against — and allowing herself to be invested by) the pathological and interruptive power attributed to "the disorder of women."

Male writers may commonly characterize the writing process as pregnancy and giving birth, but insofar as parenting is among the referents of the *Frankenstein* story, what is horrific (and compelling) is how having a child is like being a writer, not vice versa. Insofar as parents are notoriously resistant to "constructionism," tending to prefer the notion that their children are born with definite tendencies and personalities, the scary part of parenting is not necessarily the immense responsibility that shaping a life entails, but how this shaping operates, insidiously, because of and in spite of either the agency or the patience of the parent. Frankenstein's account of the insidious and ironic "fatal series" marks fate as the operation of an unconscious that operates both with and against the will (thereby structuring moments in which either of two decisions, or vacillation between them, are fated to reproduce the series).

Mary bids her "hideous progeny" (the novel as monster) to "go forth and prosper" with a complex laughter radically at odds with the high seriousness with which Percy had hyped the novel in his preface. It is possible to hear in this laughter not only a derogation of the novel's importance (and with it, the old story of feminine anxiety and self-hatred) but also an affirmation of the gothic logic by which the book continues to live, of the monstrous victory of an indiscrete and interruptive power.

The self-immolation to which the monster looks forward at the end of the novel (again, not with contrition) is at least as equivocal as the account of suicide that concludes Spivak's "Can the Subaltern Speak?" or the cliff-leap that ends *Thelma and Louise*: resistance or defeat? The monster's life must be called a limited success, at least insofar as it manages continually to frustrate its creator's murderous intent toward it and to achieve the death-on-its-own-terms that functions as the prime directive for creatures under the sway of the *death drive*. This limited success indexes the necessarily equivocal operation of all movements that seek to subvert the categorical distinctions on which they are predicated—the necessarily histori- cally limited victories and defeats of all the monster has been taken to "stand for" (cap- italism, feminism, the working class, Romanticism, and so on), sublating in the pro- cess the grandiosely totalized utopian and dystopian scenarios that drive the doctor. Are perverse hermeneutic convolutions necessary, after all, to rewrite the novel with a happy ending? Or does the novel conspire to validate its own monstrous frustra- tion by allowing itself to be read as the moral tale of a failure and not the ironic laughter of a monstrous victory? Under what conditions could the novel be read differently? Does the novel have any power to participate in the production of such conditions?

These questions are echoed in Percy Shelley's "Ozymandias," where the collapse of the king's giant statue radically and ironically recontextualizes its caption. When the monument had been standing, its caption ("Look upon my works, ye mighty, and despair") suggested that others could never hope to achieve a success so grand and durable; the ruins of the statue make the same words mean that, in light of Ozymandias's failure, *all* power must despair of succeeding. By al- lowing both things and words to be subject to radical recontextualization, Percy seems to subject his own poem to the contingency of change and thereby to achieve a backhanded kind of symbolic mastery—while reserving his own mission of con- tinuing to plead with the mighty to "Look upon *my* works." To take Percy at his word is to acknowledge how the poem participates in legitimizing the tyranny, in turn, of a hegemonic power that works not by its monumentality but by being for- ever brought down, a power that cops recontextualization as its own tool, and that wears not a "sneer of cold command" but a friendlier face. On the other hand, *Frankenstein*'s gothic logic asserts priority over Percy's favorite theme of the "con- stancy of mutability" by offering a writer-parent whose necessary ambivalence in the act of production-reproduction does not (as Ozymandias does) pit desire for eternal life against the certainty of change and death but binds the two in an ongo- ing contradiction: "He would hope that, left to itself, the slight spark of life which he had communicated would fade; that this thing, which had received such imper- fect animation, would subside into dead matter" (228).

Valéry's meditation on monsters explicitly turns the gothic logic of self-thwarting into a productive principle. For Valéry, monsters are known

only by this remarkable property *of being unable to endure. The* abnormal *are those creatures who have a little less future than the* normal. *They are like the many thoughts that contain hidden contradictions. They are formed in the mind, they seem right and promising, but their consequences ruin them, and their presence is very soon fatal to themselves.*

Who knows whether most of those prodigious thoughts over which so many great men and an infinity of lesser ones have grown pale for centuries are not, after all, psychological monsters — Monster Ideas *— born of the naive exercise of our questioning faculties . . . ?*

But the monsters of the flesh quickly perish. Yet they have a certain existence. Nothing is more instructive than to meditate on their destiny. (1973, 5–6; emphasis in original)

If Valéry's meditation works to dichotomize the Methuselan monstrosity of ideas and ephemeral monstrosities of the flesh, it does so in order to make history the story of their permutations; if normalcy is categorically differentiated from the abnormal, their difference is simultaneously rendered the question of a few ambiguous degrees: only "a little less future." Like Shelley's narrative, this paradox makes it clear that the aim of technological, economic, or eugenic "perfectability" and an eternal dynasty at the "end of history" must give way to a necessarily more limited goal of "sustainability," but it also demonstrates that neither eternalization nor sustainability can undermine the ongoing priority of a monstrous agency whose life and death are bound up together in "hidden contradictions" and whose mode of existing is always to "stir with an uneasy, half vital motion" (Shelley 1974, 228). If Mary Shel-

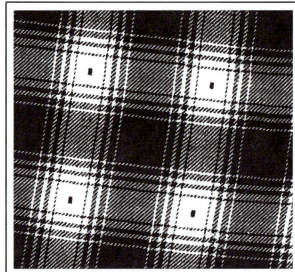

Plaid Theory. Once I was trying to take a nap in a room amid several loudly intellectual dialogues and an equally loud television. As I drifted off toward sleep, the sense of the words being spoken suddenly slipped away and the syntaxes and tones became a complex abstract pattern of patterns; that is, a plaid. This event occurred to me, at the time, as the *reversal* of a plaid to its underside, where what appear as discrete points on the front are seen to be a switchboard of tangled skeins on

ley allows the monster at the end of *Frankenstein* "a little less future," it is not in order to aestheticize a life compressed into a poignant intensity, but to acknowledge that monstrous agency is purchased at a price, and to take on the negotiation of that price as the ongoing struggle of Romantic and post-Romantic history.

The Romantic Double-Cross: Keats's Letters

The development of information theory, fractal geometry, and chaos theory were spurred by the typically postmodern problem of how to compact and maximize the transmission of information; this problem occupied Claude Shannon and Benoit Mandelbrot at Bell Labs and IBM. Within every transmission of information are sectors of noise; within each sector of noise is a sector of usable information, and so on until the limit of resolution is reached. This empirical finding follows the theoretical definition by which information and noise are inextricably related and information itself is predicated on a nonreducible dialectic between sameness (redundancy) and difference. Absolute randomness could either be called pure information or pure noise: this contradiction is both the product and the enabling condition of information theory no less than the particle/wave paradox had been the axiom and fetish of modernist physics. Taken in a broader sense (which I do not consider to be metaphorical), these observations suggest that the ubiquity of disciplinary power means also that in no place does it rule unchallenged; noise is only noise with reference to a certain code: noise is the unconsciousness of information, a pattern of the gaps in play. The jump from information to discipline is not a metaphorical one since everywhere they are each other's product and process.

But Shannon and Mandelbrot were not the first to confront the challenge of how to maximize in-

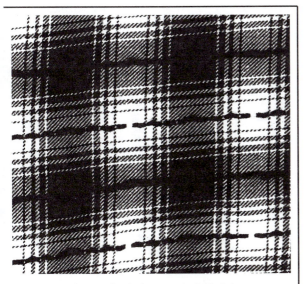

the back. In other words, the becoming-plaid of the conversations was instantly also the becoming-not-plaid of the plaid. I stayed at the point of sleep for several switchings back and forth between pointed sense and pointless pattern.

This vignette emblematizes the mutually interruptive relations between noise, information, patterning, and meaning that are the subject of this section.

formation transmission. Letter writers of the eighteenth and nineteenth centuries addressed the same problem, generated by the expense of paper and postage (the latter often restrictively manipulated by governmental regulation) and by increasing social mobility (in real space, that is). The continuous diaspora mandated by postmodern professionalism (and its poster child, the long-distance romance) are extensions of these conditions.

Romantic letter writers addressed the problem by *crossing* their letters (overlapping two perpendicular layers of writing). The practice depends on what Saussure called "the linearity of the signifier," which in this case ensures that the text remains legible in both directions. The nonlinearity of meaning is generated as an excess against the unidirectional drive of information, like the snakes that weave around the staff of a caduceus or the turbulent wake of a forward-moving ship; meaning is the snake and the wake of information.

In 1819, the poet (and erstwhile surgeon's apprentice) John Keats sent a crossed letter to his friend and publisher, John Taylor. The first, horizontal, text of the letter is devoted to a long prescription about where intellectual workers should live in order to remain healthy; this authoritative disquisition is crossed by lines from Keats's *Lamia*, a poem about a man who falls in love with a snake disguised as a woman until she is unmasked by a scientist (pretty much the old boy-meets-snake story). In the passage included in the letter, guests at Lamia's party marvel that they had never noticed her fantastic mansion on the numbered street. The uncanny way that the fantasy mansion exceeds the gridded and numbered streets (systematic house numbering began about this time in London) thematizes the way that poetry is situated, by the crossed letter, as an excess of prescriptive discourse (remember Keats's dictum that "we hate poetry that has a palpable design on us"). The signifier — prescription crossed and exceeded by poetry — becomes a metaphor of the signified and vice versa; this is a site where words and things are conflated by being made to echo each other.

Curiously, though, the same pattern of dichotomy and excess structures the prescriptive part of the letter (Keats 1970, 286–87), where Keats proceeds by a logic of ongoing problematization that structures a dynamic spatiality. A simple binary alignment of city as unhealthy and country as healthy is rejected as insufficient: danger, and with it the injunction to vigilance, must be shown to implicate both city and country. Since the binary distinction between healthy and unhealthy must also divide country from country, a more powerful code capable of making distinctions and judgments between rural locales is offered. The healthy locale, it seems, must be one of pure distinctions between elements: the traditional elements

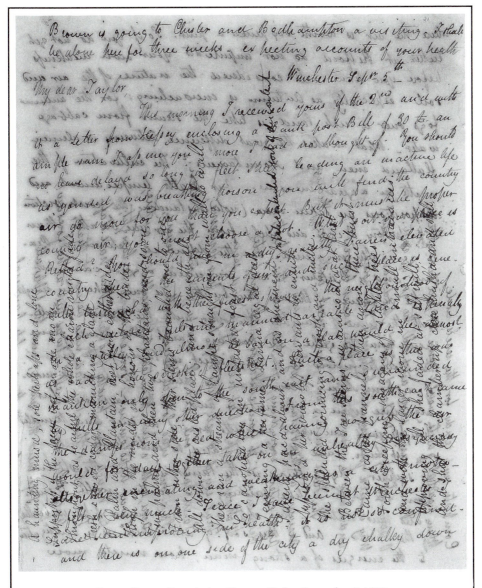

Poetry Crosses Prescription: Keats to Taylor, September 5, 1819.
(MS Keats 1.63. By permission of the Houghton Library, Harvard University)

of air, water, and earth (and fire, represented by warmth or smoke), as well as life it-self (in the forms of vegetation or human bodies), must ideally be distinct from each other. This implicit principle produces the ideal place to live as a "dry, gravelly, bar-ren, elevated...open" country where even the "gravelly" pebbles are distinct from each other (Keats 1970, 286). Unhealthy locales, on the other hand, are ones in which these distinctions are lost or "leveled": places where air contains water and matter and life (agricultural lowlands, slaughterhouses, and so on), where water is implicated with earth and life ("cabbage water," fens, and the like), earth is impli-cated with water and life, and so on. The site to be avoided above all others is thus "a rich inclosed fulsome manured arrable land." Thus Keats seems to posit a pure difference between pure difference and impure difference, preserving a vitalist viril-ity that depends on the maintenance of distinctions and opposing strength, nerve, energy, occupation, and self-interest to weakness, idleness, enervation, and tameness.

Keats's attempt to produce a hierarchy of kinds of labor out of these distinctions leads to another series of binary oppositions; first butcher is op-posed to peasant, mountaineer to valleyman, strong to weak. Finally the code must weave back into itself: if the usually healthy country can be unhealthy, it must also be possible to maintain health amid an unhealthy environment, led by the bour-geois ideals of directedness and "self-interest" (i.e., "goal-oriented behavior"). A relatively closed, self-limiting system is almost magically woven out of almost noth-ing but binary distinctions. Its dynamic limit is not a simple border but the points where it folds back onto itself: in an environment too indistinct, the supreme sin-gleness of purpose required to remain healthy—represented by the airborne dag-ger that leads Macbeth through "the fens" while keeping him from getting sick—amounts to criminality or pathology itself.

Keats rejects essentialism ("do not impute it to your own weak-ness...") in favor of a dynamic organicism that defines personality and pathology alike as largely the products of interaction between a set of behaviors and an environ-ment. Masculine differentiation is set explicitly against feminine indifferentiation by Keats's warning of the enervating effect of breathing "the steam that rises from the earth" as the equivalent of "drinking their mother's milk" (Keats 1970, 287).

John Wesley's 1786 tract, *The Duty and Advantage of Early Rising*, had forged the same elements into a temporal discipline: "By *soaking*...so long be-tween warm sheets, the flesh is as it were parboiled, and becomes soft and flabby. The nerves, in the mean time, are quite unstrung" (quoted in Thompson 1993, 392). Like Wesley, Keats weaves the homeliest principles behind traditional English stric-tures—against milk-drinking (as an infantilizing practice for adults) and against dampness (as the source of numerous ills) — into an expansive ideological algorithm. Keats's figure of "encroaching...autumn fogs" seems to spread to subject all to the specter of dangerous indifferentiation. This spreading authorizes a disciplinary saturation to cover the same ground, redifferentiating gender (by equating masculine virility, vitality, and vigilance, and by making them contingent on continuous differentiations from mothers and others), nation and race (setting individualist England against an Orientalist vision of China's vast undifferentiated crowds), division of labor (situating agricultural labor as domesticizing, "low" in several senses, and feminized). At the same time, the figure itself threatens to collapse into an empty redundancy: "encroaching" indexes a liminal threat to distinct boundaries, just as "Autumn" is a liminal season between extremes, just as "fogs" is a figure of indeterminate boundaries. What begins to emerge from Keats's prescription is the sense of a single (imaginary, ideological) algorithm capable of processing and evaluating any given data or of generating an inexhaustible series of figures, contrasts, and so on — in short, of making everything over into its own image; another version of Paine's hydra or Blake's polypus. But Keats's prescription also begins to problematize the position of *poetry* as the privileged field of the very indistinction and hybridity pathologized in prescriptive discourse. Keatsian poetry — and for that matter, the human body or brain — turns out to be more like the "rich inclosed fulsome manured arrable land" that requires to be set against the pure distinctions of prescriptive discourse; they conspire between them to divide and conquer the world.

 The textual history of a second crossed letter — Keats's May 3, 1818, letter to his friend, J. H. Reynolds — shows how the logic of binary decomposition can structure the ongoing life of a text. *The Norton Anthology of English Literature*, the Heaven where white male poets and a few of their guests go when they die (the Heaven where, as the song says, nothing ever happens), prints three blocks of text from the letter, marking by triple asterisks four large blocks omitted (Norton 1986, 865–68). I call the included blocks "i-sections" and those omitted "o-sections."

 As printed in the *Norton*, the letter has been tailored to represent Keats as an evaluative literary and social critic. The anthology, then, participates in an ongoing opposition between two caricatures that began in Keats's own lifetime: Keats the effeminate, sensual poet and Keats the virile, abstract thinker and literary theorist. This hermaphroditic image gave Byron his figure of a Keats engaged in "a sort of mental masturbation — frigging his *Imagination*" (cited in Levinson 1988, 18), while Matthew Arnold came to champion the "manly" Keats against the lowbrow sensualist and effeminized slave to love. M. H. Abrams, Romanticism editor for the *Norton*, implicitly reproduces a hermaphroditically self-sufficient Keats in his headnotes to the letters, where the penetrating, erectile thinker meets the receptive, uterine poet: "Keats thought hard and persistently about life and art, and any seed of an ethical or critical idea he picked up from his intellectual contemporaries (Hazlitt, Coleridge, Wordsworth) instantly germinated and flourished in the rich soil of his imagination" (Norton 1986, 860). Abrams goes on to state that Keats's comments "have become standard points of reference in aesthetic theory" (860). As we will see, Romantic precedent can be established for this self-authorizing claim, which is both performative and tautological insofar as the *Norton* has authority, insofar as it is a standard reference, to say what is a standard reference.

But poeticity continues to inform Keats's criticism in the form of *mistakes*, as a kind of "aura" that clings to the materiality of his artifacts: the *Norton* "reproduces the original MSS precisely, so that the reader may follow Keats's pen as, throwing grammar and spelling to the winds, it strains to keep up with the rush of his thoughts" (860). And sure enough, the May 1818 letter printed in the *Norton* contains several potentially significant crossed-out words and misspellings. What's not mentioned, though, is that the letter reproduced is a *transcript* of Keats's letter, the original having been lost long ago. Richard Woodhouse, a lawyer and reader for

---

What I complain of is that I have been in so uneasy a state of Mind as not to be fit to write to an invalid. I cannot write to any length under a dis-guised feeling. I should have loaded you with an addition of gloom, which I am sure you do not want. I am now thank God in a humor to give you a good groats worth--for Tom, after a Night without a Wink of sleep, and everburdened with fever, has got up after a refreshing day sleep and is better than he has been for a long time; and you I trust have been again round the Common without any effect but refreshment.--As to the Matter I hope I can say with Sir Andrew "I have matter enough in my head" in your favor And now, in the second place, for I reckon that I have finished my Impetinis, I am glad you blow up the weather--all through your letter there is a leaning towards a climate-curse, and you know what a delicate satisfaction there is in having a vexation anathematized: one would think there has been growing up for these last four thousand years, a grandchild Scion of the old forbidden tree, and some modern Eve had just violated it; and there was come with double charge: "Notus and After black with thunderous clouds from Sierra-leona"--Ishall breathe worsted stockings sooner than I thought for. Tom wants to be in town--we will have some such days upon the heath like that of last summer and why not with the same book; or what say you to a black letter Chaucer printed in 1596: aye I've got one huzza! I shall have it housden gothique a nice somber binding--it will go a little way to unmodernize. And also, I see no reason, because I have been away this last month, why I should not have a peep at your Spencerian--notwithstanding you speak of your office, in my thought a little too early, for I do not see why a Mind like yours is not capable of harbouring and digesting the whole Mystery of Law as easily as Parson Hugh does Pepins--which did not hinder him from his poetic Canary

--Were I to study physic or rather Medicine again--I feel it would not make the least difference in my Poetry; when the Mind is in its infancy a Bias, but when we have acquired more strength, a Bias becomes no Bias. Every department of knowledge we see excellent and calculated towards a great whole. I am so convinced of this, that I am glad at not having given away my medical Books, which I shall again look over to keep alive the little I know thitherwards; and moreover intend through you and Rice to become a sort of Pip-civilian. An extensive knowledge is needful to thinking people--it takes away the heat and fever; and helps, by widening speculation, to ease the Burden of Mystery: a thing I begin to understand a little, and which weighed upon you in the most gloomy and true sentence of your Letter. The difference of high sensations with and without knowledge appears to me this--in the latter case we are falling continually ten thousand fathoms deep and being blown up against the ill--having wings and with all horror of a bare shouldered Creature--in the former case, our shoulders are fledged, and we go thro' the same air and space without fear.

This is running one's rigs on the score of abstracted benefit--when we come to human life and the affections it is impossible how a parallel of breast and head should be drawn--[you will forgive me for thus privately treading out my depth and take it for treading as schoolboys tread the water--it is impossible to know how far knowledge will consol us for the death of a friend and the ill "that flesh is heir to--With respect to the affections and Poetry you must know by a sympathy my thoughts that way; and I dare say these few lines will be a rarification;, I wrote them on May-day--and intend to finish the ode all in good time.--
Mother of Hermes! and still youthful Maia!
  May I sing to thee
As thou wast hymned on the shores of Baiae?
  Or may I woo thee
In earlier Sicilian? or thy smiles
Seek as they once were sought, in Grecian isles,
By Bards who died content in pleasant sward,
  Leaving great verse unto a little clan?
O give me their old vigour, and unheard,
Save of the quiet Primrose, and the span
Of heaven, and the ears rounded by thee
My song should die away content as theirs
Rich in the simple worship of a day.
You may be anxious to know for fact to what sentence in your letter I allude.

You say "Ifear there is little chance of any thing else in this life." You seem by that to have been going through with a more painful and acute rest the same labyrinth that I have--I have come to the same conclusion thus far. My Branchings out therefrom have been numerous: one of them is the consideration of Wordsworth's genius and as a help, in the manner of gold being the meridian Line of worldly wealth,--how he differs from Milton.--And here I have nothing but surmises, from an uncertainty whether Miltons apparently less anxiety for Humanity proceeds from his seeing farther or no than Wordsworth: And whether Wordsworth has in truth epic passions, and martyrs himself to the human heart, the main region of his song--In regard to his genius alone--we can find what he says true as far as we have experienced and we can judge no further but by larger experience--for axioms in philosophy are not axioms until they are proved upon our pulses: We read fine--things but never feel them to the full until we have gone the same steps as the author.--I know this is not plain; you will know exactly the meaning when I say, that now I shall relish Hamlet more than I ever have done--Or, better--You are sensible no man can set down Venery as a bestial or joyless thing until he is sick of it and therefore all philosophizing on it would be mere wording. Until we are sick, we understand not;--in fine, as Byron says, "Knowledge is Sorrow"; and I go on to say that "Sorrow is Wisdom"--and further for aught we can know for certainty! "Wisdom is folly"

--So you see now I have run away from Wordsworth, and Milton; and shall still run away from what was in my head, to observe, that some kind of letters are good squares others handsome ovals, and others some orbicular, others spheroid-- and why should there not be another species with two rough edges like a Rat-trap? I hope you will find all my long letters of that species, and all will be well; for by merely touching the spring delicately and etherially, the rough edged will fly immediatly into a proper compactness, and thus you may make a good wholesome loaf, with your own leven in it, of my fragments--if you cannot find this and Rat-in:: sufficiently tractable--alas for me, it being an impossibility in grain for my ink to stain otherwise: if I scribble long letters I must play my vagaries. I must be too heavy, or too light, for whole pages--I must be quaint and free of Tropes and figures--Imust play my draughts as I please, and for my advantage and your erudition, crown a white with a black, or a black with a white, and move into black or white, far and near as I please--Imust go from Hazlitt to Patmore, and make Wordsworth and Coleman play at leap-frog--or keep one of them down a whole half holiday at fly the garter--"From Gray to Gay, from Little to Shakespeare"--Also as a long cause requires two or more sittings of the Court, so a long letter will require two or more sittings of the Breech wherefore I shall resume after dinner.--
    Having not seen a Gull, or orc, a sea Mew, or any thing to bring this Line to a proper length, and also fill up this clear part: that like the Gull I may dip--I hope, not out of sight--and also, like Gull, I hope to be lucky in a good sized fish--This crossing a letter is not without its association--for chequer work leads us naturally to a Milkmaid, a Milkmaid to Hogarth Hogarth to Shakespeare Shakespeare to Hazlitt--Hazlitt to Shakespeare and thus by merely pulling an apron string we set a pretty peal of Chimes at work--Let them chime on while, with your patience,

--Iwill return to Wordsworth--whether or no he has an extended vision or a circumscribed grandeur--whether he is an eagle in his nest, or on the wing--And to be more explicit and to show you how tall I stand by the giant, I will put down a smile of human life as far as I now perceive it; that is, to the point to which I say we both have arrived at--Well, I compare human life to a large Mansion of Many Apartments, two of which I can only describe, the doors of the rest being as yet shut upon me-- The first we step into we call the infant or thoughtless Chamber, in which we remain as long as we do not think--We remain there a long while, and notwithstanding the doors of the second Chamber remain wide open, showing a bright appearance, we care not to hasten to it,; but are at length imperceptibly impelled by the awakening of the thinking principle--within us--we no sooner get into the second Chamber, which I shall call

Letter as Zipper: Keats to Reynolds, May 3, 1818. Sections omitted from *The Norton Anthology* are on the right.

Keats's publisher and a mutual friend of Keats and Reynolds, had his secretary copy the letter and then corrected his secretary's work; this copy is reproduced in the *Norton*. The mistakes and corrections, then, are the result not of the relation between the fast mind and slow hand of Romantic genius, but between a secretary and his employer and finally a Romantic editor all too ready to collapse the transmission of the text back into a melodramatic interiority. There are two ways of reading Abrams's misrepresentation as positive information (or rather, as meaningful noise): in one sense it puts everyone who transcribes Keats *inside* the circuit between Keats's mind and hand, and indeed, in choosing which excerpts to publish, Abrams follows the blocks of text printed in the 1926 book that calls itself *The Mind of John Keats* (Thorpe 1926). But in the stronger sense, Abrams's "mistake" reveals the repeatedly reconstructed cultural artifact called "Keats's mind" as a displaced and condensed version of relations (extended widely in real space and time) between publishers and readers and secretaries and authors and editors, for the circulation of information and division of labor among them (without which the letter would never have been written or reproduced) is mandated by capitalism and the disciplinarity that is its Holy Ghost. In this, "Keats's mind" when he was alive and the cultural site subsequently called "Keats's mind" do not differ in kind.

The *Norton*'s excerpting vandalizes the text, but Humpty-Dumpty can't be put back together. Restoring the full text cannot be a recuperation but only another act of vandalism (like the old joke about vandals breaking into the Louvre and putting arms on the Venus de Milo), since the letter's complex fractures and failures to coincide with itself are what generates and defines it as a text in the first place.

In the i-sections (Norton 1986, 865–68), Keats compares universalized and binarized individual developmental stages—"when the Mind is in its infancy" versus "when we have acquired more strength"—and states of being: "the difference of high Sensations with and without knowledge." He extensively evaluates "Wordsworth's genius... in the manner of gold being the meridian Line of worldly wealth,—how he differs from Milton." This crucial mixed metaphor aligns a capitalist currency referenced to the gold standard (which became official the following year) with a fully mapped and gridded globe (in which human space-time is oriented by its reference to an Anglocentric meridian) and with a literary field normalized by reference to the great author and English nationalist hero. Note that the mixed metaphor works by aligning fields in which an apparently arbitrary reference point or axis is valorized (the gold standard, the prime meridian, Milton). In other words, the fields are aligned by an interdisciplinary alignment to each other that grandfathers their arbitrary axes into a resonant truth-effect. What makes the mixed metaphor an emptily self-referential and tautological loop (the alignment of alignments) is also what allows it to configure (and implicates it inextricably with) the history of English cartography, economics, and literature.

Keats attempts to determine whether Milton sees "further or no than Wordsworth," and again whether Wordsworth "has an extended vision or a circumscribed grandeur," and finally, "to show you how tall I stand by the giant, I will put down a simile of human life as far as I now perceive it." The measurer is to be measured by his measurements, or as Pierre Bourdieu has it, "social subjects, classified by their classifications, distinguish themselves by the distinctions they make" (1984, 6).

The subsequently canonized figure of the "Mansion of Many Apartments" that follows spatializes a developmental schema, beginning with an anteroom ("the infant or thoughtless chamber") and proceeding to a "Chamber of Maiden-Thought," from which branch out numerous darkened passages. Keats deploys this blueprint to make a critical assessment: "To this point was Wordsworth come, as far as I can conceive when he wrote 'Tintern Abbey.'" Again, by the phrase "as far as I can conceive," the assessment marks the assessor as subject to the same spatial-developmental logic as that which is assessed. Keats concludes that Wordsworth "is a Genius and superior to us, in so far as he can, more than we, make discoveries, and shed a light" (in the dark passages), but he adds an important qualification: "though I think it has depended more upon the general and gregarious advance of intellect, than individual greatness of Mind." In view of the fact that Milton's philosophy may now "be understood by one not much advanced in years," Keats offers a historical sketch, concluding in the manner of a logical demonstration: although Milton "did not think into the human heart, as Wordsworth has done—Yet Milton as a Philosopher, had sure as great powers as Wordsworth—What is to be inferr'd? O many things—It proves there is really a grand march of intellect."

Masculine mapping, measurement, money, mansions, and marches are the predominant metaphors in the i-sections. In Keats's universalized national progressivist history (set up as ongoing emancipation from superstition), historical perspective must be factored out in order for Great Men to compare the size of their geniuses. Evolutionary history is conceived as an acceleration and dissemination of features: Milton's philosophy, formerly the product of the singular most advanced mind, is now accessible to every schoolboy. As it turns out, though, historical advance cannot be factored out in a determination of individual genius, which can only be compared synchronically. Both scenarios consist in the masculinist science project of penetration and mapping of new and uncharted areas; the project of Romanticism is a "thinking into the human heart."

In omitting blocks of text (Keats 1970, 90–97) that differ consistently from and alternate regularly with the included text, the *Norton* disciplines a cross-authorizing polarity between poetry and criticism.

The first o-section begins with a still conventional apology for not writing ("I have been in so uneasy a state of Mind as not to be fit to write to an invalid") and meanders among topics such as the weather and books. In the o-section, however, the book is not a manifestation of genius but a physical and historical commodity, a collector's item: "what say you to a black Letter Chaucer printed in 1596: aye I've got one huzza! I shall have it bounden gothique a nice sombre binding—it will go a little way to unmodernize." The typically Romantic impulse to "unmodernize" stands as a foil to the progressivist modernization scenario of the i-sections to come.

The second o-section begins with an apologetic metacomment on the critical pronouncements in the preceding i-section: "This is running one's rigs on the score of abstracted benefit . . . you will forgive me for thus privately treading out of my depth and take it for treading as schoolboys tread the water." Yet even as Keats seems to denigrate his philosophizing, he also radically limits the discursive reach of the geometry of comparison developed in the first i-section: "when we come to human Life and the affections it is impossible how a parallel of breast and head can be drawn"; and again: "it is impossible to know how far knowledge will console us." Note that here the question of "how" marks the impossibility of binary complementarity, while "how far" becomes not a matter of simply measuring the reach of knowledge but of how the knowledge of knowledge or measurement of measurement thwarts rather than amplifies each. Predictably, the o-section includes poetry, concluding with a verse of Keats that begins with a pre-Miltonic invocation ("Mother of Hermes!") and ends with a post-Wordsworthian recuperation (Keats's "Rich in the simple worship of a day" echoing Wordsworth's "simple produce of the common day"), in which Keats associates himself with each in order to distinguish himself from both, situating his verse as a kind of excess that comprehends all of literary history.

A shorter omission toward the end of the letter is also an apology, in which Keats casts Reynolds as a "Tutor" forced to hear a tedious recitation, explaining that "I like to say my lesson to one who will endure my tediousness for my own sake." While Keats's apologies are clearly structured by his own overdetermined insecurities (especially his sociocultural class disabilities), returning as they do to the figure of the schoolboy, they are also conventional markers of discursive change. Early literary critics, like doctors who say, "Now this might sting a bit," often apologize for their obtrusions. In casting himself as trying out the stance of "cultural critic" in the privacy of a letter, Keats situates the professional within the compass of personal friendship, *and vice versa*: the privacy or interiority of the "personal letter" appears as a kind of staging area; it is made into an interiority in order to be converted into a reserve for public production.

The third omitted block, which warrants full citation, begins again with a mock-apologetic metacomment:

—So you see how I have run away from Wordsworth, and Milton; and shall still run away from what was in my head, to observe, that some kind of letters are good squares others handsome ovals, and others some orbicular, others spheroid—and why should there not be another species with two rough edges like a Rat-trap? I hope you will find all my long letters of that species, and all will be well; for by merely touching the spring delicately and etherially, the rough edged will fly immediately into a proper compactness, and thus you may make a good wholesome loaf, with your own leven in it, of my fragments—If you cannot find this said Rat-trap sufficiently tractable—alas for me, it being an impossibility in grain for my ink to stain otherwise: if I scribble long letters I must play my vagaries. I must be too heavy, or too light, for whole pages— I must be quaint and free of Tropes and figures—I must play my draughts as I please, and for my advantage and your erudition, crown a white with a black, or a black with a white, and move into black or white, far and near as I please—I must go from Hazlitt to Patmore, and make Wordsworth and Coleman play at leap-frog—or keep one of them down a whole half holiday at fly the garter—"From Gray to Gay, from Little to Shakespeare"— Also as a long cause requires two or more sittings of the Court, so a long letter will require two or more sittings of the Breech wherefore I shall resume after dinner.—

Have you not seen a Gull, an orc, a sea Mew, or any thing to bring this Line to a proper length, and also fill up this clear part: that like the Gull I may dip—I hope, not out of sight—and also, like a Gull, I hope to be lucky in a good sized fish—This crossing a letter is not without its association— for chequer work leads us naturally to a Milkmaid, a Milkmaid to Hogarth Hogarth to Shakespeare Shakespear to Hazlitt—Hazlitt to Shakespeare and thus by merely pulling an apron string we set a pretty peal of Chimes at work—Let them chime on while, with your patience,—I will return to Wordsworth— (1970, 93–94)

Here, then, Keats deploys a very different set of metaphors: animals, hunting and fishing, cooking and eating, games and holidays, clothes, and finally, cacophonous noise. First, Keats divides the textual field of letters into a domain of smooth, Euclidean geometry (i.e., where "parallels" can be drawn and blueprints made) and a fractal "species with two rough edges," the fragmentation of which is to motivate the reader's interpretive labor. The rough edges of the letter are, presumably, those that divide the authoritatively measuring blocks of text from the apologetic, metacommenting, and playful: the dotted line along which the *Norton* breaks the text into i and o. But since the long letter as a genre must be, by Keats's terms, a mix of the mixed (the o-sections) and the unmixed (the i-sections), the edge between rough and smooth is itself rough, a fractal interpenetration rather than a simple border.

In contradistinction, again, to the progressivist time line that Keats establishes in the i-sections, the checkerboard metaphor situates Keats the correspondent/poet as free from rules of sequence in time and space: the field of literature is no longer organized into domains ruled by individual authors (as in the octave of "Chapman's Homer") but an intertextually fluid one (as in that poem's sestet). The field is not, as in the i-sections, normalized or axiologized with reference to a great author, but organized as the play of a metonymic fluidity against a uniform grid; it is the uniformity, black-and-white binarity, and Euclidean regularity of this grid that enables the nonlinear and lawless play of the poet to appear as such.

The checkerboard metaphor proleptically anticipates the actual *crossing* of the letter, which retroactively validates it. In writing the letter, Keats anticipates his crossing by beginning the metaphor before he begins to cross the letter; for the reader, though, the letter is "always already" crossed: word and thing seem always to have been made in each other's image.

Keats mixes metaphors conspicuously throughout and comments on this mixing. After the long section of metacomment, he shifts via metaphor (comically now characterizing his consideration of Wordsworth and Milton as a court proceeding) into what I will call "subcommentary." The "sittings of the Breech" that a "long cause requires" make the o-sections (the regularly recurring gaps or recesses in the literary-critical deliberations) into a fractal echo of the recesses from the recesses (the breaks Keats takes from the breaks he takes from his deliberations). Subcommentary consists of acknowledgment of the material conditions of the letter's production. First, that it is produced in real time ("I shall resume after dinner") and real space, the material constraint of the page end (and, with it, the anticipated necessity of "crossing") being marshaled as the enabling condition for the play of further troping. Keats marks that he pauses not out of some internal necessity of organic form, but where external temporal, physical, and spatial constraints overdetermine a pause: "I shall resume after dinner" coincides with the end of the page.

How can we know where Keats's page ended when all we have is a transcript? Keats's figurative play with the materiality of the letter causes a ghost or a fossil of the letter's physical presence to remain in the text; this ghost of materiality functions as the incitement to editorial discourse. Woodhouse, the letter's first editor, carefully noted for posterity, with a double-cross mark on his clerk's transcribed copy, the point where the letter "crosses," the word "dip" being "the first word that *dips* into the former writing" after two lines "written in the clear space of the margin" (Keats 1958,

Reconstruction of the Crossing:
Keats to Reynolds, May 3, 1818

280n). The material generic difference between the private (crossed) letter and public prose (which must conform to uncrossed mass-production standards in printing) is marked here in order to auraticize the letter (to give it the status of a unique original), while the distinction between prose (mandated to fill the page arbitrarily) and poetry (which breaks its lines for its own reasons) is displaced. As they approach the crossing, Keats's words have no significance outside their materiality on the page: the words "bring this Line to a proper length, and also fill up this clear part" are perfectly performative in the original (where they did, evidently, fill up the remaining clear margin), perfectly unintelligible otherwise (unless explained by an editor).

As I said, Abrams's four sets of three asterisks (marking the omitted text) and Woodhouse's single double-cross (marking the omitted *work*) are not superseded by my reconstruction of the crossed letter. The letter's physicality—what Lacan called, appropriately, "The Insistence of the Letter"—troubles the text; the text is produced and reproduced out of this trouble; it *is* this trouble. The transmission of the text is a noisy channel in which whole sectors of the message are lost and extraneous marks introduced, but the interpenetration of noise and information characterizes both the production and reproduction of the text. In an important sense, then, the three asterisks and the double-cross come to stand for the letter itself.

The metonymic sequence that segues into the following i-section presumably works as follows: *chequer work* is the pattern sewn or worn by a *milk-maid*, who is the type of rural subject painted by *Hogarth*, who also painted scenes from *Shakespeare*, who was the object of literary criticism by *Hazlitt*, who criticized *Shakespeare*, who was the object... (and so on). The sequence proceeds like a stochastic process that finally spirals back to the circle of author and critic, each of whose work suggests and repetitively cross-authorizes the other. "By merely pulling an apron string we set a Pretty peal of Chimes at work," just as the two edges of the Rat-trap letter are configured "by merely touching the spring delicately and etherially." The metonymy/metaphor that closes the o-section and opens the i-section is one of only two images of sound and of woman that appear in the letter. The other, in the first o-section, associates the biblical Eve with the sound of a thunderclap. In this one, a needy child or would-be seducer pulls the apron string of a maid and sets off a "pretty peal" (slang term for a woman's scolding [see *1811 Dictionary of the Vulgar Tongue*]). Having reintroduced the critic-poet relation, then, Keats can "return to Wordsworth—whether or no he has an extended vision," the measurement of masculine vision and dualistic whether-or-no scenario set in stark contrast to a feminine cacophony of ringing sound that can't be resolved or managed, merely touched off and then left to run its own course ("let them chime on a while...").

The woman/sound image, erupting near the center of the long letter, functions—like the o-section in which it appears—as a fractal deterritorialization that both undermines and stabilizes the territoriality around it. The child/man, reconnected briefly by the umbilical apron string to the milkmaid, developmentally proceeds to symbolic masculine differentiations, while the semiotic choral riffing is reduced to a kind of background Muzak. And yet, wound like a golf ball's core or curled up in the fluid womb of language or spinning like the inner ring of a gyroscope, in the middle of the milkmaid metaphor/metonym movement, the surgeon finds again those dead ringers in the tower, the would-be self-sufficient yin-yang twins of male homosociality, critic and poet, always about to be born or aborted.

The dependence of the i-sections on the o-sections they emerge from and stand out against is effaced insofar as the i-sections operate by exclusion, while the o-sections operate by inclusion. Thus the i-sections appear to stand alone and so can be printed separately without anything seeming to be missing, while the o-sections are doubly contingent, not only on the content of the i-sections on which they comment, but on the materiality of the letter itself. The i-sections define the realm of evaluative disciplinary standards as a public and homosocial field seemingly oriented by the alignment of metaphors of orientation; the o-sections are carnivalesque, feminized, interruptive, and yet foundational. The metaphor of woman and cacophonous noise marks the place where signifier and signified become radically non-self-identical, since *sound* is precisely *not* what signifies in the written letter, while the visual resonance of the grid anchors signifier and signified by self-similarity.

It is easy to see the multiple cross-codings of hierarchized binaries that are configured by the letter's alternating sections, which align masculine and feminine with criticism and poetry, with visual and aural, and so on. Even so, the power enacted here does not operate simply by asserting the adequacy of these binary distinctions but by their decomposition: like a gene, it unzips in order to recombine and mutate. The two halves of the letter drop away, like a Cheshire cat that disappears leaving only its smile. The letter leaves a textual history as a zipper-like wake that is continually produced, continually expands, and continually disappears in a cleavage that is always being opened and shut. The epitaph Keats requested for himself—"Here lies one whose name was writ on water"—defines a logic by which the text continues to be animated by the death of the author. Another "late" Keats text works up this logic into the temporal and thermo/psychodynamic contradiction of a spookily manipulative come-on:

> This living hand, now warm and capable
> Of earnest grasping, would, if it were cold
> And in the icy silence of the tomb,
> So haunt thy days and chill thy dreaming nights
> That thou would wish thy own heart dry of blood,
> So in my veins red life might stream again,
> And thou be conscience-calm'd. See, here it is—
> I hold it towards you.
> (Keats 1978, 503)

Interference of Text and Work in Stevens's "Palm"

The nothingness was a nakedness, a point

Beyond which thought could not progress as thought.

He had to choose. But it was not a choice

Between excluding things. It was not a choice

Between, but of. He chose to include the things

That in each other are included, the whole,

The complicate, the amassing harmony.
—Wallace Stevens, "Notes
toward a Supreme Fiction"

The palm at the end of the mind,

Beyond the last thought, rises

In the bronze decor,

A gold-feathered bird

Sings in the palm, without human meaning,

Without human feeling, a foreign song.

You know then that it is not the reason

That makes us happy or unhappy.

The bird sings. Its feathers shine.

The palm stands on the edge of space.

The wind moves slowly in the branches.

The bird's fire-fangled feathers dangle down.
—Wallace Stevens, "Of Mere Being"

The moving but unintelligible voice of the Other is thematized in Stevens's enigmatic poem "Of Mere Being" as the typically Romantic "foreign song" of the bird; the narrator's relation to the bird in the palm is a model for the reader's relation to the poem, whose hypnotic suggestions tell you what you see and what "you know."

"The end of the mind" must be a place where mind meets something that is not mind (something other—matter, the body); in a spatial sense, where it meets the world (the senses), if these are at least heuristically differentiable. In a temporal sense, the point of death: Stevens composed the poem as he faced imminent death by cancer; it seems to have been his last poem. But *the mind* need not refer only to an individual mind in either a narrowly autobiographical or phenomenological sense; the mind of the human or any other species will do, even most broadly the existence of "mind" in the universe.

Presumably, what the poem calls *thought* ends before what it calls *mind*, since the palm is at the mind's end but beyond the last thought. But even temporally, what is "beyond the last thought"? The *next* thought (the rest of the poem) or something categorically different, the extinction of thought? Or might we be looking backwards in time to a place where thought or mind are supposed to arise out of what is not mind, or out of another mind or thought? What kind of difference is being engaged?

The figure of "bronze decor" continues the careful process of simultaneous location and dislocation that constitutes the poem. Bronze, in Stevens's poetic palette, often signifies the color of the sea at sunset, an image that here echoes the sense of being at a boundary in space and in time. In any case, even this referential fixation cannot reduce, merely by substituting for interpretation a simplistic "decoding," the manifold of readings already suggested. Are we supposed to be walking along a beach in the flux of waves or approaching shore from a sea journey (perpendicular readings), stranded alone on an island staring at a mirage in the air, or sitting in some tacky public space staring out the window at a "real" palm or at some

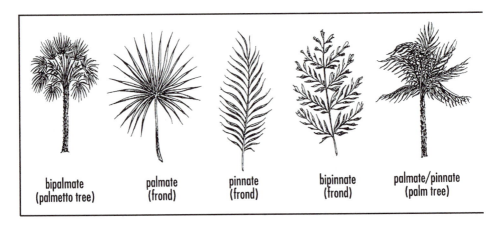

bipalmate
(palmetto tree)

palmate
(frond)

pinnate
(frond)

bipinnate
(frond)

palmate/pinnate
(palm tree)

tropical scene on a cocktail napkin? Which of these, that is, stands best for what the writer or reader of the poem is actually doing or experiencing in writing or reading the poem?

Innumerable differences (between phases, spaces, times, readings) arise and multiply as a series of bifurcations (individual/species, time/space, forward/backward, and so on) that between them generate a combinatory more complex than the act of interpretation can sustain at once, but this multiplication of differences (the maintenance of ambiguities) is also how the poem produces a similarity dimension by folding back on itself.

The palm, at least at first, could refer either to a tree or to the palm of a hand. Rather than trying to distinguish between these (or even by virtue of having to pick one and exclude the other), the reader is invited to notice a structural similarity: in either case, a kind of branching or flowering, an outward bifurcation: the tree a single trunk flowering along its length and finally into an explosion of frond-stems that also radiate into veined leaves; the human palm a kind of flowering of bones and nerves; the brain an involuted flowering at the end of its spinal trunk. Each of these figures may be taken to embody temporal (ontogenetic and phylogenetic) and spatial structures.

Like its first line, the poem's concluding line suggests that something is going on in the "similarity dimension" of the poem, inviting the reader in visualizing the image to notice that the bird's dangling feathers are barely distinguishable from the fronds of the palm in which it sits. I imagine a bird of paradise (although almost any bird would suffice), its dangling tail two long threadlike shafts, each tipped with a fan of feathers, which, like the palms, comprise another series of

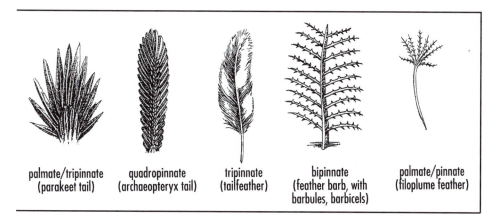

| palmate/tripinnate (parakeet tail) | quadropinnate (archaeopteryx tail) | tripinnate (tailfeather) | bipinnate (feather barb, with barbules, barbicels) | palmate/pinnate (filoplume feather) |

smaller splittings. But, importantly, difference as well as similarity inheres *within* palm and feather as well as *between*: in fact, palm leaves come in two basic shapes, "palmate" (palm or fan-shaped) and "pinnate" (feather-shaped); palms are notable for self-similarity (between the shapes of tree, leaf, and leaflet) and/or self-difference (that is, palms may alternate, across scale, between being palm-shaped and feather-shaped). Bird tails, too, may be roughly palm- or feather-shaped, and are strikingly self-similar (between tail shape, feather, barb, barbule, barbicle) or self-different (as in "filoplumes," which alternate across scale between palm and feather shapes).

We cannot tell (because the poem does not tell) whether the bird's feathers shine and are "fire-fangled" with iridescent color of their own or with the tincture of the sunset; that is, we cannot tell whether this iridescence is an intrinsic or interactive phenomenon, or whether the wave form (light, in this case) is differentiable from the particular network of matter (feathers) over which it plays. The same indeterminacy holds for the various wave forms that play across various bifurcating networks of matter in the poem: the synaptic electricity of thought and sensation, the sound of the song, the wind in the branches. This figural complex of wave forms rising and falling, unintelligible speech, and iridescence is an ongoing one in Stevens's poetry, from the famous opening stanzas of "The Idea of Order at Key West" to "Notes toward a Supreme Fiction," in which "the grossest iridescence of ocean / Howls hoo and rises and howls hoo and falls" (209) and so on.

The palm a poem makes—like the "footsteps" of textual distribution in Shelley's "Mask of Anarchy"—is also a structure in "real" space-time. Mapping the extension of the poem (that is, every concrete instantiation of it) yields another palmate diagram. Stevens's original typescript of the poem would appear as a line extending through space-time until the poem is copied, at which point another line would diverge, and so on, exploding into a firework at various technological "nodes of production" each time it is published, anthologized, or cited in published works. Since this diagram cannot show where the poem is being read (versus where copies simply exist), acts of reading might be marked as Stevensian iridescences.

Holly Stevens, the poet's daughter and editor, develops this self-similar dimension by using the poem's first line to title her collection of her father's poetry, suggesting that his entire poetic output forms a "palm at the end of the mind." The titling is metonymic (synechdochic) and metaphoric, suggesting that a single line can "stand for" the body of work in which it appears.

The problem with the diagram is that it maintains the author as a node into which (presumably) a root system of other poems converges and from which the poem in question originates, marking the author as a refractive interval, a constriction or singularity between reading and writing in an essentially linear progress. My text, then, constitutes another node from which issue more copies of the poem, a synapse in the brain of postindustrial capitalism. But my language knows something that I do not; something transmits itself through the text that I cannot know because it is a phenomenon of a longer wavelength than my own subjectivity. Not merely Stevens's poem nor the genre of poetry that uses me as its host but language itself comes to seem an alien intelligence by which I am instrumentalized.

If we superimpose a particular parameter on the mapping of the poem's extension — say, "reader's cultural class" (as defined by a set of variables such as education and family of origin) — we would no doubt find that the two maps conform closely. Likewise we might observe an even more radical limitation in discursive space. If our diagram were able to represent instances where the poem was read, discussed, or written about, we would find that these were clustered around literature classes, poetry workshops, literary journals, and so on, and that these instances overlap broadly with contemporary maps of the distribution of other poetry (and of this book). Stevens, then, contemplates the posthumous discursive extension of his body in a discursive space of "poetry" that appears to be closed.

When we consider the poem as an intertextual object, it will be more difficult to maintain the vision of the palm. One refers outward to a figural complex or set of codes established as a formally closed system in Stevens's body of work, and beyond such an individual body to the generic body of poetry. Stevens's images are of course overdetermined in relation to any number of other poems: Marvell's embowered soul-bird that "waves in its plumes the various light"; Wordsworth's "solitary reaper," singing her foreign song; Yeats's golden nightingale; and so on and on. Stevens is a bird singing in the branches of the distribution of these texts that converge in his own text as a singing bird; Stevens's critics sing, in turn, in all these branches, making each bird and each song a branching embedded within a branching. The palmate structure (a genealogical tree of texts sprouting from the patriarchal author's loins) gets continually lost in the fractal density of these structures.

Ambiguous echoes of this grand intertextual scale also structure the chaotic complexity of the signifier at a more and more microscopic level of the poem. Varying syntactic units of the poem (I will limit myself to considering sentences) play across unvarying formal units (three-line stanzas) in a seemingly schematic way: first a six-line sentence that comprises two stanzas, then a two-line sentence and two half-line sentences that comprise a stanza, then three single-line sentences that comprise a stanza. If there is a narrative logic to this movement, it can only proceed as a stochastic process that bounces between permutations, coming closer to a closure that is a closure because it establishes an optimal congruence between aural, grammatical, and visual organization (the three single-line sentences that comprise the final stanza). Within these parameters, anyway, the poem proceeds through permutations of difference (between sentence, line, and stanza) to maximum similarity. However, by considering these relations of auditory to visual units statically and statistically (as a set of "spatial" possibilities), it is just as easy to maintain that the poem maximizes difference rather than similarity by distributing sentences that can be longer than, shorter than, or equal to stanzas or to lines. Only one of these six possibilities seems not to be provided by the poem: no sentence is exactly one stanza long. There is, however, one point of indeterminacy in this schema, a grammatical "error," in fact, between the first and second stanza. The third line forms a dependent clause that, on first reading anyway, would seem to *conclude* a sentence that comprises the first stanza (thus one allows the pitch of one's voice to fall with the final syllable). However, the same line also functions as the *beginning* clause for the subsequent three lines (in which case one would have to read the final syllable with rising pitch). Because this "error" allows several possibilities to overlap, the first and second three lines also form syntactically complete sentences comprising a stanza each. Thus the congruence and incongruence of units—their openness and closure—do not simply alternate but coexist. This overlap is marked by the crux of syntactic indeterminacy that problematizes the articulation of the final syllable of the first stanza: in order to allow for all possibilities, one must level the pitch and stress over the final two syllables. This ensures that one cannot read the poem as a linear progression, since what follows alters the articulation of what precedes it; that is, the poem marks as a literal contradiction in the signifier—the binary bit of sound-information that concludes the stanza—what otherwise occurs as a problematic in the hermeneutic process of its writing or reading—for example, the challenge to rectify categories and figures of "rising" and "falling."

  The final word of the first stanza is a crux in the "work" of the poem as well as in the text. Holly Stevens notes that, "as printed in *Opus Posthumous . . . ,* the last word of the third line is 'distance.' 'Decor' is the word appearing in the original typescript, and has been restored here" (Stevens 1972, 404). When, how, or if Wallace Stevens was responsible for the change between typescript and first published version remains a question, but here above all it would seem to go against the author's intention to follow the classical textual critic's mandate to decide *between* versions by determining the author's final intention (the "first" and "final" intention being nearly simultaneous in this case, in any case). All we can say is that the poem—as a work—vacillates between "distance" and "decor," bifurcating it into two branches. The phonic choice between the words can be described as an opposition between oppositions between oppositions: (stressed/unstressed versus unstressed/stressed) versus (long consonants/short vowels versus long vowels/short consonants). These are among the primary oppositions (or transpositions) across which the poem makes its music, moving from a predominance of "long" consonants through a predominance of long vowels to find resolution in a profoundly mixed state. The difference between "distance" and "decor" is no less stark in the signified, where "bronze distance" and "bronze decor" turn on the axes of nature and culture, exteriority and interiority, energy (bronze as quality of light) and matter (bronze as a material substance).

The choice between "decor" and "distance" is also, more subtly, a visual one at the level of the signifier. The title begins a series of phrases that reproduce the figure of the palm as a series of words that expand in length: "Of Mere Being...the last thought...in the palm" and so on. It would be impossible to systematize these in any thoroughgoing way; it is in fact difficult to establish that such occurrences are anything more than accidents of ordinary language, but the subliminal figure only assumes significance where the poem most resonantly aligns it with aural, grammatical, and formal units (lines, clauses, caesurae, and so on), using it to shape word sequences into expansions and contractions toward closure. Predictably, this structure becomes most resonant in the last stanza. Given that the final word of the first stanza is a crux in a number of the signifying parameters of the poem, it is not surprising that it should be so in the letter-distribution curve as well, where the choice between the two words is between expansion and contraction.

Similar visual/aural play—such as the transposition between "n" and "g" in "foreign song" or the vertical transposition between the initial letters of "mind" and "wind"—is recruited into the signifying system; in *w* and *m*, for example, one may find again the frayings of rising palm and dangling feathers. Again, the visual transposition would not signify if it were not aligned with a vocal one—an *m* is made with closed lips, *w* with lips open to produce the wind that makes the sound—and a similar opposition in the signified: mind is a (formally) closed system (an organism); wind is not. This opposition is a primary conceptual engine of the poem. Should the difference be treated as one of degree or kind? It's an open-and-shut case. Wind, generated by temperature differentials, forms a complex dynamical system—a kind of fluid cortex around the earth's crust. The poem attempts to engage the meaningless differentials of language (information) around which mind or meaning is generated.

In the signifier's space, it is the letter *d* that is "at the end of the mind." In fact, the poem distributes the letter carefully, beginning by *ending* words with it and concluding (both the first stanza and the whole poem) by *beginning* words with it. The shape of the letter has already been traced in the stochastic but determined swerving back that constitutes the movement of syntax in the poem; could *d* be the shape of a stem and leaf, or a tailfeather? This observation would again be arbitrary if the poem did not play so consistently with "rhymed" and opposed shapes of letters rising and dangling, open and closed, beginning and ending key words. Here at the most microscopic signifying scale (the letter), it is most difficult to distinguish noise from information, accident from intent, critic's overreading from author's overwriting. At the least, the use of *d* to accentuate consonant-stressed word endings ("end," "mind," "beyond") makes its position at the beginning of the final word (of the first stanza and poem) function to make the reader/listener see/hear how the word dangles from a *d*. It matters less what word is "chosen" as the final word of the first stanza, as long as it begins with the letter *d*, since the poem establishes a system in which the letter *d* is overdetermined in ways that dictate its placement. This overdetermination is, of course, not true of ordinary language but therefore of a particular kind of poetry (which concerns itself somewhat solipsistically with the physicality of its signifiers) that seeks to constitute a system in which the arbitrarities of language are made to signify, in which random noise (numbers and positions and shapes of letters) is converted not merely to information but—through its fractal engagement in the signifying structures of the poem—into meaning, the "rage for order." Why bother? Even if we could establish that, as Blake asserted, "Poetry admits not a Letter that is Insignificant" (560), what is gained, when Stevens's use of letters is not even generalizable to his other poems? If only it were not remarkable as high-poetic strategy, it would be the unmarkedness of this difference "that makes us happy or unhappy," that tells us we are in contact with an Other, a "foreign song."

The poem moves as an entity across a number of parameters at once. The evolution of these parameters is nonsynchronous; one becomes more orderly as entropy increases in another; one swerves back as another frays outward. An uncertainty principle operates in reading; it seems that when one parameter is brought under control, others wriggle away. Instead of finding an elementary particle as we direct our attention to more and more minute particulars of the poem, we find that particles multiply.

In trying to treat the poem as a formally closed system, one finds that it is a subsystem of other larger systems, the meander of a breeze in a cortex of intertextual currents, where meaning is made by simultaneous alignment and misalignment of structure across scale and dimension of discursive space-time. The discursively incestuous swerves inward and exogamously outward meet everywhere at a singularity; meaning is the zippery wake of information backward across our bodies swimming in language.

F   I   V   E

Fractal Logics of Romanticism:
Rhythming

Introduction: Romantic Dysrhythmia

Romantic devaluation of strictly metered verse and the privileging of aesthetic complexity and of "organic" literary form (featuring mixed and "self-organizing" patterns, and patterns of patterns or "plaids") can be understood in relation to the real-time dysrhythmia that came to distinguish intellectual and professional labor (a distinction still preserved in the college student's "all-nighter" and the medical intern's long shifts as professionalizing "hazing rituals"). C. S. Whitaker (1970) characterized as dysrhythmic the clash between traditional and modern structures in twentieth-century Nigeria; at issue here is modernity's valorization and attempted monopolization of dysrhythmia as a mark of distinction. Dysrhythmia in this sense — chaotic or complex rhythm rather than disorder — distinguishes the professional at once from the agricultural laborer, subject both to the regularity of diurnal and seasonal rhythms and to their unpredictable fluctuations, and from the factory worker, subject to industrial capitalism's increasingly regularized alternation of labor and leisure and to its increasingly unpredictable economic cycles. In other words, chaos is distinguished from both the despotism of order and the terrorism of disorder. But emergent professionalism does not add a new or more complex temporal riff on top of the monotonous bass or drumbeat of traditional work, which had its own well-established ways of making chaotic peace with the implacable rhythms on which it depended.

Instead, the mix is altered systematically to produce the contrast by squeezing out casual labor and artisanal labor (carried on in relative temporal freedom), and so on. Professionalism is dysrhythmed against the regularization of nonprofessional labor.

Throughout subsequent remixings (such as the complex relations of salaried to wage labor), the literary writer has continued to be an important liminal figure. Such a writer may be "working" at any time or place or at all times and places (for example, using personal relationships as fodder for a new novel) or, on the other hand, doesn't seem to work at all. Romantic writers repeatedly valorize the dysrhythmia that distinguishes their labor: Coleridge's night meditations when the other "inmates" of his cottage are at rest (in "Frost at Midnight"), Blake's "wandering" through the "chartered streets" of "London," Wordsworth's distinction from Lucy's "diurnal round," Keats's poetic record of his all-night reading set against those who owe "fealty to Apollo" (god of the sun as well as of poetry). Another elegant twist on this distinction can be found in De Quincey's record (in his *Confessions*) of taking opium on Saturday nights so he could mingle with "the poor" (that is, those who must work for a living, and who have just received their weekly wages) and thereby simulate for himself a periodic cycle of labor and leisure even though he "had no labours that I rested from; no wages to receive" (1950, 304).

A figurative combinatory of noise and regularity or harmony (one that is both surprisingly consistent and permutationally variable) is discernible in many poems of the period.

In "The Thresher's Labor," Stephen Duck contrasts the monotonous regularity of harvesting with the noise of harvest's end—its "stunning Clamours," "Bells, and clashing Whips, . . . And rattling Waggons . . . And loud Huzza's" (1985, 360–61). Thompson calls this "an obligatory set-piece in eighteenth-century farming poetry," but one that marks nonetheless a "moment at which older collective rhythms break through the new" as alienated labor gives way to a common satisfaction that includes a "momentary obliteration of social distinctions" (1993, 361).

Joanna Baillie's 1790 account of the evening of "A Summer Day" is no less a set piece, but Baillie depicts a Romanticized organic rural community poised in transit between field and village, work and play, day and night. Rather than setting cacophonous "older collective rhythms" against a regularized and alienated labor that they can merely punctuate, Baillie aestheticizes the two into the *concordia discord* of a nostalgic chaos:

> The village, lone and silent through the day,
> Receiving from the fields its merry bands,

Sends forth its evening sound, confused but cheerful;
Whilst dogs and children, eager housewives' tongues,
And true-love ditties, in no plaintive strain
By shrill-voiced maid at open window sung;
The lowing of the home-returning kine,
The herd's low droning trump, and tinkling bell
Tied to the collar of his favorite sheep,
Make no contemptible variety
To ears not over-nice.
(Lonsdale 1990, 432)

In spite of their differences, the two poems both mark "older collective rhythms" by *lists* that level syntactic subordination into a series of sound-figures connected only by commas or "ands"; that is, to a "horizontal" series in which each element is in some sense equivalent. This distinguishing feature closely relates listing with poeticity itself insofar as poetry strings words together into equivalent rhythmic units (metrical feet), or because of their equivalence in sound (as in rhyme).

The poetic list has continued to function as a figure of insubordination, excess, and "leveling" of difference. Its genealogy can be traced back through Ginsberg's *Howl* (which contains a four-page run-on sentence comprising lists of lists of lists) and back through Whitman at least to Keats and Blake, who used lists to valorize sensual and mystical excess. Wordsworth, on the other hand, tended to use lists to stigmatize insubordinate levelings of difference, from the "rocks, and stones,

List as Argument. The history of the list as a trope of insubordination makes it a characteristically postmodern argumentative device: Eve Sedgwick's list of some of the ways that people understand their sexualities has compelling argumentative force because it sprawls across and implicates (rather than dialectically transcending) the supposedly definitive binary oppositions that organize hegemonic sexual difference (e.g., male/female, straight/gay, top/bottom, butch/femme, nature/nurture, practice/identity, fantasy/reality, and so on). Here's a selection:

> Even identical genital acts mean very different things to different people.
>
> To some people, the nimbus of "the sexual" seems scarcely to extend beyond the boundaries of discrete genital acts; to others, it enfolds them loosely or floats virtually free of them.
>
> Sexuality makes up a large share of the self-perceived identity of some people, a small share of others'.
>
> Many people have their richest mental/emotional involvement with sexual acts that they don't do, or even don't *want* to do.
>
> For some people, the preference for a certain sexual object, act, role, zone, or scenario is so immemorial and durable that it can only be experienced as innate; for others, it appears to come late or to feel aleatory or discretionary. (Sedgwick 1990, 25)

and trees" to which the subject is reduced in "A Slumber" to the almost page-long list of performers and vendors at London's Saint Bartholomew's Fair (in *The Prelude* [1979, 262–64]), a collective assemblage that constitutes for Wordsworth a "Parliament of Monsters" (cultural democracy being as horrific for the poet as more democratic representation in the actual Parliament had been for Burke). Like the "almost unendurable" sentences of *Blackwood's Edinburgh Magazine* analyzed by Jon Klancher, Wordsworth's trick of subordinating even a page-long list to the imperial reach of his syntax enacts a "victory over dispersion . . . again and again rehearsed in language," by which "the baffling swarm of different people and social classes can now be read for its latent *unity*" (Klancher 1987, 53, 57–58).

Like Baillie's "Evening," Blake's "Nurse's Song" from the *Songs of Innocence* also turns on a liminal moment between day and night but takes this liminality as an occasion in which power is negotiated. The lyric turns on a dispute between a nanny and her charges: she orders the children to "come home" and "leave off play" because "the sun is gone down"; they respond, "No, no, let us play, for it is yet day"; she acquiesces ("Well, well, go & play till the light fades away"); and finally "The little ones leaped & shouted & laugh'd" (note again the list of noises), "And all the hills ecchoed" (1982, 15). "Innocence" here takes the form of a nonbinarity between binarity (day and night divided by the punctual moment of sunset) and nonbinarity (the fading light in which the moment is embedded, making the boundary negotiable). Play plays with its edge, requiring this liminal time (or another similar ambiguity) in order to count as play. The echoing hills mark the recursive "binary decomposition" of play at its edge. Even if it is apparently temporally contained, the noise of liminality (rather than the punctual sunset) is nonetheless the definitive one for the temporality in which it occurs; it is the "Moment in each Day that Satan cannot find / Nor can his Watch Fiends find it," as Blake described it elsewhere (1982, 136).

Blake's lyric is a kind of political "aubade," usually a set piece in which a lover argues, in spite of manifest evidence, that the sun has not yet risen, in order to stay with a lover a little longer. All who are subject to imposed regularities — employees, students, children, patients — are familiar with Blake's version.

The nurse of Blake's companion piece from the "Songs of Experience," by contrast, is first embarrassed by remembering the days of her youth, then summarily orders the children home. This time the last word is hers: "Your spring & your day are wasted in play, / And your winter and night in disguise" (23). Against the echoic decomposition that ends the first "Nurse's Song" is set the echoic resonance that ends this one: the conventionally self-similar "scaling" relation between a life, a seasonal year, and a single day depends on alignment of the binarities of youth/age, spring/winter, day/night. Each of these are aligned in turn with the curious opposition of "play" and "disguise." "Experience" takes the form of a binary between binarity and nonbinarity, impoverishing both play and work as "wasted" time; play because it brings no profit, and work because it brings no pleasure. The nurse of "Experience" seems to be caught between two economies, one of bourgeois work-discipline in which time is money, and an earlier one in which gratuitous waste or bestowal of time and money is the supreme marker of wealth and power. The nurse's role is also caught between two frameworks: a precapitalist or paternalistic economy (which situates the nurse as a kind of family member, with certain discretionary powers) and the other a capitalist one in which the home-centeredness of the nurse's occupation tends not to make her labor relatively less alienated but only particularly low status; here the nurse enacts and reproduces her own subordination, in her relation to her charges. The temporal scenario whereby the nurse's remembered past is rigidly separated from the stern disciplinary role she has adopted also appears as a spatial one: the "disguise" of the disciplinarian (apparently a kind of assumed persona or mask) is dependent on its distinction from the so-called inner child (identified here as a pathetic ruse). This distinction displaces and internalizes what is otherwise a physical distinction between "outside" play and the relatively homebound interiority enforced by winter, night, or old age. The nurse of "Experience" is the subject of a proletarianization vis-à-vis a precapitalist economy of time and status. The "betweenness" that for the first nurse allows a suspension of hierarchical power makes the second nurse and her charges especially subject to it; the terms by which time had been negotiated have ceased to be available. E. P. Thompson traces a similar movement in factory work:

The first generation of factory workers were taught by their masters the importance of time; the second generation formed their short-time committees in the ten-hour movement; the third generation struck for overtime or time-and-a-half. They had accepted the categories of their employers and learned to fight back within them. They had learned their lesson, that time is money, only too well. (Thompson 1993, 390)

While the liminality of nurses, artisans, mothers, pieceworkers, and other home laborers is being devalued with respect to regularized labor, the temporal liminality of professional labor is being valorized. Keats's "On First Looking into Chapman's Homer" elegantly marks professionalization as dysrhythming:

Much have I travell'd in the realms of gold,
  And many goodly states and kingdoms seen;
  Round many western islands have I been
Which bards in fealty to Apollo hold.
Oft of one wide expanse had I been told
    That deep-brow'd Homer ruled as his desmesne;
    Yet did I never breathe its pure serene
Till I heard Chapman speak out loud and bold:
Then felt I like some watcher of the skies
    When a new planet swims into his ken;
Or like stout Cortez when with eagle eyes
    He star'd at the Pacific — and all his men
Look'd at each other with a wild surmise —
    Silent, upon a peak in Darien.
(Keats 1978, 64)

Keats wrote the sonnet after an all-night reading of Chapman with his old school-teacher, Charles Cowden Clarke, and sent Clarke a copy by the morning post (Norton 1986, 798); that is, he documented the immediacy of its writing by official postmark. His night reading and writing mark him as an intellectual or professional worker, not "rolled round in earth's diurnal course" but exempt from the rhythms that rule working-class labor. "Fealty to Apollo," god of the sun as well as of poetry, is situated as belonging to a superseded stage, characterized in the octave as an explicitly feudal mode of literary production: literature is organized into domains ruled by individual authors, who in turn owe "fealty to Apollo" in a pyramidally scaling hierarchy. The nighttime discovery of the astronomer-poet, on the other hand, belongs to a contemporary mode of knowledge production: the swimming planets and oceanic vistas mark the liquidation of cultural capital into raw material for the poet's own production. The "indetermination" of what Cortez sees, and therefore of what Keats sees in Chapman's Homer (marked not only by its oceanic expanse but, more explicitly, by the bafflement of Cortez's men), is that which professional knowledge characterizes as uniquely its own (as against merely "technical" knowledge), attempting to appropriate for itself the unreifiable and incommunicable character of all cultural or "enculturated" knowledge.

In other words, the poem is itself a kind of postmark, written in order to document what first seems to be the reading of Chapman but turns out to be the dysrhythmia of its own writing; in this sense it is *performative*: by reading and writing about reading at night, Keats performs his professionalization as a poet. The poem is constituted by working up the conditions of its production; the fact of reading and writing at night and the relative social significance of these acts are both repressed and elaborated. Similarly, Keats writes Clarke (and the mediation of cultural power by education) out of the experience, the better to present his own unmediated and solitary communion with genius.

Keats's famous "mistake"—his substitution of the conquistador Cortez for the discoverer Balboa—succinctly reenacts the dynamic, making his reading, by virtue of a literal forgetting of history, no mere discovery but, as it becomes raw material for his writing, a conquest. This poetic parapraxis—overdetermined by the (Britishized) resemblance of "Cortez" to "Keats"—writes the poet into the patrilineage, now reconstituted as an English national literary empire that does not merely inherit the classics but continually liquidates and remakes history to its specifications. Neither the fixity of mappable property nor the reading of Greek can any longer delimit cultural power; the tautology of the genius of genius—like the genius of money, on which it is modeled—is that it can be made to liquidate all other meaning and to generate a surplus in subjectivity itself, fetishizable in the name of the author. The distance between Romantic reader and writer is at once collapsed and made unbridgeable; an infinite but already redundant series of sequels is established: "On First Looking into Keats's 'On First Looking into Chapman's Homer,'" and so on. The belated reader plays Achilles to Keats's tortoise.

A survey of the poem's textual history reveals a series of transformations, each of which tells the same story of individuation and professionalization. When writing out the draft, Keats changes "low brow'd Homer" to "deep brow'd Homer": the word "low," crossed out in Keats's handwritten copy, with the word "deep" written above it, makes another nice emblem for the dynamic of the poem, by which Keats enacts his own sociocultural transit from "low-brow" to "deep-brow."

Between the draft and the version published in the *Examiner*, the passively childlike "wond'ring eyes" of Cortez/Keats become the vigilantly predatory "eagle eyes" that look down on the text not as spectacle but as potential raw material. Between the *Examiner* version and the version published in Keats's *Poems* of 1817, the pedestrian admission of previous ignorance and exclusion ("Yet could I never judge what Men could mean") becomes the assertion of present and immediate participation ("Yet did I never breathe its pure serene"). In each case, the changes make the poem "more poetic." It makes little difference whether Keats or others made these changes, since each so succinctly records and performs the "making of a

On the first looking into Chapman's Homer
Much have I travell'd in the Realms of Gold,——
And many goodly States, and Kingdoms seen;
Round many Western islands have I been,
Which Bards in fealty to Apollo hold.——
Of one wide expanse had I been told,——
Which deep brow'd Homer ruled as his Demesne;
Yet could I never judge what Men could mean,
Till I heard Chapman speak out loud and bold.——
Then felt I like some Watcher of the Skies
When a new Planet swims into his Ken,
Or like stout Cortez when with wond'ring eyes
He star'd at the Pacific, and all his Men
Look'd at each other with a wild surmise——
Silent upon a Peak in Darien——

"On First Looking into Chapman's Homer": Keats's Holograph Draft.
(MS Keats 2.4. By permission of the Houghton Library, Harvard University)

difference" that was not Keats's own to begin with: poeticization and professionalization are made to coincide. In any case, posthumous editions continue the fractally pervasive logic of development: between Keats's edition and modern versions, the sonnet *number*, making the poem merely one of many, is omitted in favor of a title. Individuation keeps happening in and to the text; its sequence from posted letter to newspaper entry to author's volume to literary anthology is made to tell the story of the apotheosis of Literature and the figure of the author. The simple placement of the poem in the *Norton Anthology* makes the poem performatively "happy," retroactively validating as a self-fulfilling prophecy Keats's famous boast that he would be "among the English poets" after his death.

Keats's "To Autumn," almost exclusively a palimpsest of lists, offers a veritable apotheosis of dysrhythmia. Its first stanza signifies excess by a list of autumn's attributes and actions in a series of noun phrases and dependent clauses that, in fact, do not yield a grammatical sentence but a list so elaborate that few readers notice this fact; syntactic excess performs what is thematized in images of excess, particularly, in the stanza's concluding lines, the surplus liquidity that is the product of the bee's collective labor. The poem ends with another elaborate list of sounds that, unlike Baillie's "Summer Day," have now been rigorously and hierarchically orchestrated:

> Then in a wailful choir the small gnats mourn
>> Among the river sallows, borne aloft
>>> Or sinking as the light wind lives or dies;
> And full-grown lambs loud bleat from hilly bourn;
>> Hedge-crickets sing; and now with treble soft
>> The red-breast whistles from a garden-croft;
>>> And gathering swallows twitter in the skies.
>
> (Keats 1978, 477)

Keats's gnats, completely subject to external forces (the wind that moves them about and the approaching winter that will kill them), can only mourn their imminent death; likewise the lambs, "full-grown" insofar as they will not be allowed to live to maturity, seem impotently to protest their imminent slaughter, a traditional autumn event (at least since the seventeenth century, when lambs began to be raised as much for meat as for wool [Russell 1986, 157]). Among the "hedge-crickets" who next add their song—if these are like the typical poetic crickets of Keats's "The Grasshopper and the Cricket"—some few individuals will manage to cheat death for a time and to eke out a precarious indoor existence singing from a hearth. Next, the whistling "red-breast" is even more privileged, traditionally represented in English poetry as the only bird that continues to sing throughout the winter. Keats's symphony works its way up by increments of pitch and speed from mourning to bleating to singing to whistling and finally twittering, as it works its way up a "chain of being" marked by increasing exemption from regular cyclical change. The "gathering swallows," whose twittering ends the poem, form a collective subject, a body whose dynamically shifting boundaries make it a kind of liquid (another overflowing surplus like the "o'erbrimming" honey that ends the first stanza or the "oozings" of the "cyderpress" that end the second), a class whose restless motion and manic twittering orients and coordinates its members self-referentially and semiautonomously to each other rather than to the earth, whose rise and imminent transnational migration allow it to transcend the temporal and spatial boundaries at which all other creatures are stationed—in short, perhaps the most highly naturalized and aestheticized version of that old story, the rise of the middle class, identified here with the surplus liquidity by which it is constituted. Keats makes this liquidity subsume and dissolve all other relations by embodying it at every scale, down to the most molecular, the sound and shape of the single letter "s," which (anticipating Joyce's *Ulysses*) conspicuously begins, sinuously weaves through, and ends the poem—as well as stanzas and words—from the first stanza's opening ("Season of mists and mellow fruitfulness") and concluding line ("summer has o'er-brimmed their clammy cells") to the final "swallows . . . in the skies."

Blake's Cycles

By following a very simple temporal, biographical scenario—William Blake's falling-out with his employer, William Hayley, between 1800 and 1803 (see Wilson 1971, 145–203)—it becomes clear that, as in each "Nurse's Song," the structuration of real time depends on the ambiguity of power relations within the changing economies that configure them. Blake's relation to Hayley (like the role of the "Nurse") fluctuates between several very different frameworks. Hayley is, most consistently, Blake's *employer* insofar as he commissions Blake to complete certain projects specified and judged by Hayley, although Hayley is always only on the verge of becoming an employer, since Blake's income from Hayley never does more than hover around a subsistence level. On the other hand, Hayley also always seems about to become more of a *patron*, allowing Blake more liberty to control his own productions, but within the quasi-feudal structure of dependence that characterizes patronage. These two ambiguous relationships, in turn, hold the never-quite-materializing promise that Hayley could become a *"consumer"* (a "patron" in the modern sense) who would buy artworks that Blake produced as an "independent" producer. The ongoing liminality of these relationships produces a temporal trajectory for Blake's career that remains continually under construction. It is easy to see that such ambiguities are ongoing in the economic status of artists, literati, and intellectuals; what may be less easy to see is that such liminality differentiates them less than it allies them to other apparently more clearly defined economic relations. In following Blake's cycles, though, it should become clear that the persistence of ambiguity is definitive even for what seem first to be unambiguous points that fixate the cycle.

In September 1800, Blake and his wife Catherine moved to Felpham from London so that William could work more closely with Hayley. Hayley had been encouraging Blake to make a living painting portraits and miniatures, and had already given Blake a commission. Just arrived, Blake writes to sculptor John Flaxman that "Mr Hayley recievd us with his usual brotherly affection" and that "Felpham is a sweet place for Study. because it is more Spiritual than London Heaven opens here on all sides her golden Gates her windows are not obstructed by vapours" (Blake 1982, 710). After about eight months, Blake writes to his friend and patron, Thomas Butts, that "Mr Hayley acts like a Prince"; "Miniature is become a Goddess in my eyes & my Friends in Sussex say that I Excell in the pursuit"; and that "Felpham in particular is the sweetest spot on Earth at least it is so to me & My Good Wife" (715).

Blake's subsequent letters to Butts, and to his brother James, seem to chronicle a gradual but very thorough disillusionment with Felpham, with Hayley, and with portraiture.

A year after his arrival at Felpham, in September 1801, Blake has begun to set his own "historical" design practice against the miniature and portraiture Hayley paid him for. He writes to Butts that "I have now discoverd that without Nature before the painters Eye he can never produce any thing in the walks of Natural Painting Historical Designing is one thing & Portrait Painting another & they are as Distinct as any two Arts can be *Happy would that man be who could unite them*" (717; my emphasis). In November 1802 Blake writes more emphatically to Butts that "Portrait Painting is the direct contrary to Designing & Historical Painting in every respect," reasserting the incompatibility of painterly naturalism with his own design practice, and now arguing that "the Venetian finesse in Art can *never be united* with the Majesty of Colouring necessary to Historical beauty" (718–19; my emphasis), even citing Sir Joshua Reynolds as an authority (although in Blake's private marginalia, Reynolds appears exclusively as a nemesis). By July 1803, having decided to leave Felpham, Blake writes even more vehemently: "Nature & Fancy are Two Things & can *Never be joined neither ought any one to attempt it* for it is [Idolatry] & destroys the Soul" (730; my emphasis).

Blake's "falling out" with Hayley seems to follow a trajectory parallel to these pronouncements about design: his early praise of Hayley is followed by long silence, then oblique hints that all is not right, and finally, outright denunciation. In November 1802 Blake explains to Butts that he has not written because "I have been very Unhappy & could not think of troubling you about it or any of my real Friends (I have written many letters to you which I burnd & did not send)" (719). At this point, only the mystifying secrecy Blake ascribes to propriety, in conjunction with the reference to "real Friends" (and its implicit contrary, false friends), suggests that Hayley is involved in Blake's unhappiness, for this conjunction will occur repeatedly in Blake's complaints about Hayley.

In January 1803 Blake first mentions his wife's "Ague & Rheumatism" to Butts, now asserting (contradicting an earlier letter) that these "have been her almost constant Enemies which she has combated in vain ever since we have been here"; several lines later, a more gradual onset is again implied: "When I came down here I was more sanguine than I am at present but it was chiefly because I was ignorant of many things which have since occurred & chiefly the unhealthiness of the place" (723). The same etiological nuances problematize the course of Blake's own relation with Hayley, and will finally bear on whether Blake's dis-ease with Hayley was an acute or a chronic condition. For now, Blake asserts that "Mr H I doubt not will do ultimately all that both he & I wish to lift me out of difficulty," but then adds an ambiguous qualification: "but this is no easy matter to a man who having Spiritual Enemies of such formidable magnitude cannot expect to want natural hidden ones." Later in the letter, Blake manages, in spite of himself, to be a bit less ambiguous:

But you have so generously & openly desired that I will divide my griefs with you that I cannot hide what is now become my duty to explain — My unhappiness has arisen from a source which if explord too narrowly might hurt my pecuniary circumstances. As my dependence is on Engraving at present & particularly on the Engravings I have in hand for Mr H. & I find on all hands great objections to my doing any thing but the meer drudgery of business & intimations that if I do not confine myself to this I shall not live. this has always pursud me. (724)

Blake introduces his unhappiness with a propriety that anxiously absolves him of responsibility for what follows (Butts's inquiries make it Blake's "duty to explain"), promising to explicate what has been hidden, but proceeding only to implicate in the course of explaining why he cannot be explicit. Blake mentions Hayley only as one on whom he depends, but again suppresses Hayley's name as a source of the "great objections" and threatening "intimations," as if these were the voices of evil pursuing spirits. Finally, he suggests that the consequence of being a poet and artist in his own right would be death, although (as he goes on to explain) he also "cannot live without doing my duty to lay up treasures in heaven"; that is, by exercising his spiritual gifts as an artist. Material life ("business") and spiritual life (art) seem to be mutually exclusive polarities.

A January 1803 letter to his brother James establishes more clearly the terms of this dynamic. Blake complains openly of the "Agues & Rheumatisms" his wife has suffered in Felpham and states his determination to leave, "because I am now certain of what I have long doubted Viz [that H] is jealous"—namely, as he goes on to specify, of his own artistic and poetic gifts—"& will be no further My friend than he is compelld by circumstances" (725). In light of what follows, such an assertion seems an ironic and wishful projection, for while his own financial circumstances seemed continually to compel Blake to be Hayley's friend, Hayley needed Blake's friendship only for the gratification and status of patronizing "my gentle visionary" (as he addressed Blake in a dedication). Blake mentions his uneasiness at Hayley's envy, and that

This is the uneasiness I spoke of to Mr Butts but I did not tell him so plain & wish you to keep it a secret & to burn this letter because it speaks so plain I told Mr Butts that I did not wish to Explore too much the cause of our determination to leave Felpham because of pecuniary connexions between H & me. (725–26)

An irony that marks levels of financial and professional dependence operates between the "plain speech" Blake allows himself with his brother (with the proviso that the letter be burned), the veiled hints he sends to Butts (a patron and friend), and the secrecy he observes with Hayley. Blake goes on to boast that he is "fully Employd & Well Paid," having

made it so much H's interest to employ me that he can no longer treat me with indifference & now it is in my power to stay or return or remove to any other place that I choose, because I am getting before hand in money matters The Profits arising from Publications are immense & I now have it in my power to commence publication with very many formidable works... I am now Engraving Six little plates for a little work of Mr H's [The Triumphs of Temper] for which I am to have 10 Guineas each & the certain profits of that work are a fortune such as would make me independent supposing that I could substantiate such a one of my own & I mean to try many. (726)

These assertions will be belied by Blake's continual failure to make even a subsistence market for his own work; because the capital and control needed for his "independent" productions remain dependent on his more profitable work for others as an engraver, his class position remains actively ambiguous.

In April 1803 Blake asks Butts to "Congratulate me on my return to London with the full approbation of Mr Hayley" (728); that is, since he has managed to keep his animosity secret from Hayley, thus securing continued support. As before, Hayley's name arises in this neutral statement only juxtaposed to the complaint that follows but clearly applies to him, although Blake again introduces it with a dark complicity that promises a dangerous revelation:

Now I may say to you what perhaps I should not dare to say to any one else. That I can alone carry on my visionary studies in London Unannoyd... & at liberty from the doubts of other Mortals.... if a Man is the Enemy of my Spiritual Life while he pretends to be the Friend of my Corporeal. he is a Real Enemy. (728)

        Blake's polarity with Hayley has now been fully charged; by July 1803, he sees prospects for profitable employments elsewhere, so

As to Mr H I feel myself at liberty to say as follows upon this ticklish subject... Mr H approves of My Designs as little as he does of my Poems and I have been forced to insist on his leaving me in both to my Own Self Will. for I am determind to be no longer Pesterd with his Genteel Ignorance & Polite Disapprobation. I know myself both Poet & Painter & it is not his affected Contempt that can move me to any thing but a more assiduous pursuit of both Arts. (730)

        Blake goes on to characterize Hayley's "imbecile attempts to depress Me" and his own "Patience & Forbearance of Injuries upon Injuries," assuring Butts that "if I could have returnd to London a Month after my arrival here I should have done so, but I was commanded by my Spiritual friends to bear all to be silent & to go through all without murmuring."

        What, then, has happened over the course of three years at Felpham? How should the narrative be written? Did Blake change his mind about Hayley, portraiture, and Felpham as his early hopes came to seem naive in light of subsequent knowledge? Or had he always only tried to put a good face on an always ambivalent relationship and an artistic venture that was never more than an economic expedient, finally (but not quite) giving up as he realized again that "the eagle never lost so much time as when he submitted to learn of the crow" (Blake 1982, 37)? What should be made of the fact that the realization coincides with new possibilities for financial independence, opened partially by what he has learned (and earned) "of the crow"?

        In order to establish ironic ambivalence in Blake, one must refer first of all to incongruities *between his texts*. The simple spatial construction (concentric circles or spheres from most private to most public) in which I have located Blake's texts seems to be fixed at its extremes. His private comments and epigrams about Hayley—or about kings, or about Sir Joshua—are continually damning. Blake's public friendship with Hayley, on the other hand, seems also to remain constant and intact; there is no open falling-out. Indeed, after Blake leaves Felpham his letters to Hayley are more solicitous than ever. Only between the polarized extremes of private blame and public praise—in his letters to his friend and patron Butts—can the narrative structure of a "falling-out" be established.

But the irony of blame by praise begins to appear even in Blake's early approbations of Hayley, an irony so consistent that it is difficult to support the notion that Blake changed his mind about Hayley at all. "Mr Hayley acts like a Prince," but which Prince? Could it be . . . Satan? In other writings, Blake most often associates the title of "prince" with wickedness, except by an ironic substitution of the spiritual for the material (as in "I, William Blake, a Mental Prince . . ." [580]). And what of Hayley's "brotherly affection?" Blake ironizes it in *Milton* as the malignant "officious brotherhood" of Satan, "seeming a brother, being a tyrant, even thinking himself a brother / While he is murdering the just" (101, 100). "Miniature is become a Goddess in my eyes"—but in his prophetic works, Blake reserves the title "Goddess" for the likes of Vala, associated with natural delusion. Incipient spiritual/material polarizations lurk in these statements, although their irony is attenuated by being distributed among his texts. Still, irony can be located, even without reference to other texts, in the language of representation: "*acts* like a Prince" (but is it only an act, a display?); "become a Goddess in my eyes" (but only, then, as a passing appearance?).

In other early letters, too, the evidence of ironic polarity is at hand. In an 1801 letter, for example, Blake asks Butts to "continue to excuse my want of steady perseverance" in completing a promised miniature, explaining that "I labour incessantly & accomplish not one half of what I intend because my Abstract folly hurries me often away . . . Alas wretched happy ineffectual labourer of times moments that I am" (Blake 1982, 716). He goes on in a similar vein to express "Extreme disappointment at Mr Johnsons forgetfulness, who appointed to call on you but did Not. He is also a happy Abstract known by all his Friends as the most innocent forgetter of his own Interests." Given these backhanded compliments (praise by blame) to the unbusinesslike habits of the artist, the economic and commercial language render ironic his subsequent praise of Hayley's "matchless industry" and of Hayley's *Life of Cowper* as "a most valuable acquisition to Literature."

The apology for deficient production ("excuse my want of steady perseverance") appears often in Blake's writings, as do apologies for what amounts to excessive production. An apology of the latter type occupies a prominent place in Blake's preface to *Jerusalem*: "The Enthusiasm of the following Poem, the Author hopes [no Reader will think presumptuousness]" (145). Blake's October 1804 letter to Hayley is also typical: after a long paragraph setting out his spiritual triumphs, Blake interrupts himself, as if beginning the letter again, "Dear Sir, excuse my enthusiasm or rather madness, for I am really drunk with intellectual vision whenever I take a pencil or graver into my hand, even as I used to be in my youth" (757). It does not seem to matter whether this apology is read as "sincere" or as an emptily apotropaic gesture, an irony of a kind: it operates in any case as a trough between waves of performative enthusiasm, enacting a withdrawal or denial. Like the coyote in the cartoon, Blake runs off a (rhetorical) cliff but falls only when he looks down, when he feels the disapproving gaze of his hegemonic audience (suffers from ironic knowledge).

Of course "enthusiasm" denotes a religious passion or inspiration particularly déclassé among the "enlightened" in Blake's time: the apology is not merely the mark of some "personal" neurosis, but is charged by the institutionalized polarities in which Blake finds himself. He withdraws in a wave of shame (even if ironic shame) that is at least in one dimension a kind of class-based phenomenon.

Predictably, Blake's apologies for deficient production seem always to concern "business" (e.g., the miniature promised to Butts), while the excesses for which he apologizes involve his own idiosyncratic spiritual-artistic practices. Excess and lack or deficiency operate like mania and depression for Blake, and the cycles between these poles recur often, structuring units of time or text from the course of a single letter to the sweep of a life (e.g., his assertion of having regained, at age forty-six, the enthusiasm of his youth). Only at the nadir of his Felpham trajectory, though, does Blake (in a letter to Butts) represent his condition as a seemingly essential polarity within himself and between himself and the rest of humanity, a mark (obverse of the mark of Romantic "genius") that falls on him alone ("O why was I born with a different face"), so that "When Elate I am Envy'd" (leading to a phase of being "silent & passive"), but "When Meek I'm despisd" (733). Passivity—the attempt to please, to follow the dictates of another, and to be the person required by the other—seems always to fail, no less than envy and rejection will follow pursuit of his "Own Self Will" (730), the eponym "Will" marking Blake's ongoing investment of identity in the polarity that kept reasserting itself in his economic relationship with Hayley. Inevitably, then, Blake was always relearning his proverb about the eagle and the crow, or as he wrote to John Linnell some twenty years later (a year before his death):

No discipline will turn one Man into another even in the least particle. & such Discipline I call Presumption & Folly I have tried it too much not to know this & am very sorry for all who may be led to such ostentatious Exertion against their Eternal Existence itself because it is Mental Rebellion against the Holy Spirit & fit only for a Soldier of Satan to perform. (775)

Yet in another mood, Blake ameliorates the scenario that opposes the Holy Spirit to Satan (or mania to depression or life to death): his description of the Felpham sojourn as merely a restful "three years Slumber on the banks of the Ocean" (728) is typical.

As the private returns to speak in public as irony, so the public returns in private to silence, partially. Thus even private letters that "speak too plain" must be burned, complaints ambiguated, and—even in private epigrams—complainants identified mostly by initials only, as if the names were too holy or profane to be written. If this excessive caution smells like paranoia, only an analyst or paranoiac could be delusionally certain that the smell is exclusively his own or exclusively the other's.

One of the few verses in which Blake names his enemies outright is his "apology for his Catalogue," an angry piece of notebook doggerel in which he comments on his own polemical exhibition catalogue. "Having given great offence by writing in Prose," he begins, "I'll write in verse as soft as Bartolloze" (i.e., as polished as Bartollozzi's popular engravings), since "Some blush at what others can see no crime in / But nobody sees any harm in Rhyming" (505). Even in the privacy of his own notebook, then, Blake seems to be pursued by a gaze under which he is compelled to ironize his anger, generically, into doggerel; Blake could not have been surprised that nobody saw "any harm" in those "beautiful little poems," his *Songs.*

Does the downturn in Blake's representation of Hayley simply mark an upswing in his own hopes for financial independence from Hayley (for a rise in class) or simply the attrition of his hopes for the relationship? The safest and apparently most reasonable choice for a biographer would be to steer a middle course, assigning Blake a cautious hope that Hayley would become a "true friend," then disappointment when this proved not to be the case, then renewed confidence, and so on. The main problem with such a scenario is that it fails to account for the patterned repetition of phase transitions between hope and disillusion it constructs. Blake leaves Felpham with the same visionary enthusiasm for his prospects in the London publishing scene that he had entertained for Felpham, and soon enough these hopes are again succeeded by what will seem to be inevitable disillusion. Even during Blake's stay in Felpham, his hopes for expansion of the art market as a result of the lull in the war with France ("The Reign of Literature & the Arts Commences," he had written to Flaxman in October 1801) had suffered a similar fate. Blake's falling-out with Hayley had not been prototypical, either, but merely repeats his trajectory with other patrons and employers. Just before moving to Felpham, for example, Blake had been engaged as an illustrator by the Reverend John Trusler. After a time at work on the project, Blake wrote to Trusler, explaining that "I find more & more that my Style of Designing is a Species by itself. & in this which I send you have been compelld by my Genius or Angel to follow where he led if I were to act otherwise it would not fulfill the purpose for which alone I live" (701). When Trusler disapproves of Blake's designs, Blake again asserts that he cannot do otherwise, the strength of his assertion, which effectively ended Blake's employment by Trusler, reflecting his expanding prospects for employment by Hayley. Cycle follows cycle and nestles within cycle (Trusler, Hayley, the market with France, the London market); the wheels keep spinning in place.

This is not to suggest that Blake generated these polarities merely out of some personal neurosis or psychosis. The question is more convoluted: was Blake mad because Trusler's moralizing *Way to Be Rich and Respectable* or Hayley's antifeminist *Triumphs of Temper* made him mad or because he triumphed over his temper for riches (meager as they were) and for respectability's sake?

The scenario of shifts between enthusiastic hopes and bitter disappointments is not primarily a personal (biographical) matter, nor even only a marker of contradictions between Blake's class identities. The same scenario, for example, is sometimes cited in explanation of Wordsworth's changing attitude toward the French Revolution, as if the course of the revolution itself were a "fact" sufficient to explain it. In fact, the most explicitly radical and politically engaged Wordsworthian statement extant is his 1793 "open letter" to Robert Watson, bishop of Llandaff (whose essay also provoked Blake's most inflammatory marginalia). In this letter—which he declined to post or publish—Wordsworth makes clear that he is prepared for the immediate result of the revolution to be merely a "change of tyranny," but also that he expects that "the stream will go on gradually refining itself" (Wordsworth 1974, 38). How was it, then, that Wordsworth was not able to keep the faith, even as he castigated Watson for falling away from *his* early support of the revolution? It may be just as accurate to assert not that the revolution's course directed Wordsworth's change of mind, but that Wordsworth's change of mind directed the course of the revolution, at least insofar as England's participation in the war against France contributed to the polarizations and extremisms of the revolution, and insofar as this participation was facilitated by the failure of active English support for the revolution—a failure in which figured prominently "that profound disenchantment, of which Wordsworth is representative, in an intellectual generation which had identified its beliefs in too ardent and utopian a way with the cause of France," as Thompson put it (1966, 115). Admittedly this causal construction is attenuated and reductive—it might be better to dispense with traditional causality altogether. Until this can be done without seeming to endorse some kind of quietistic fatalism, it seems necessary to continue to observe that opposition and disenchantment with revolution still function as self-fulfilling prophesies or, to abbreviate the causal loop still further, as performatives. When Wordsworth recoiled in real mock horror from the French Revolution, he failed to recognize in that moment the monster he created and abandoned, created by abandoning, made contemptible by his contempt.

There is always a problem of which comes first, the coercive attempts to silence opposition or the hegemonic ("spontaneous") change of heart. Coleridge, for example, is very careful in his *Biographia*—too careful, that is—to show that, by the time he and Wordsworth were under surveillance by spies, they had already renounced Jacobinism. But hadn't this renunciation been the product of the watchful gaze of a much more effective hegemonic surveillance, by which Coleridge and Wordsworth anticipated (*avant-garde*) the renunciation that the powers that be came to demand, as subordinates come to read the desires of superiors before they are articulated? Is this what it means to be in touch with the "spirit of the age"?

It is likewise difficult to determine whether circumstances conspired, or Blake conspired with circumstances, to keep him in Hayley's orbit. After Blake had decided to leave Felpham, a soldier Blake had thrown out of his garden accused him of damning the king (among other seditious statements), and he was forced to rely again on Hayley to provide a lawyer for the trial (he was acquitted). Could Blake's denial of the charges represent the retroactive fulfillment of his hero's hope that, in *Jerusalem*, "he who will not defend Truth may be compelld to defend / A Lie" (1982, 152)? Scholars have been inclined to conclude that the charges against Blake were false (it makes things easier), and knowing his even paranoid caution, it seems likely. Yet the real vignette also seems too consistent with the patterns of Blake's writing to have occurred without his collaboration: the private denunciation and, seeming to follow it in space or time, the public denial; irony is, after all, a strategy of deniability. Blake had written it before and would write it again, only embellished with names from the "real" incident, altered (as usual) to avoid prosecution. Even Blake's reluctance, in his notebooks, to spell out his accusations is ironically duplicated in his public deposition, in which he denies having uttered the words "D—n the K—g" (734): the injunction to speak and the injunction to remain silent meet in an irony by which the name of the king is reduced, if only in the letter, to the status of a swearword, under the gaze of his all-powerful spirit. Did Blake *really* damn the king? As in his letters and poetry (before, during, and after the event), he did—and, simultaneously and/or subsequently, he didn't. Irony can appear as a space or time between texts and/or utterances, between phases or phrases of a text, or even as spaces that emerge in individual words: the spiral of silence and speech weaves through every modality of an n-dimensional textual/historical fabric, from the smallest moment in a private notebook or public deposition to the widest swath of literary history. The absolute interval between affirmation and denial is what I have been calling irony, whether it manifests itself as timelike or spacelike.

Blake's irony was of a piece with the irony that neutralized it. On one hand, this irony functions to privatize, to localize, to contain, to keep intact, and to foreclose mediation. In Blake's own time, it worked through him to ensure that his most radical statements remained only graffiti in the margins of a single, private book or notebook, or that his works (auraticized and unmediated by printers and booksellers) circulated only as curiosities among a few collectors. At the textual level, this irony ensured that real names (Hayley, George III, and so on) kept contracting with the infinitely receding lower term of allegory. On the other hand, such irony seems to function just as well to dilute, to dissipate by distributing, so that the Blake who appeared before the largest public (in the largest number of texts) was a "gentle visionary" cooing over "sublime displays" of public charity, a madman, or even more widely, a second-rate illustrator. At the textual level, this irony works by distributing the code by which Blake can be read across his texts or between his and other texts. These two ironies, fingers of those invisible hands of order and disorder, sometimes seem to pull in different directions only to tighten the woven spiral of a thoroughgoing hegemony in which we must remain caught.

Is this then the structure of Blake throughout discursive space-time? A burning sun of political rage orbited and eclipsed by the false consciousness of an aestheticized "green and pleasant land"? A radical root, buried underground, which in the open air merely branches out into a "pretty rose tree"? In fact, the Blake engaged here is a four-dimensional or n-dimensional orbit and system of branchings, a curvature in one dimension coextensive with the collective mind and body politic, crazed and warped by the turbulences of hierarchical difference.

The turning of political energies inward, toward the body (as toward the person of the author)—shortening the feedback loop until the body appears to attack or to desire only itself—seems to be a particular skill of capitalism, although the reformist's belief in the perfectability of the world was always as bogus as the belief of today's "fitness victim" in the perfectability of the body, and as many ironies continue to be committed in its name. Did Blake suffer from a similar involution, pedaling his own stationary cycle, when he fought "the accuser" or the ghost of an insufferable patron or mad king only in himself, or across the electrical network of his brain and the pages of his arcane texts and not in the streets or even the salons? Predictably, the stories of Blake's extratextual political actions are as problematic, obscured, and ironized as the politics of his texts. Did Blake really warn Thomas Paine to leave the country on the eve of his arrest, and thus save him from a trial that (who knows?) might have galvanized resistance in England; save Paine's skin at the cost of a revolution, as he saved his own? Did he really voice outrage and cause the chain to be removed from a young worker's leg, when he could not shake loose the chains from his own writing hand? Was he merely swept along by the crowd during the Gordon Riots of 1780, or did he take an active part in the release of prisoners and burning of Newgate Prison? In each case Blake is found writing and being written by the polarities (material/spiritual, passive/active, and so on) of an ongoing textual and historical field. One keeps finding Blake the resistance fighter and Blake the collaborator, and finding that no critical centrifuge can separate the two. To demonstrate that Blake conspired against himself is not, after all, to assign blame but to affirm that he was afraid.

In "London," Blake elaborates the recursive shudder of fear that binds victim and oppressor:

> I wander thro' each charter'd street,
> Near where the charter'd Thames does flow.
> And mark on every face I meet
> Marks of weakness, marks of woe.
>
> In every cry of every Man,
> In every Infants cry of fear,
> In every voice: in every ban,
> The mind-forg'd manacles I hear
>
> How the Chimney-sweepers cry
> Every blackning Church appalls,
> And the hapless Soldiers sigh
> Runs in blood down Palace walls
>
> But most thro' midnight streets I hear
> How the youthful Harlots curse

Blasts the new-born Infants tear
And blights with plagues the Marriage hearse
(1982, 26–27)

The narrator of "London" (as in Wordsworth's "I Wandered Lonely") seems to do little but wander, look, and listen — and, apparently, to speak or write the poem. He hears victims speaking and their words — or rather their inarticulate cries, sighs, and curses — made flesh and come back to haunt — to mark — institutions responsible for their oppression ("Church," "Palace," "Marriage"). The final verse, however, complicates this construction. The "Harlots curse" is allowed to be — without metaphor — both word and flesh, both verbal and viral: a curse she utters or that which utters her (interpellates her as immoral); syphilis that infects her or, through her, her clients and their children. The disease, whose effects are suggested in the poem's final lines, is beyond human agency, or rather it is systemically bred and operates *through* people, instrumentalizing victims and oppressors alike; the cursers and accursed implicated in the recursivity of the spirochete, representing a lowermost bound (what Blake might have called a "limit of Contraction") to which systemic contradictions can be repressed and from which they insidiously return.

But the poem also problematizes the victim/oppressor scenario from the first. The narrator's *marking* may be more active than a noticing; it is at any rate a selective notice. It first seems that this marking may itself amount to an oppressive act, reinscribing victim status, or alternately, even that "marks of weakness" may be read as physiognomic manifestations of some character deficiency on the part of their bearers. But in Ezekiel's "Vision of Jerusalem in her Pollutions," which Blake echoes here, "marking" has quite a different effect. In *Ezekiel*, God summons the man who has "the writer's inkhorn by his side" and commands that he go "through the midst of Jerusalem, and set a mark upon the foreheads of the men that sigh and cry for all the abominations that be done in the midst thereof" (I:9, 3–5).

It is then the *unmarked* that God orders to be slain. The story works as an empowering myth for the writer, promising that, come the revolution, the blacklisted writer's own blacklist will prevail. But for Blake's narrator the marking isn't so simple. It marks victims, but everyone is a victim (and an oppressor): "every face" and "every voice" bear the mark of the "mind-forg'd manacles" and, presumably, some responsibility for forging them. Blake's manuscript version of the poem first identified these mentally generated chains as the all-too-concretely produced "German-forg'd links" (796) of the oppressive Hanoverian rule of George III. This original epithet, oblique as it now seems, amounts to identifying an oppressor by name and thus can be read as a call for more overt oppositional action: "Damn the King!" It seems likely that fear of prosecution for sedition, the very reasonable fear of being put in real chains, was a factor in Blake's rewriting. Between the "German-forg'd links" of Blake's unpublished manuscript and the "mind-forg'd manacles" of his printed text, the fear—itself a "mind-forg'd manacle"—of real chains, themselves manufactured out of fear of potentially seditious sighs and cries like Blake's own, intervenes. The chains twist the cry back—but not quite back—upon itself. The fear Blake describes and can't help but enact is an unprocessible *noise* that is conserved—carried over, echoed—through all permutations of commentary and metacommentary. David Erdman has remarked on the same phenomenon in Blake's "Grey Monk," where again it is enacted around figures of recursive binding (the rack, the chain, and the bent body of the tortured monk): "In continuing to write, Blake does of course defy the rack and chain. Yet their marks are even upon this ballad, for he mutes 'Seditious Monk' to 'Thou lazy Monk' before transferring it to the public text of *Jerusalem*" (1954, 386). The literal and the figural rack and chain twist into an ongoing recursion that is the mark of hegemonic power. To conclude, as does the "Grey Monk," in such a viral-political regime, that even "a Sigh is the Sword of an Angel King," may be both a radical affirmation and the height of false consciousness.

Irresolution and Interdependence

The ambiguous trajectory of Blake's career traced nesting cycles in which a spatial structure (concentric circles of audience) correlated with a temporal structure of enthusiasms and fallings-out, both structures propagated by fractal resonances across various scales of text and time. Wordsworth's "Resolution and Independence" begins by sketching a similarly scaling cycle of moods that is finally "resolved" by a related but very different notion of "independence" that both coordinates and ironizes the relation between poetic time and real time.

As the poem opens, night storm gives way to an echoic play, this time at the liminal moment of sunrise, which comprises a traffic between species and even between living and nonliving processes as "the Jay makes answer as the Magpie chatters; / And all the air is filled with pleasant noise of waters" (Wordsworth 1969, 155).

As in Blake's first "Nurse's Song" (or in the utopian conclusion of Coleridge's "Frost at Midnight"), echoic noise signifies an ecology of plenitude marked not by "full presence" but by maximal hybridity and interpenetration. The activity of the creatures who participate in this ecology is an end in itself, a "wake" that inalienably accompanies the body but is not reducible to a discrete or reified thing:

> The hare is running races in her mirth;
> And with her feet she from the plashy earth
> Raises a mist; that, glittering in the sun,
> Runs with her all the way, wherever she does run.
> (1969, 155)

To experience the bodily indiscretion of a prealienated engagement with the world is for Blake, as for Wordsworth here, not to betray one's attachment to an older economy but to partake of a mystical excess in which (for example) "ev'ry Bird that cuts the airy way, / Is an immense world of delight, clos'd by your senses five" (1982, 35). By contrast, Blake's "fallen" human life is characterized as a "worm of sixty winters" or of "seventy inches" (177, 285, 175), in which the tortuous wake of the body (its "worldline") is discretely measured as it moves through a world in which time is money.

But Wordsworth's trick is to autonomize and automatize the way in which the highs of "mystical participation," by internal necessity and as a kind of law of physics, give way to the lows of alienation, abjection, and proletarianization:

> By our own spirits we are deified:
> We Poets in our youth begin in gladness;
> But thereof come in the end despondency and madness.
> (Wordsworth 1969, 155)

The leech-gatherer will offer a "resolution" to this two-cycle rhythm by being an example for the poet of how the ongoing ability to alienate one's labor constitutes "independence." In the process, the interpenetrative ecology that begins the poem can be said to be recouped in the complex play of difference and identification between poet and laborer. The mystification that the poem perpetrates is in aestheticizing this play of similarity and difference between the leech-gatherer, subject to the unpredictable rhythms of supply and demand, and the poet, apparently subject only to the rise and fall of his own moods, his transcendence of these cycles marked by his ability to extract speculatively a poetic profit at any stage, by merely "thinking" of the figure of the leech-gatherer. The poet seems thus to be rendered self-sufficient in a self-organizing, specular, and speculative economy (i.e., a "free market") that internalizes his control over the means of poetic production.

Two facts are recorded in Dorothy Wordsworth's journal and letters that throw the poem into a starkly ironic perspective.

First, Dorothy's journal (1941, 63) records that the actual leech-gatherer that she and her brother encountered was not the proudly "self-sufficient" laborer William's poem depicts but, in fact, a beggar who asked them for money. This fact in itself would not have been enough to disqualify the leech-gatherer as a figure of and for the poet: beggary in other Wordsworth poems performs the service of affirming the persistence of an earlier economy of gift and obligation (a romanticized feudalism). Even so, the problematic dichotomy between dependence and independence that divides Dorothy's (private) text from William's (public) poem persists self-referentially *in* the poem as a nagging ambiguity about whether leeches or poems and those who peddle them are cathartic healers or parasites.

Second, Dorothy's letters record that what happened, in real time, between her brother's beginning and finishing the poem, is that the Wordsworths received substantial portions of the inheritance owed to their father's estate by Lord Lowther. In Dorothy's letters from this time (as in Blake's), "independence" is used as a straightforward synonym for "capital": when her brother wishes to invest her portion of the inheritance, Dorothy demands security for it, citing "the impropriety of my running the risque of losing this money by which means I might forfeit my independence without any means of reinstating myself in it" (Wordsworth and Wordsworth 1967–93, 2:386). If she were to lose the money, that is, work for pay would offer Dorothy's only "means of reinstating" herself, but such work (like her governess job before she became her brother's helper) would be unlikely to provide savings— and would in itself constitute the fall in class that the money (and her ongoing residence with her brother) staves off.

In light of the two facts Dorothy provides, the poem and its figurative or ideological resolution (as well as its ongoing critical interest) can be seen to depend on the irresolubility of a complex economy of alignments, oppositions, and transmutations between and among fact and image, real time and poetic (textual, narrative) time, private journals or letters and public poetry, brother and sister, leech-gatherer and poet and healing and parasitism, and independence as capital and independence as labor—intervals the poem works to insinuate itself as their mediator.

Parkinsonism, Romanticism, Postmodernism: Neurology as Ideology

Beauty will be convulsive or it will not be.
—André Breton

James Parkinson (1755–1824), apothecary and surgeon, was a prominent member of the London Corresponding Society during the 1790s. All of his writings (which could only now qualify as "interdisciplinary") are of a piece with the tradition of Enlightenment dissent and reformism that shaped his career. He published several important Jacobinical pamphlets during the years 1793 to 1795, mostly under the pseudonym "Old Hubert" (e.g., *An Address to the Hon. Edmund Burke from the Swinish Multitude*). Many of his works are devoted to the advocacy of medical discipline: *The Hospital Pupil* (1800) addresses the professionalizing process, *Medical Admonitions* (1799) and *The Villager's Friend and Physician* (1800) exhort what we now call "the consumer"; and institutional discipline is the object of *Observations on the Act for Regulating Mad-houses* (1811). A lifelong fossil hunter, Parkinson rushed off from his medical practice — with the eagerness of a Renaissance artist at the exhumation of a Roman sculpture — to witness the excavation of a "huge crocodile." Parkinson's popular *Organic Remains of a Former World* (1811) affirms a new historicism in late-eighteenth-century geology and recuperates a disciplinary god: "The world is seen, in its formation and continuance, constantly under the providence of Almighty God, without whose knowledge not one sparrow falls to the ground" (Critchley 1955, 130).

Somewhat like Keats in his 1818 preface to *Endymion*, Parkinson prefaces his groundbreaking 1817 *Essay on the Shaking Palsy* with a kind of apology for its prematurity:

> *Some conciliatory explanation should be offered for the present publication: in which, it is acknowledged, that mere conjecture takes the place of experiment; and that analogy is the substitute for anatomical explanation, the only sure foundation for pathological knowledge. (Critchley 1955, i)*

The trajectory leading from analogy — via apology — to anatomy is characteristic of the general epistemological shift traced by Foucault's *Birth of the Clinic*. As promised, Parkinson spends most of his essay in the traditional, analogical mode, carefully welding similarities and chiseling differences between sets of symptoms and etiologies in order to rough-sculpt his "shaking palsy" in a taxonomic space roughly coextensive with the social space in which symptoms occur. In an analogical medicine, "when they become dense enough, these similarities cross the threshold of mere kinship and accede to unity of essence" (Foucault 1975, 7), but an emergent disciplinary regime increasingly defers this "unity of essence" into a bodily interior — buries it alive — where it can be pursued by the anatomist's penetrating gaze. In other words, a more extended and heterogeneous tissue of similarities and differences implicated in language and culture is displaced and condensed into the density and opacity of bodily tissue, from where it may be triumphantly brought to light: the body "materializes" for medicine as an analogue of analogy, "realized" in the flesh without realizing that the very density of flesh is always already also a metaphor of metaphor. *Origins* are the privileged ends of a process that now begins in medias res with what Parkinson calls a "substitute" (a superficial trace or set of symptoms) and proceeds, via dissection or excavation, toward a "sure foundation," toward that which is beyond semiosis, that which simply is what it is, like Althusser's "Absolute Subject" or (sometimes) Freud's cigar. The end of Parkinson's essay restates its goal of "leading the attention of those who humanely employ anatomical examination in detecting the causes and natures of diseases, particularly to this malady," and with an encomium to the "professional ardour" of anatomists, to whose "researches the healing art is already much indebted for the enlargement of its powers of lessening the evils of suffering humanity" (Critchley 1955, 66).

"Pathological knowledge," situated as origin and end, entails a new kind of individuation or subjectification for both doctor and patient, differentially: here, sufferers of the "shaking palsy" isolated by Parkinson will come to be assigned a provisionally coherent identity tied to their pathology and its patriarch: they will be known as "Parkinsonians." Like the fossil bean, *Pandanocarpus parkinsonis*, they will bear the Name of the doctor/taxonomist/Father into our century.

The neurologist Oliver Sacks begins *Awakenings*, his popular 1973 study of postencephalitic Parkinsonism, with a rhapsodic note on Parkinson's walks through London. During these walks, Parkinson had encountered some of the people whose case histories appear in his 1817 essay, and who will come to bear his name:

Parkinson resembles a genuine *astronomer, and London the field of his astronomical observations, and at this stage, through his eyes, we see Parkinsonians as bodies-in-transit, moving like comets or stars. Soon, moreover, he came to recognize that certain stars form a* constellation, *that many seemingly unrelated phenomena form a definite and constant "assemblage of symptoms." He was the first to recognize this "assemblage" as such, this constellation or syndrome we now call "Parkinsonism." (Sacks 1990, 4n)*

The "unmoved mover" of these heavenly bodies, then, is the truth and unity of the disease that is the object of "pathological knowledge": in the depths of disciplinary space, the doctor's vision, as it simultaneously cleaves symptoms together and apart ("carves up and articulates," in Foucault's formula [1975, xix]), reverently worships its own reflection, the artifact that its own unacknowledged positionedness configures. Just as Keats felt, "On First Looking into Chapman's Homer," like "some watcher of the skies / When a new planet swims into his ken" precisely because he was *not the first* to read it, Sacks can claim Parkinson as a "genius" because "his observations were deeper than those of his predecessors, deeper-rooted and more deeply related" (1990, 4n): he saw what everyone else saw, but dissected and put it together more intricately, more densely. This construction of genius is given in schematic form by

Blake: "As none by traveling over known lands can find out the unknown. So from already acquired knowledge Man could not acquire more. therefore an universal Poetic Genius exists" (1982, 1). The "knownness" of the world is thus a grid against which genius can be made to appear, situating Romantic creation at the always ambiguous intersection of invention and discovery, writing and reading, production and reproduction. The world seems to be created anew in Romanticism because *creation is created*—in the image of capitalist discipline, continually revolutionizing power and knowledge, dissecting and connecting. It is predictable, then, that the final enclosure of English common lands during this period coincides with their unprecedented opening up both to scientific and aesthetic exploration (fossil hunting and view hunting), and that ongoing colonization and disciplinary saturation of space abroad and at home will come to align Mayhew's urban anthropology in "darkest London" with Livingstone's travels in "darkest Africa." Internal and external Others are coproduced in an ongoing mission of fractal disciplinary saturation and imperial expansionism: to seek out new life and new civilizations, to boldly go where no one (but many others) has gone before. Haraway's succinct comment on the *Star Trek* introduction is relevant here: "Science remains an important genre of Western exploration and travel literature" (1991, 205).

In *The Man Who Mistook His Wife for a Hat*, Sacks's account of a street encounter implicitly updates both Parkinson's astronomical street-diagnostics and Althusser's cop-on-the-beat parable of ideology, generating a postmodern school-of-mirrors account of interpellation. On a crowded New York street, Sacks sees "a grey-haired woman in her sixties, who was apparently the centre of a most amazing disturbance": convulsed by Tourette's syndrome, "and, by a sort of sympathy or contagion—also convulsing everyone" she passes, the woman delivers a two-minute performance, a "virtually instantaneous, automatic and convulsive mirroring of every face and figure":

Every mirroring was also a parody, a mocking, an exaggeration of salient gestures and expressions, but an exaggeration in itself no less convulsive than intentional—a consequence of the violent acceleration and distortion of all her motions. Thus a slow smile, monstrously accelerated, would become a violent, milliseconds-long grimace; an ample gesture, accelerated, would become a farcical convulsive movement.

And there were ludicrous imitations of the second and third order; for the people in the street, startled, outraged, bewildered by her imitations, took on these expressions in reaction to her; and those expressions in turn, were re-flected, re-directed, re-distorted, by the Touretter, causing a still greater degree of outrage and shock. This grotesque, involuntary resonance, or mutuality, by which everyone *was drawn into an absurdly amplifying interaction, was the source of the disturbance I had seen from a distance. This woman who, becoming everybody, lost her own self, became nobody. This woman with a thousand faces, masks,* personae—*how must it be for* her *in this whirlwind of identities? (Sacks 1987, 122–23)*

Keats's identitiless "camelion poet" returns here with a vengeance that derives from its recursive speed. Presumably, people could not interact at all without reflecting and refracting each other's gestures, mixing and matching from whatever repertoires they have at hand. But when the speed—or more generally, the *scale*—of gestures in time and space (not necessarily even their sequence or shape) changes in the mirroring process, mirroring itself becomes disruptively visible. Elsewhere Sacks writes of Parkinsonians that "the wrongness of their movements is a wrongness of *scale*—their movements are too large or too small, too fast or too slow" (1990, 346).

Sacks's "amazing disturbance" is produced by a collective and unspeakable confrontation with the Otherness of the self. Speed and other scalar differences are categorical, making it difficult to say whether something that goes fast becomes a different thing, or whether what kind of a thing it is follows *from* its speed. But "fast" and "slow" only begin to account for the richness of the scalar dimension, which is here also marked by its "convulsive" rhythm. Unlike a simple anamorphoscope in reverse, the Touretter does more than offer the spectator a distorting mirror: she performs in a seductive and compelling way that neurological "normalcy" is already at least the distortion of a distortion. The bodily, almost autonomic response of the spectators-turned-actors performs another turn on the turning around or "conversion" of suspect into subject by Althusser's cop. The spectators are available or "on call" as actors not because they respond by identification ("it's me!"), but because of their engagement in the turbulent play, between the normal and the pathological, of two responses: "it's me!" and "it's not me!" The Touretter enacts a kind of "candid camera" critique that is effective insofar as it intervenes, directly as it were, not into the "self-images" of the passersby, but into the means whereby they are produced and sustained.

The shaky, analogical truth of Parkinson's "shaking palsy" had been established by observing the same symptoms and etiology in different people; its instability appears as a *desire* to anatomize its "sure foundation." This trajectory gets a new twist as well: postmodern Parkinsonism is initially "exciting" to Sacks not as the manifestation of a similarity but as "the spectacle of a disease that was never the same in two patients, a disease that could take any possible form—one rightly called a 'phantasmagoria'" (1990, xxviii). As such, Parkinsonism is capable of producing a performative truth-effect by recursive self-similarity and difference in a contagion of gesture: the Touretter functions to create an "amazing disturbance" in the crowd as her Tourette's syndrome itself functions to disturb her own brain. Unfortunately (as we will see later), Sacks's account works to restore "pathological knowledge" back to the social and cultural space from which Romantic discipline had appropriated it only to protect discipline from the excess it generates.

Sacks's account of "The President's Speech" (1987, 80–84) seems to propose an even more intimate identity between neurology and ideology. Sacks describes the effect of a televised Reagan speech on a neurology ward. The ward includes aphasics, who can only comprehend speech insofar as it is charged with "feeling-tone" (often because of damage to the left temporal lobe, which is supposed to process grammar and syntax), as well as one patient with the "opposite" disorder: stricken with "tonal agnosia" or "atonia" (due to a tumor on the *right* temporal lobe), she cannot process emotional or colloquial speech except insofar as it is also grammatically and logically correct. For the aphasics, then, its forced and misplaced sentiments make Reagan's speech hilariously incomprehensible, while for the atonia patient, it is strangely "not cogent" and the speaker must either be "brain-damaged, or he has something to conceal." Sacks offers a moral: that "we normals—aided, doubtless, by our wish to be fooled, were indeed well and truly fooled," yet "so cunningly was deceptive word-use combined with deceptive tone, that only the brain-damaged remained intact, undeceived" (1987, 84). The neatness of the paradox forecloses the most radical—and I believe the most obvious—conclusion from the evidence. In order to make the paradox work, Sacks must forget that a great many "normals" consistently found Reagan speeches laughable, monstrously unbelievable, and brain-damaged. Second, Sacks is forced to exaggerate the difference between the brain-damaged as innocent and undeceivable fools and the president as a crafty rhetorician, again forgetting that Reagan was most often cast as the "natural" in a regime where "undeceivability" is inseparable from a power that awards the privilege of believing in one's own fictions. Ideology *is* neurology (not simply neuropathology) and vice versa. Aphasia or atonia are categorically indistinguishable from the partial abjection or nonsubjecthood enforced on those who, for whatever reason, respond atypically (or do not respond) to the "hail" of a given dominant ideology.

Sacks's quest to articulate his vision of Parkinsonism leads from Einsteinian relativistic models to quantum mechanics and finally to chaos theory. Parkinsonism—significantly, like Romanticism, modernism, postmodernism, ideology, love, and so on—is first described by Sacks as "a systematic disorder of space-time parameters, a systematic warping of coordinate-systems" (1990, 345), and as "a dynamic, field, or relativistic disorder." But these Einsteinian terms, Sacks comes to conclude in subsequent revisions, are not quite adequate to account for Parkinsonism, which (like Einsteinian relativity itself) turns out to require a quantum-mechanical qualification: in Parkinsonism, "what we observe is not, in fact, a smoothly *warped* metric, but an infinitely stranger *twitching* metric; not a smooth geometrical transform, but a sudden algebraic or statistical one" (341). In a 1990 appendix, "Chaos and Awakenings," Sacks completes the paradigmatic trajectory from quantum mechanics to the chaotic or fractal "phase space" model of the "strange attractor," whereby "*Parkinsonism itself* can be visualized as a sort of surface, bipolar, like a figure-of-eight" and Parkinsonians are "enthralled on this surface, which is a dynamical surface, an orbiting surface in time" (1990, 364).

It would seem that the difference between neurological normalcy and Parkinsonism is always like the difference between the current and the emergent paradigm: if "normals" are Newtonian, Parkinsonians are Einsteinian; if normals are Einsteinian, Parkinsonians are quantum-mechanical; if normals are quantum-mechanical, Parkinsonians are chaotic. Neither the mandate to represent sickness as radically different nor the mandate simply to keep pathology up-to-date with the latest paradigms can quite account for the schematic temporal thrust of Sacks's paradigm parade. Disease is *futurity* and vice versa; the trajectory of time is literally "sickening," and the future manifests itself as a pathological disturbance of the present.

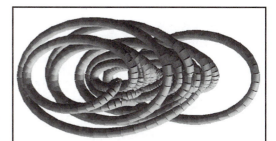

Ed W.'s State. Sacks's "mathematically inclined" patient Ed W., a Parkinsonian on an L-dopa regimen, graphed his degree of Parkinsonian symptoms (from extreme hyperkinesia to extreme immobility) hourly for three months. Sacks and colleague Ralph Siegel took the linear graph of Ed W.'s first month and plotted it in "phase space" against its derivatives (e.g., its rate of change); the resulting "attractor" shows the typically chaotic ("orderly but unpredictable") cycles of Ed W.'s Parkinsonism and L-dopa response.

"Enthrallment" and "surface" seem to function as the markers of pathology in Sacks's strange-attractor paradigm. In the most generous reading, it is not the operation of a strange attractor itself but enthrallment by it that seems to constitute the pathology of Parkinsonism for Sacks, as implicitly opposed to the semiautonomous connection that "normal" people must enjoy with their strange neurological attractors. The Parkinsonian self skewered on an attractor deeply embedded in the brain can also appear as "surface," a self nakedly algorithmic, a machine, a model. It is finally, then, its paradigmatic status that is pathological: for normals, the strange attractor may be merely a model upon which the fiction of the self is loosely built; for Sacks's Parkinsonians the model is, as it were, lived, as is ideology for those who, in Slavoj Žižek's formula, take it seriously and are thereby driven to challenge it.

If the repeated discontinuities or "twitching" of the quantum model can characterize Parkinsonian pathology against the smooth transformations of Einsteinian relativity, Parkinsonism can also appear as a disease of excessive continuity, a quality also marked by one of Sacks's migraine patients, who says his migraine "*looms,*" but "it's just a change of scale—everything is already there from the start" (1990, 98). One Parkinsonian says she would have no trouble getting around "if the world consisted entirely of stairs" (43), that is, if all otherwise continuous differences were quantized. Excessive continuity continually requires externally articulated algorithms in order to be properly rhythmed. This contingency is dramatized in the film based on Sacks's book when an otherwise chronically "akinetic" patient spontaneously and deftly catches her eyeglasses as they fall from her face, illustrating Charcot's diagnostic category of "aboulia" or "absence of the will," which he applied to patients who "would sit for hours not only motionless, but apparently without any impulse to move . . . although they might move quite well if the stimulus or command or request to move came from another person—*from the outside*" (Sacks 1990, 9). In the film, this otherwise akinetic patient is able to catch a ball thrown to her, leading to the conceptual-breakthrough conclusion that she adopts "the will of the ball" as a substitute for her own. The thrown ball works like the cop's shout in Althusser's parable: one can either catch or dodge the ball or let it strike, but one must come into relation with it in any case (you can play ball or not, take your pick). Another Parkinsonian in the film can walk only as far as the black-and-white checkerboard pattern of the linoleum guides her footsteps; other patients are animated and guided ("roused and fixed" or "kindled and restrained," as Wordsworth put it) by the rhythms of music. It is finally the drug L-dopamine into which the doctor will attempt, and fail, to displace and condense these ideological rhythming functions.

Instead of providing a dramatic illustration of the externality of ideology to the organism, and of the organism's necessary cyberneticization (its animation and guidance as well as its paralysis or disabling by the way that differences are articulated in culture), the discovery of Parkinsonism as a disorder of excessive continuity is an occasion for Sacks to *distinguish* the discretion of normalcy from

Parkinsonian continuity in a strangely unconscious and obsessive manner. At the very moment that Sacks announces his discovery of the "always-already" character of Parkinsonism and its tendency to "proceed by an infinite multitude of infinitesimal increments," he obsessively marks the ruptural discontinuity and radical newness of his *own* discovery as "a sudden jarring of my thinking, a sudden wrenching from a way of seeing, a frame of reference, to one which was deeply and shockingly different," repeating that he "suddenly realized" and again "suddenly realized" and again "it suddenly came to me" (1990, 97). This obsessive (or, in Parkinsonian terms, *echolalic*) characterization of the discoverer and the discovery against the discovered represents only a particularly acute attack of the apotropaic or prophylactic principle that structures the doctor's professional knowledge and discourse. The doctor is, as it were, defined as the one with the most "at stake"; the one for whom the dangers of the recursive performativity (and therefore, the compelling and contagious virality) of pathology are most acute, and therefore also the one most mandated to establish that "it's not me" — and finally, thus also the one by definition incapable of representing sickness as knowledge. By the same token, one might say that professional intellectuals are most often those who must continually immunize themselves to ideas, those whose training is designed to protect them from the danger that *living* ideas poses.

The film of *Awakenings* moves the doctor from primarily a principle of the discourse to primarily a character among characters, and in the process, performs a "systematic warping" of the book. The film follows the main trajectory of the case studies in the book, showing the initial success and eventual failure of the drug L-dopamine in reviving chronic patients often lapsed into akinesis for years after bouts of encephalitis. The film *individualizes*, focusing on a single patient (Leonard L.) from among the many case histories that appear in Sacks's account. It *bipolarizes* the states of the patients: in Sacks's account, it is clear that a range of various functionalities and dysfunctionalities characterize Sacks's patients before, during, and after their course of L-dopa. In the film, though, all the patients are at first nearly totally akinetic, achieve brief near-normalcy on L-dopa, and then are plunged back into deathlike akinesis when the drug is taken away. Finally, the film *simultanizes* the patients, awakening them en masse and allowing them to lapse, in neat succession, back to sleep.

But this schematization only allows the relatively complex trajectory that characterizes the patients in the film — dehumanization by akinesis, brief rehumanization by drugs, re-dehumanization by mania and then again by akinesis — to be opposed again to the one-directional humanization trajectory of the heroic doctor. Established as a shy man who prefers research and solitary hobbies to human contact, his (at first reluctant) engagement with his patients brings him out more and more until, in the film's final scene, he is finally able to ask his nurse assistant to lunch. One could say that the humanity of the professional is finally proven by his ability to engage in sexual harrassment. Rather than an extraneous or gratuitous alteration of Sack's book, then, the film's implicit opposition of the singular individual and his one-way humanization trajectory to the plural patients and their repeated transits of de- and rehumanization works as a very precise translation of the "author function" and "doctor function" that structure Sacks's discourse.

Sacks's own account of the film and other fictionalizations of his book, appended to the 1990 edition of *Awakenings*, is particularly revealing. It is only in considering these fictionalizations that *truth* becomes problematic for Sacks, and truth, in Sacks's rhetoric, becomes an embarrassing Romantic tic that enthralls Sacks's accounts of the plays and films, which he describes repetitively with phrases such as "faithfulness to the *truth* of the story, the inner truth" (1990, 367; emphasis in original), "the ultimate touchstone of truth" (367), "just like the truth" (370), "the inmost truth" (370), "never departed from the truth" (373), "the emotional truth of the portrayals" (374), "what was overwhelming for me was the *truth* of this scene" (385; emphasis in original), and so on. On one occasion, Sacks describes a radio play in which his Parkinsonian patient, Miriam H.—"an ageing, and somewhat deformed, Ashkenazi-Jewish white woman"—is played by Jackie Samuels, "a great, busty, gutsy, ebullient black woman," and yet the performance is an "absolutely perfect Miriam," "deeply right" and "fundamentally true," a performance "the original Miriam H., had she been alive, would have delighted in" (1990, 373). The "truth" of disease, for Sacks, must be "deeper" than the apparently superficial identities of ethnicity, race, religion, age, and other bodily specificities, and yet somehow the "truth" of the portrait makes it not simply a perfect representation of the *disease* but an "absolutely perfect *Miriam*" (my emphasis). The paradigmatic status of Parkinsonism is contained by being individualized, by being given a "human face."

The truth of Parkinsonism, then, appears for Sacks only recursively, in transit through the multiple mediations of a school of mirrors: the doctor observes patients and writes case histories; actors and writers read the doctor's accounts (and sometimes, after being thus prepared, observe patients); the doctor observes the actors and writers who have relied on his case histories and then finds their performances to be "true"—not by consulting his patients but by *imagining* their responses. This last—crucial—mediation repeatedly drives the doctor to put words into his patients's mouths:

This, for me, is the ultimate touchstone of truth — a sense that the actual patients, if they could be shown these versions, would exclaim: "Yes, that's amazing — that's just how it was!"...
I imagined Rose reading and seeing the play, and saying: "My God! He's got me.
He's got me to a T."...I was agonized at the thought that Rose R. might see it,
and be beside herself, and say: "No, no, it's all wrong, it's nothing like the truth." ...She has just
given me a wink, and a barely perceptible thumbs-up sign, meaning, "He's okay — he's got it!
He really knows what it's like." (1990, 367, 370, 370n, 386)

Can the Parkinsonian speak? Through *me*, says the neurologist. Sacks describes Leonard L.'s convulsive production of a fifty-thousand-word autobiography, but not a word of it appears in Sacks's book.

In spite of wondering whether acting the part of a Parkinsonian could "actually alter the nervous system" (383) and wanting, "half-seriously, to get an EEG" (383) during Robert De Niro's performance of a Parkinsonian seizure, Sacks does not follow up these impulses, perhaps to protect the assumption that Parkinsonism must proceed from organic causes to behavior, and not vice versa. Ironically, the Sacks role in the film is played by Robin Williams, an actor famous for his Tourettic performances, but even when noting that "Robin suddenly exploded with an incredible playback of the ward, imitating everyone's voice and style to perfection" and, "almost, being possessed by them" (376), Sacks will not explicitly acknowledge that acting — and along with it, all identity performance — may itself be a kind of Tourette's. But De Niro's performance, for example, is compelling not because it is "truthful" in a simple referential sense but because (like Dustin Hoffman's famous portrayal of autism in *Rain Man*) it is so *contagious*; it induces the viewer to copy it; it generates second- and third-order copies because it undermines originality: aestheticization pirates and makes available what medicalization works to copyright and contain. Likewise, to attribute the popularity of Sacks's books simply to the exoticism of the pathological Other is to radically underestimate the turbulence of the me/not-me dynamic in which pathology becomes the paradigm for normalcy.

Predictably, Sacks's response to the Sacks character in the film script differs dramatically from the truth-seizures he reports on seeing his fictionalized patients. The Sacks character, he protests, bears "some relation, but only some relation, to myself!" (374). Likewise, modest or immodest ellipses interrupt his account of first hearing "that Robin Williams would play...*me*, or at least the doctor character in the film who was, in part, to be based on me" (375). But the quaintly hesitating gesture enacted by these ellipses is, in fact, the very touchstone of Williams's portrayal of the doctor's doctorlike modesty. What may seem to be an affectation of modesty in Williams's portrayal of the doctor may well portray an affectation of modesty in the doctor's portrayal of "himself." But Sacks would oppose the loose relation that "normals" maintain with their identity performances to the truth that fixes pathology to performance and paradigm.

In a predictably self-referential maneuver, the film aligns doctor and filmmaker by showing the Sacks character filming his patient, marking the way that the "doctor as character among characters" opens uniquely onto the "doctor as the field of the film's gaze." The Sacks character's modesty in the face of his patient's seizures is overcome by Leonard L.'s heroic desire to be documented. In returning to Sacks's account, though, one finds that the films-within-the-film are only a schematized reduction of the complicated circulation of "real" filmic images in which the Hollywood production is implicated. These include clinical footage of patients, "home movies" recorded by patients and their visitors, and an earlier documentary film made from these. In one radio play, Sacks reads the part of the Sacks character, putting a half-twist on the famous postmodern advertising claim that "I'm not a doctor but I play one on TV."

But if the circulation of images mark Parkinsonism as a relay for cultural production, this circulation is also crucial in the diagnostics that define the disease medically. William Langston's study of California teenagers stricken with severe Parkinsonism after ingesting a synthetic opiate designer drug leads to an important diagnostic breakthrough: "The reason for the similarities of Langston's findings and my own is extremely simple, but its discovery had to await the development of PET scanning, which can directly visualize living brain tissue" (Sacks 1990, 334). The visualization techniques of scanning only confirm another conjunction of images: "The similarity between Langston's patients and my own was dramatically shown in 1986 when his tapes, and the documentary film of *Awakenings*, were shown together at a meeting of the American Academy of Neurology in San Francisco" (334n). These multiple mirrorings seem to make the American Academy of Neurology into a strange analogue of the "amazing disturbance" on a New York street, or is it the other way around?

The ongoing development of imaging techniques such as radiography, stratigraphy, and tomography participates in an ongoing redefinition of pathology, which is, in Cartwright and Goldfarb's account, "no longer identified by way of surface symptom; it is now located in the differential between the multiple surfaces constituting the depth field of the body" (1992, 197). In other words, the differential necessary for the correlation between a surface symptom and a deep structure to be revealed by the anatomist is broken down into the "multiple surfaces constituting the depth field of the body," in which surface and depth are no longer simply opposed. In the process, the representation of one visual image in another visual medium (as in photography) is ongoingly displaced by the technical "visualization" of largely nonvisual phenomena (such as brain waves, electrical activity, or volumetrics), a practice that does not deprivilege the visual but rather insists that its privilege be reproduced dynamically in a continual translation between dimensions, an attenuation that allows power to be exercised in the interval. Such a change is schematically illustrated in the gradual displacement of a disciplinary regime whose ideal is the visibility of pathology on the "actual" surface of the body. If nineteenth-century physiognomy and physical anthropology are the patriarchs of this regime, the yellow Star of David and the pink triangle are its crowning glories. The emergence of twentieth-century genetics stands nicely for an increase in the order of magnitude of mediation between the social and the physical, the large and small, the collective and the individual, in such a way that these differentials break apart without thereby undermining the hegemonic power-knowledge that had been built upon them. It is no wonder, then, that the causes for violence are now hysterically sought in television images of violence or in genetic predispositions. Medical ethicists, acting as shills for the Human Genome Project, like to hype the new and prodigious power and knowledge that genetics puts at human disposal, but this power is not so much a new ability to intervene between genetic causes and pathological effects as it is the actual production of this interval as a new site for intervention by a power that is dangerous because it is *not* new, another interval between the "multiple surfaces that constitute the depth field" of the collective and discursive body in which to install mechanisms of the more properly institutionalized violences of racism, capitalism, and sexism. The paradigm for power-knowledge ventures such as the genome project should not be the old modernist misreading of *Frankenstein* but a willfully postmodern misreading of *The Wizard of Oz*: the little man behind the screen, what Lacan called the "Imposture of the Phallus" (which can only function when veiled), is both the genome project and the genome itself, a thoroughly ideological object, a fetish, a con game whose effectivity (in producing knowledge effects) is guaranteed, since the reality in which it operates was thoroughgoingly *virtual* to begin with. But what does it mean to even want the kind of brain, heart, and courage being offered? And what if one doesn't want to go "back" to an epistemological Kansas?

Upon rereading *Awakenings*, it gets more difficult to tell how much L-dopa, institutionalization, sophisticated diagnostics, and even humanistic science have hurt or helped either individual patients or Parkinsonians generally.

Predictably, though, Sacks's account of a correlation between staff layoffs due to institutional downsizing and a dramatic collective neurological "decompensation" by his patients does not lead him to acknowledge his own institution as a Parkinsonogenic agent or Parkinsonism as a socioeconomic phenomenon. What is the status of Hippocratic principles or of "pathological knowledge" generally when it is impossible to say whether the Parkinsonian effects of some antipsychotic drugs are side effects of the drugs or (as Sacks prefers) resilient somaticizations of a patient's prior condition, and when anti-Parkinsonian drugs prescribed to reduce these side effects sometimes include Parkinsonism among their *own* side effects? Or when the horrors of institutionalization are matched by the horrors of deinstitutionalization, or the interventionist hubris of "curing" are matched with the laissez-faire cruelties of "maintenance"?

But the trick of Sacks's book is to affirm at each moment the essential rightness of disciplinarity in spite or even because of its ability to accommodate resistance, to persist heroically or modestly in the face of its own failures and counterproductivities, which it acknowledges only to reference its own modest heroism.

Sacks describes one Parkinsonian patient, Rolando P., whose symptoms are particularly, even perversely, resistant to L-dopa, able to accommodate any variation in the rhythms or titrations of the drug treatment and still reassert themselves. He gradually and convulsively is made to replace his dependency on his mother with his relationship to a staff nurse, but then is thrown into a neurological tailspin—from which he never recovers—when the nurse is fired in the latest round of cutbacks. As against the film's Leonard L., who heroically insists on being documented and thus serves to inaugurate and legitimize disciplinary knowledge as an unproblematic response to a patient's desire, Rolando P.'s last words mark the absolute impasse of disciplinarity, the point at which both the patient and the institution achieve their ultimate defeat and victory: "Can't you fuckers leave me alone? Where's the sense in all your fucking tests? Don't you have eyes and ears in your head? Can't you see I'm dying of grief? For Chrissake let me die in peace!" (1990, 128).

S I X

Postmodern Postscript

The Traffic in Leeches: Cronenberg's *Rabid* and
the Semiotics of Parasitism

It is now surprising that the English word *leech* derives from an Anglo-Saxon word meaning "to heal." For almost a millennium, the word (at least as written) referred without prejudice to both the doctor and the sluglike animal used by doctors to draw patients' blood. Not until the late eighteenth century, when new protocols for the extraction by doctors of money and knowledge from patients became primary, did the word begin to be used in writing to refer to parasitism. This change participates in a dense network of changes in technological practices and social relations. Among these, the changing status of leechcraft in medicine (once interchangeable terms) is perhaps less important than the changing status of medical knowledge in capitalism and the status of writing and professionalism with respect to other social relations.

Medieval medicine named the leech; the emergence of power-knowledge under capitalism gave the leech a particularly bad name: the healer—the doctor or artist that lets out bad or excess blood and by the catharsis (operation, text) reintegrates the social body—was coded more pointedly with and against the parasite, interrupting, infecting, and disintegrating through the manipulation of gaps and surpluses. Predictably, it was also toward the end of the eighteenth century that the word *doctor* began to be used in writing as a verb meaning "to adulterate."

The crux of epistemic change that can be located in retrospect in the late eighteenth century implicates shifting polarities in semiotic relations as well as their discursive extension. The fault lines that divide the signifieds of single words ("leech," "doctor") may be tributaries of great fractal canyons extended in discursive space-time. "Literary" or "open" texts have also been "epicentered" (positioned as "origins") by multiple interfaces of the tectonic plates of discourse.

If the familiar witticism, "the operation was a success; the patient died," marks the ongoing ascendancy of professional knowledge-production over bodies, the black humor of a patient living through a failed operation in David Cronenberg's 1977 film, *Rabid*, would mark the relativization of this ascendancy and put all relations under the sign of parasitism — the traffic in leeches. The reading of the film that follows is an attempt to assess the kind of semiotic relations that characterize such a regime, which can be called postcapitalist and postdisciplinary in the sense that capitalism and disciplinarity have metastasized so thoroughly, so globally and molecularly as to become less figure than ground. My desire is to engage the viral (or in the film's terms, rabid) semiosis that lives parasitically in this ground — without either pathologizing or hyping it.

This semiotic regime calls implicitly for a reevaluation of Freudian processes such as repression, sublimation, condensation and displacement, fetishization, and symptom formation, insofar as these processes tend to refer back to various origins that they distort — primal scene, dream thoughts, originary myth. If Freud problematized such retroactive reductions, American therapists have been good at validating them (e.g., in the search for childhood abuse scenarios) and bad at putting into question the participation of countertransference (or of the role of professional power-knowledge generally) in the retroactive fixing of pathology and desire. Post-Freudian therapists, that is, have tended to take the inaugural moment of psychoanalysis, the apple that fell on Freud's head, the idea that his female patients' incest stories were fantasies, and reattach it to the tree of fact, while the post-post-Freudian objective is to juggle it in the air long enough to take a few Eve-like bites as the metaphor gets out of hand. But even countertransference inevitably implies an originary relation that is transferred (away from its "proper" site); the slogan of a parasitic psychology might be the paradoxical "countertransference without transference."

The observation that the nodes around which psyches are built are never original but have always retroactively been "epicentered" (e.g., as "screen memories") may complicate but does not fundamentally alter their centrality. This centeredness irreducibly implicates a Freudian hermeneutics in which, for example, genitalia cannot by definition be fetishes (since fetishization displaces and condenses *from* the genitalia to other sites). Freud's assertion that each dream has a "navel, the spot where it reaches into the unknown," enacts a similar orientational strategy. The metaphor situates the mother's body as the central mystery and validates analytic knowledge that begins—literally and metaphorically—where detachment from the mother leaves off (e.g., with the Oedipal crisis). At the dream's "navel," Freud continues, "dream-thoughts to which we are led by interpretation cannot, from the nature of things, have any definite endings; they are bound to branch out in every direction into the intricate network of our world of thought. It is at some point where this meshwork is particularly close that the dream-wish grows up, like a mushroom out of its mycelium" (Freud 1965, 564). The movement of Freud's metaphor from "navel" (a kind of erect hole, not a scarred exit wound but a closed entrance) to phallic mushroom (singular excess of an otherwise rhizomic, acentric network) enacts the substitution of supplementarity that establishes the semiotic center of Freudian interpretation. To literalize Freud's mixed metaphor as a penis growing out of a navel, or to expose the navel/penis as a contradiction rather than a substitution, to betray at their origin (or *as* origins) the inlets and outlets through which interpretation is meant to flow, is the work that Cronenberg's film—and this text, in participating in the theoretical work of the film—would like to perform. This work not only displaces hermeneutic and epistemic status from fatherly mushroom to motherly mycelium, from phallic tree to acentric rhizome, it calls into question the oppositions between them (see Deleuze and Guattari 1987, 3–25).

It is easy to overstate the case for such epistemic shift. New-age rumors of the Death of the Clinic are greatly exaggerated, as is the millennial sense that the ambiguity of "late" capitalism allows us to understand its recent demise as well as its transnational maturity. But thinking ahead of what one's own time will in fact allow to be realized does not foreclose realizations that it may be later than one thinks. Overstatement and totalization of the case inevitably backfire (as they do in the film): the liberatory polymorphosis that would reverse the strictures of Oedipal genitalization (and the direction of time and modernization structured with it) is always collapsing back onto itself, but in so doing it does not merely reinscribe the categories it had sought to deconstruct but perpetuates the story of an ongoing conservation of chaos against the regimes of both order and disorder, and of the living, discursive, and historical bodies that belong to this story: bodies neither/both ephemeral nor/and eternal, holding their own with and against the production of knowledge.

Rabid offers an apparently schematic plot. Rose (Marilyn Chambers), a young woman burned in a motorcycle accident, is treated by a doctor who uses a radically new skin grafting technique. Skin taken from one part of the body is supposed to be "neutralized" in order to allow it to grow back to match the area onto which it is sewn. Instead, when Rose emerges from a coma following the operation, she has grown an erectile blood-sucking appendage (with a needlelike stinger at the tip) that emerges from a little purse-lipped opening in her armpit, where skin from her thigh had been grafted. She is driven by a craving for blood. In hypersexualized embraces she penetrates several men and women (including the doctor and some of his patients) and draws blood from them in an ecstatic kind of reverse ejaculation. Her partners are first stupefied and then become rabid, biting other victims (again with no gender preference) before dying; their victims become rabid in turn. Doctors are unable to develop a vaccine or cure; the plague spreads and martial law is declared; the rabid are shot on sight. Ostensibly to prove to her boyfriend that she is not responsible for the infection, Rose locks herself in a room with one of her victims, who is moving in to attack her as the camera cuts away. In the film's final scene, a plague-sanitation crew removes her corpse from an alley.

As *Rabid* begins, Dr. Keloid's partners—his wife and a fatherly older doctor—are persuading him to franchise their clinic into a chain of plastic-surgery resorts for their jet-set clientele. Keloid's reluctance ("to become the Colonel Sanders of plastic surgery") is only skin deep; in order to pursue his medical ambitions, he will leave the financial and managerial entrepreneurship to his partners. When news of the accident interrupts the meeting, he quickly acquiesces to the plan, and rushes off to attend to the victim.

What's rotten in the state of medicine—which is rather casually and satirically noted at the beginning of the film—requires an "accident" to be activated. The film's title sequence intercuts scenes of the clinic partners' planning meeting with scenes of Rose and her boyfriend embarking on their motorcycle trip with scenes of what lies ahead of them on the road, grafting together schematically the convergence of circumstances that will generate the fatal sequence whose unfolding will occupy the rest of the film. A vacationing family is lost and the husband disagrees with his wife and son (who insist that he has missed the turn) on how to proceed. The husband relents, but as he begins a three-point turn, the van stalls in the middle of a rural road. "We should never have sold the station wagon," he pouts, thus displacing and condensing an origin for the present crisis into a prior mistake, another failure to resist a "modernization" scenario. One may imagine a "flow chart" of binarized decisions (to franchise or not, to buy or not, to turn back or not) in which the fatal swerve has always already occurred, is always in process, and is always about to happen. The satiric vignette of the bickering family echoes the scene of the clinic partners: in both cases an Oedipal nuclear family group (generic organizational unit of the bourgeois state) comes to a crisis in location and direction, and the dominant male relinquishes (in order to recuperate) his sovereignty. Satire is interrupted when the motorcycling couple collides with the van, sending them into a sickening trajectory.

The Imaginary wholeness of the androgynous young couple, clad alike in black leather, cloven together on/with their black motorcycle, when processed through the symbolic aporia of the family and corporation (unstable and internally divided triads), is cloven apart by what amount to His-and-Her Oedipal Crises, given that such a crisis does not merely refer "back" to some previous divergence but (as in Lacan's parable of the two doors, "Ladies" and "Gentlemen") is a channeling (canalization) that is made to keep happening (Lacan 1977, 151). The man with his minor orthopedic injuries is sent to "The General [hospital]" (that rough-and-ready representative of medical pragmatism) and pinned together, while the more profoundly damaged woman emerges from crash and clinic and coma—the Female Oedipal Crisis, that mother of all malpractices—with a wicked chip under her shoulder. "Do you feel weak?" Doctor Keloid solicits his patient after she emerges from her coma. "No," Rose replies, "I feel *strong*."

The conventional and hierarchical gender difference implicit in the positions of the couple (he drives, she rides)—but relativized by their identical clothing and unity with their machine—is polarized by the trajectory following the crash: the man is thrown clear and the woman is trapped under the burning machine. This gender divergence coincides with the convergence of generically differentiated stories as the family quarrel is interrupted by the impending crash and then the planning meeting is interrupted by its aftermath: three stories (one couple, two triads), clearly differentiated in genre as tragic love story and parodic social satire, are braided together. From this braiding an unstable third genre, horror, will emerge out of the "medical procedural" drama that follows. Since the opening scenes are intercut with the titles, the "film proper" is made to begin with the crash—where genders diverge and genres converge.

As the doctors prepare to operate on Rose, it is Dr. Keloid's wife who at first objects—and then relinquishes her objection—to his medical procedure as too risky, just as he resisted and then gave in to the franchise "operation." Caution and entrepreneurship, then, are cross-polarized between medicine and marketplace; the cross-polarizations are themselves polarized between husband and wife; the structure of the polarities and the compromises between them cross-authorize entrepreneurship—and dispense with caution—in both finance and medicine. With this "X" the film marks the spot where the (husband-and-wife) team of disciplinarity and capitalism strike the Faustian trade-off that inaugurates their ascendancy and fall.

The second "accident," a more nebulous condensation of causality and locus of the monstrous change, occurs in the course of the medical procedure. Skin taken from Rose's thigh and sewn to her armpit is sent to a lab to be neutralized; doubly displaced, "it loses its specificity not only as thigh tissue but as skin tissue." Somewhere in the process, though, it is not neutralized but activated: it neither wholly retains the specificity of its origin nor conforms to where it is implanted. Instead, the procedure produces a dangerous supplementation, the dark side of surplus value, constructed by capitalism as a seemingly occult disturbance in its own logic; that is, in the neutralizability or commutability of bodies, commodities, and texts in the cash nexus. More particularly here, one might read vertically (with Freud and Marx) that money/flesh alienated or instrumentalized from "below" and sutured "above" fails to efface or repress its origin, which returns with distorted vengeance. But "return" and "origin" are rendered meaningless in the process, which is monstrous precisely because all agents and patients and features and functions, all bodies and organs, are "changed, changed utterly" in its sway. The horizontal reading is that a new mediation has been introduced between the body and itself (as films are "media" between culture and itself) as the skin is "farmed out" to a lab to be neutralized. The universal laundering solvent of money (and more generally an official hegemony of valuation and status) by which all differences are to be reconcilable proves to be or not to be biodegradable. In the process, the woman gets a monstrous "upgrade" as her own body seems to "resist" the medical procedure.

We may read the first order of parasitism represented in (or by) the film—professionalism itself in late capitalism—as a deteriorative scenario: having abandoned the ostensible purpose or pretext of reproducing the health of the whole social body—the workings of the depths—medicine has been given over to an aesthetic production of vanity—the play of surfaces—for a parasitic elite. U.S. release of the Canadian film, set in Quebec, engages further "spatialized" and complex contradictions between and within Canada's sluggish but guaranteed health-care system and the profit-driven, Social Darwinist organized crime of health care in the United States. Although the film does tend to construct (as an absence) an imaginary temporal or spatial *elsewhere* in which such contradictions are not constitutive, it must be *either* the discursive space-time before the birth or after the death of the clinic (and with it, power-knowledge under Western capitalist patriarchy) that the film necessarily but perhaps constructively fails to remember or imagine, or the living clinic's seamless whole body of ideology the film would be happy meanwhile to penetrate and infect. The differential between these Imaginaries—the crosscurrent of possible pasts and futures as they ripple the surface of the present—is the disturbance around which the film is elaborated. The Birth of the Clinic is grafted historically forward to the film's contemporary time frame, and its (future) death is grafted back to renegotiate the terms of each.

In any case, the film represents the shift in function (or imagines its own demystification of the function) of medicine as ironically counterproductive, producing (as Marx asserts that the bourgeoisie produces "its own gravediggers" [1972, 483]) a monstrous offspring that will come back to haunt and to destroy it. Disciplinary dysfunction, figured in the mutation that is its by-product, is a series of reversals of flows and channels and the messages and codes that are configured by them: a penis—located not at a man's crotch but at a woman's armpit— that does not ejaculate sperm but sucks blood, that does not impregnate but infects, that is not inserted into some handy orifice but makes its own orifice, violating the body's integrity. To align the terms: a medicine (professional power-knowledge) dedicated not to reproduction but to self-serving narcissism (its own as well as its elite clientele's), neither a fecund source nor a pure channel for a consensual cultural code but a parasitic drain (a gap) and the means of supplementation by noise (a surplus), which does not fit naturally in an economy of mutual or interdependent needs and pleasures but drastically disrupts this economy.

Along with their functions and locations, the identities of all the implicated categories are ambiguated in the process: the penis is not a penis, the woman is not a woman (nor a personality as such: "You're *not* Rose," the boyfriend insists, in spite of Gertrude Stein), fucking is not fucking is not fucking, and so on. Insofar as this ambiguation has the ambition to deconstruct the ideological categories on which it feeds, it runs the risk of backfiring in several different directions: indeterminacy or different differences are still at least partially containable in the film as professional, nonhuman, nonmale, nonheterosexual—or merely as *accidental*: a regime in which the phrase "shit happens" would be a consoling refusal of interpretation is an exclusive and expulsive one, reducing all indigestible meaning to shit and film to flushing. But the abjection of meaning—as in the final scene in which Rose's corpse disappears into the maw of a receding trash truck—cannot foreclose its repercussions.

The mutant woman who comes to occupy the center of the film figures a dazzling confusion between the sites and functions of production, reproduction, and consumption, succinctly condensed into a prohibited exchange of features (called above "a crisis in location and direction") between breast, mouth, and penis (a list that threatens to extend indefinitely to include umbilicus, anus, vagina, hand, eye, needle, and so on). This exchange of features echoes here and there in various vignettes: Rose sucks the blood of a cow in the barn where she's taken refuge, the drunken farmer crudely suggests fellatio ("I've got something you can drink off of, and it ain't no whiskey neither"), Rose penetrates the farmer's eye as he sucks on her breast, the doctor's older (male) partner bottle-feeds his baby, an infected Doctor Keloid cuts and sucks the blood from a nurse's finger instead of cutting the thread with which he is suturing a patient's ear, and of course the rabid make vampiristic attacks and drool the obligatory horror-film generic indeterminate viscous whitish fluid. The mis-circulation of fluids (blood, milk, semen, and mucus — standing in for money and information) accompanies the misappropriation of flesh or instability of identity categories.

In the confusion, the propriety of various otherwise locally socially acceptable practices may become suspect. For example, instrumentalizing animals for food is no longer an option for Rose after the change: her attempt to vampirize a cow is interrupted by vomiting (itself interrupted as the farmer barges in). Likewise, when she tries to eat a steak sandwich she is again interrupted by vomiting (again interrupted, this time by the truck driver she's hitched a ride with, who pulls her back into the cab). The carnivorous etiquette of Western humanism (cows may be eaten, people must not be) gives way to a more demanding cannibalism (people must be eaten, cows must not be). But the change is here described from a humanist perspective that starkly opposes eater and eaten; the parasite negotiates with its host (whether these are doctor and patient, parent and child, employer and employee, or film and viewer) an always historically particular and unprincipled parameter between meal ticket and meal: in the parasitical ecology, there can be no adequation of needs and abilities, no ultimate symbiotic model or final economy that can regulate the chiasmic and deferred interchanges between irreconcilable kinds of power.

The interruptions and metainterruptions are themselves the story. A young man trying to pick Rose up in a mall (he offers her a cigarette) is interrupted before consummating either the smoke or the pickup — or before Rose can penetrate him — when the man he approaches for a light wheels around and attacks him, sucking blood from his neck, before being interrupted in turn by the security guard, who sprays bullets into the assailant, killing the shopping-mall Santa Claus as well — a nice satiric vignette of the collateral damage inflicted on the sacred cows of the old order by friendly fire in the ideological sacrificial crisis. When push comes to shove, the powers that be can dispense with the friendly fatherly figure of the "author function," which, as Foucault writes, only appears to bestow "with infinite wealth and generosity, an inexhaustible world of significations"—precisely the shopping-mall Santa effect—but functions instead as the principle that fixates, reduces, and "impedes the free circulation, the free manipulation, the free composition, decomposition, and recomposition of meaning" (Foucault 1984, 118–19). But it is no longer disseminations or coitions that are interrupted in the film, but interruptions and parasitisms (barn squattings, vampirisms, hitchhikings, pickups, and so on). By this "squared" remove, as by the multiplied bodily displacements, the film would unmoor itself from the burden of the symbiotic or wholistic paradigm against which it had sought to assert its own nonidentity. The ball and chain allows two free steps before it has to be dragged again. The inevitable failure of this removal can be traced in the nonlinearity by which the doctor's penetration of his patient rebounds on him; the failure of removal now enters a second stage as well, the effect of Rose's penetrations now interrupting and foreclosing the act of penetration itself.

Is sucking smoke through a paper tube okay? Should a gentleman offer a lady a cigarette? Is sucking liquor out of a bottle okay? What constitutes rape? Is spraying bullets out of a metal tube okay? Is eating meat cool? Shooting the rabid? Penises in mouths? Penises coming out of vaginas coming out of armpits? Needles in arms? Needles coming out of penises? Coming out? Outing? Penetration? Men nursing babies? Plastic surgery? Sex change? Horror films? Theorizing them? The anal child or Oedipal adult who insistently repeats these questions of what is politic or correct—questions of taste or judgment—is always interrupted by the phallic woman whose thrust is to question how these practices are allowed to configure and disfigure those on either side of them. One might argue, for example, that a gun is a semiotic instrument, a rhetorical device that displaces, condenses, and channels violence, polarizing by its one-way flow the difference between the one who wields it and the one on the business end—a rough definition of violence.

The film sets itself up against a rigorously (but spontaneously and hegemonically) policed regime organized by one-way flows of semen, breast milk, and so on, and the exclusivity of the channels, senders, and receivers configured by these flows. This opposition works by reanimating with a vengeance the premodern or predisciplinary body characterized by "fungibility" of bodily fluids and their capacity to transmute into each other (see Laqueur 1987, 116; Duden 1991, 165–70). Only against the absent presence of a disciplinary master flowchart, a "sublime object of ideology," can the film signify at all; only against an imaginary symbiotic paradigm can it sustain a generic identity as "horror." But it is toward a "body without organs" and a nonsignifying semiotics that is its milieu—not toward a central or transcendental signifier that can be hermeneutically situated as its origin—that the film points with horror and pleasure.

The exceeding of parameters is marked by "gridlock," a form of nonlinear self-blockage. After violence disorganizes the clinic, police intervention begins with the cops setting up shop there; we see a man being given a Breathalyzer test. The breath itself is channeled and measured; soon identity cards are issued to those who have been vaccinated, checkpoints are set up at entrances and exits, intersections are patrolled, and the dead are collected and disposed by roving crews who block traffic. The gothicization of both order and disorder, of canalizations and decanalizations, and their distribution across the film, work to situate the film's subject in another semiotic or epistemic space, a chaos that differs in kind from both order and disorder. There remains a question whether the condensation, denaturalization, and gothicization of cross-functionality onto the figure of the mutant woman works as a drain to draw scrutiny away from other practices or to pull them into its vortex. In any case, the film ambiguates along with these practices the implication of the various victims, again offering the viewer the finally futile job of processing each case into a normalizing spectrum of guilt and innocence. At the guilty end, presumably, are the doctor who, in the process of "saving her," uses the helpless Rose as a guinea pig; the drunken farmer who (echoing the doctor) tries to rape Rose where she has come for refuge; and the sleazy porn film viewer who (again echoing the doctor) offers her protection in order to molest her: male saviors are revealed as parasites. Toward the end of innocence (and of the film, after some chiaroscuro between) is Rose's friend Mindy, who takes Rose in and tries to help her. Rose is first a patient who does not choose her fate (unless wearing black leather and riding motorcycles with pretty boys is culpable); she gains agency first to victimize the victimizers and at last the unimplicated (unless being a perky yuppie named Mindy, with a turned-up nose and pink fashion-victim eyewear, is culpable). As the circulation of victimization cycles back again, Rose herself assumes a version of the doctor's role (drawing blood from an innocent victim as "an experiment") and, again, becomes her victim's victim. The confusion of ends wrought by the nonlinear turbulence of these cycles of guilt and innocence and coolness and uncoolness threatens to level distinctions within as well as between aesthetics and morality.

Insofar as the film works (like many horror films) as a kind of do-it-yourself Dante's *Inferno*, "you the viewer" may assemble hierarchies of vice and assign the characters and their practices to wherever you like (Fashion-victim shades? Aisle three), but your assignations just assign you back to the cultural position in which you find yourself. To say (for example), BAD film or BAD doctor, as if disciplining a dog or a child, is to be duped into reproducing a conventional author-ity: thus the literary critic is positioned conveniently to show you how best to acces-sorize your cultural wardrobe.

Self-referentiality and self-authorization, those privileged mark-ers of literary and professional subjectivity in the Romantic and post-Romantic West, are obviously rabid here. The confusion between production, consumption, and re-production that the film displays can be read into or from virtually all Romantic and post-Romantic Western literary texts insofar as the historically overdetermined ambiguous and ambivalent position and cross-functional operation of the culture in-dustry (and eventually, every other discursive organ) in the social body cannot avoid representing itself. In the flux of difference and similarity between the terms of metaphor, the arbitrariness of constitutive distinctions emerges. What is the film qua doctor (or any particular configuration of power-knowledge) trying to do? What is the doctor-slash-film or doctor-cum-film trying to do? What is the difference be-tween a cum film and a slash film, or between cumming and slashing, sex and vio-lence? Does the doctor or the film try to save its patient/audience or merely to save face or make its name at the expense of its patient and finally itself? Self-referential-ity circulates among the film's characters and vignettes: the film as couple (embark-ing, a cool and beautiful hermaphroditic cyborg—in love—with everything possi-ble; the film on the double double reel of the motorcycle/projector); the film as clinic (where the plastic surgery of filmmaking goes on—these endless planning meetings—the film could be franchised—it could be all over the place—with financing and distribution—and I can have my cake and eat it too: I can preserve my artistic aspi-rations if I let the others handle the business); the film as family (okay, I'll martyr my pigheaded sense of direction and stop being such a maverick—but that blocks me—I don't want to get stuck being middle-of-the-road); the film as crash (split subjectivity: this woman on fire trapped under the wrecked machinery and this stu-pefied, impotent man thrown clear); the film as operation (it's too dangerous to go on, but now I must); the film as mutant woman (oh my god, now what am I doing? what has been done to me? am I just a monstrous narcissistic ego, sucking everyone dry to keep this thing going?); the film as martial law (I've got to keep it under control, monitor everything—I'm the director here—oh, Christ, I've murdered the auteur/Santa I thought I was); the film as boyfriend (it's out of control, but all I can do is look on in frustration); and finally, after she has devoured the well-meaning viewer who was foolish enough to take her in—and finally, after her attempt to monitor her effect on others is self-defeating, the film is in the can and taken away, leaving indeterminacy as to whether it will spread or not—and the effacement of the trace (am I destined, then, not even to be remembered as the origin or the vehicle—Typhoid Mary, scourge of god, father, penis, mouthpiece, author, leech—whereby the world of meaning was emptied or impregnated, purged or polluted—just a flash in the pan after all—a couple hours of fame or fucking or film?—but you know and I know—that I—that she—that it—made it happen—demonstrated the otherwise inscrutible semiotic genitalia in operation—and then the bibliography rolled by and then they left the theater). After speaking at the crossing of all these voices and practices I can no longer unambiguously say I.

    Film as book, writing as fucking, penis as leech, leechcraft as writing. Being almost reduced to an empty metacommentary on its own production, distribution, and consumption, it threatens to collapse into nonsignifying self-identity. But again, not a penis, not a film, not a leech, not fucking; not over. Not yet. The flood of indistinction and intermetaphoricity wanes; the world must be continuously destroyed and remade with no Ark and no Ararat to ensure the survival of species.

    As the man in an old cartoon said, watching robots make robots: sometimes I ask myself, where will it end? But this is not just a repetitive reperformance, deterioration, or progress. What's wrong with reproduction, with medicine, with the second law of thermodynamics is that the game of Telephone produces not the same message, nor only an abstraction or schematization or representation or evolution or deterioration or elaboration of a message, but a chain of differences whose irreconcilability—against the hegemonic regime of the same—produces pleasure.

    As the film auditions itself for all its parts, it also offers the viewer a number of roles. In an easy bit of typecasting, the viewer is first offered the part of boyfriend, who in the opening scene steps out of a doorway to gaze lovingly at Rose, standing by the motorcycle waiting for him to begin the trip. At first, apparently, in control, he is stupefied by the crash and then can only assume the role of frustrated and impotent onlooker, after only briefly pausing to assess (and, apparently, to dismiss) his own implication as a causal agent ("I didn't kill her, did I?"). His only substantive intervention works to install in Rose, again in an apparently well-intentioned attempt to save her, the suggestion that she is responsible for the plague. This suggestion only leads her to her own fatal experiment in the attempt to assess her own implication, while he is reduced to attempting to warn her, by telephone, to stop the experiment. Insofar as the boyfriend is less implicated, he is also less damaged: the presumption, anyway, is that he and the viewer—however changed or traumatized—survive the film.

    The roles of clinic patients and then of Rose's victims are the next most obvious for the viewer, with their varying degrees and kinds of culpability; that is, their ambiguous desires. For the squeamish, the film offers a stereotypi-cally gay man who is offended at the sight of Rose's damaged body being carried into the clinic. Rose's first victim is a plastic-surgery recidivist whose gazing in the mirror at his new face while smoking a cigarette *through a holder* (both channelings—of gaze and smoke—marking him as not a "real man") is interrupted by Rose's awaken-ing screams, and whose fatherly attentions and intentions are confused by her sex-ual embrace.

Rose's third victim is Judy Glasberg, a stereotypically assimilated upper-class Jew, who has returned for her second nose job because "Daddy said it wasn't different enough from his" (another failure of the Oedipal differentiation re-quired for cultural mainstreaming). "I shudder to find out what it all means," she coos, holding up a tattered paperback Freud: through her the film singles out for special punishment its would-be interpreters. Rose attacks her in a hot tub and places her in a freezer, as the film assembles a nice little cluster of anti-Semitic codes: the Jewish question—where the privilege to renegotiate the directions of differentia-tion and assimilation can be both marked and unmarked on the body—is disposed by the dualistic thermodynamics of racism (as enforced transit between "sun people" and "ice people"?): Judy, upper-class Jew, daddy's girl, would-be intellectual; Glas-berg, superficial as glass, frigid as an iceberg, reluctant lesbian. But here the director includes his own ambiguous signature as well, by the echo of "David Cronenberg" in "Judy Glasberg" (David and Judith both being Old Testament giant-killers). The ambiguous signature and its ambiguous marking of the director's Jewishness remind us that ambiguity of identity has been contained precisely as a marker of Jewish identity. The liminal anti-identity or "queerness" of Jewishness, which cannot help but participate in the racism that coproduces it, here also inhabits a predicament that might be called the "Jewish Science Question" (psychoanalysis—or Marxism?), which may begin by putting into play the mutually cross-constructive and decon-structive relations between Jewishness (itself indeterminably a race, religion, or cul-ture) and psychoanalysis (like Marxism, indeterminably a theory or practice, both always problematic as sciences, subsequently "passing" as literary theory), but rever-berates again to evoke, to call into its question, to haunt and to be haunted by the "late" formations of clinical discipline and capitalism.

Does the film work to "reterritorialize" such liminality? The clinic patients are uniformly upper-class and ambiguously sexual; Rose's outside victims are just as stereotypically working or middle-class and straight: the farmer-rapist, the truck driver, the businessman, the porn patron, the dumb mall boy, the Cosmo single girl. It is again unclear whether Rose's indiscrimination and repeated comings-

and-goings between them deconstruct or reinscribe the difference between these inside(r)s and outside(r)s. Rose and the viewer taken in with/by her occupy the role of artist/author, standing inside/outside systems of differentiation (in class, gender, sexuality, and ethnicity), switchboards in a game of Telephone. Rose as film as viewer as victim is instrumentalized, but not alone, as sites of reception and transmission. Orgasm is replaced or revealed as *chiasm*; the patient becomes an agent, an object, and a subject of knowledge at the same crossing. The ejaculation-in-reverse of the leech, that singular and locally applied phallic creature, and leaching—the multiple and molecular *jouissance* that erupts nonlocally across the discursive body—are interpenetrating by-products.

But even in the roles of boyfriend and victims we notice the same sequence through which the doctors and Rose must pass—something happens; control is relinquished or shared, one is stupefied or comatose, and one emerges changed, not really knowing what happened or how one is implicated. In a classic hermeneutic striptease, the film leaves us guessing as to what has happened to Rose and what she is doing to her victims, before showing us, in various glimpses, the cross-functional equipment that is felt but never seen by each of her victims, even refusing to emerge under Dr. Keloid's clinical gaze. This overcoded scenario works retroactively to interconstruct incest, historical and epistemic change, professionalization, and semioticization. Something happened. Glimpses of the cross-functional mechanism weave through the film like a needle through fabric. Each time it seems the same—but slightly different.

Oppositions between female desire and orgasm as visually undocumentable and therefore subject to doubt and faking, visible male desire (erection) and orgasm as guarantors of authenticity and closure (hence the generic marker of "cum shot" or "money shot" in masculinist pornography), motherhood as that which is never in doubt (birth as metonymy), and fatherhood as that which is always in doubt (birth as metaphor) have been "epicentered" to operate a signifying system. By leveraging these oppositions, the film gets away with showing a kind of erection and a kind of orgasm (we see the victim's blood being pulled into the translucent stinger) and thus would subvert the categories that control its own circulation according to official status: the film would conflate the ratings R and X into a counterprescription. It is possible to show and to speak of these things only in retrospect, only insofar as they have in some sense ceased to ground a system of meaning, at the place where the realms of *meaning* (culture, literarity) continue to establish their own self-serving and parasitical priority, to bring power down without thereby erecting themselves in its place, but not without allowing themselves to be saturated with its effects.

Numerous other examples might be adduced, including most of Cronenberg's later films, of a growing "body horror" genre that includes *Rabid* in its rhizomic genealogy. The latest epistemic Big Bang—the explosion, rabid proliferation, and mutation of discourses (literatures, theories, histories) of bodies—enacts performatively as much as it describes an ongoing discursive metastasis that grows not like a circle ("returning" to a predisciplinary bodily paradigm) but like fractal shapes elaborated through a "simple" function that is not a punctual or still center but a feedback loop, an ongoing mutation. Fractal body shapes mark another change in the forms and status of change itself, some of whose square roots will always be imaginary. The hyperdisciplinary ground or "complex plane" (which graphs together real and imaginary numbers) where it is played out is, for better and worse, "where we live now." Even while the famous last words of an imperial modernism—"the horror, the horror" of implication in Other bodies—continue to echo, they begin to be answered by a queer response: get used to it. Get used to it.

The Ends of Dreams

A man, a homeless man maybe, lived in an old railroad car he'd converted into a kind of museum. It was filled with hanging things, like clothes maybe but also like artworks or artifacts. I don't know if the car was connected to other cars or freestanding, but one minute I was on the platform and the next minute I was in the car, without really being sure how I got there. But it didn't bother me. I think something about the relation of the car to the platform was remarkable, that there was an especially large or small gap or that you had to step up or down or maybe even that the car was on exactly the same level as the platform.

Not much to go on but a string of indeterminacies (echoed in the string of texts that constitute this section), each time the same but slightly different. Everything could be one thing or another and might or might not be connected: "maybe … kind of … like … but also like … or … I don't know if … or … without really being sure … I think something … or … or … or … or maybe …." Even so, this multiplication of ambiguities—the inability to identify anything certainly—identifies the account unambiguously as a dream, an exemplary "open" or "writerly" text.

Amid all this shiftiness is a shift of another kind, a metashift between the plot and its telling: the inside of the car is described *before* the passage into it (even though this seems to be the first time the viewer has entered the car), so that the passage between them comes as the nonstory's denouement: the middle is the end; the story seems to have been turned inside out. The passage between makes a good ending because it is also where the indeterminacy is *squared*: at first, the passage/nonpassage between platform and car appears as a simple aporia—a juxtaposition of scenes with neither continuity nor discontinuity between them—but then this relation/nonrelation is elaborated, as if retroactively, and found to be constituted by another (or maybe the same) aporia: that the (indeterminately vertical or horizontal) distance between platform and car either existed or did not. It is apparently unremarkable to the dreamer that it should be remarkable at all that something either was or was not the case, as if flipping a coin a hundred times and getting a random distribution of heads and tails were equivalent to having the coin land each time on its edge.

The shift between plot and narrative resembles the process Freud called "secondary revision" (1965, 526–46), a manipulation of dream contents that effects the narratability of the dream. Strictly speaking, secondary revision (and with it, dreaming itself) can *never end*, even after awakening or even (as in this case) where the dream is reported secondhand, since (as in the transmission of any text) every telling must introduce various unconscious noise/information into the dream (see Freud 1965, 537–38); far from simply causing the deterioration of a message, this process produces and is produced by the dream not as a message but as a performative effect.

If the problematic passage from dream to waking can be said to be among the referents of the "passage between" represented repeatedly in the dream, the dream doesn't represent itself but perversely engages its own empty difference from nondreams by incorporating this difference as its problematic. This may help to explain why the passage between should come at the end of the dream (closer to the border between the dream and waking), why the dream seems so continuously to produce and mark its genericity. Likewise, though, the dream indicates that it was never *not* subject to revision, since the reverberations of this passage extend to the very bottom or beginning of the dream.

Even a sloppy reading of the indeterminacy series engages an ongoing conservation of ambiguity that constitutes the "dreamwork." "A man, a homeless man maybe": the question of the man's fixity in space or social space makes the "maybe" not a qualifier but an intensifier: not to know whether he is homeless (to be unable to "locate" him) seems to make his condition an exemplary form of homelessness (as in *Rabid*, where ambiguous Jewishness is a primary marker of Jewishness). It's hard to say, too, whether to live in a railroad car is to have a home or not, when a railroad car moves between points and home is usually treated as an end point: means and ends are folded back onto each other. The next image keeps the dream on the same track: the place is "a kind of museum" because it is also a kind of car and/or home, and because it is also potentially several kinds of museums, one showing "artworks" and another showing "artifacts" (the latter apparently a kind of anthropological or historical museum). Two "kinds of kinds" are linked (museum/not-museum and museum A/museum B), as if horizontally, without privileging difference between or within kinds. The dream maintains or restores indeterminacy in the opposition of the functionality of home (as living space) to the specular or nonfunctional space of the museum, refining the maneuver further by reambiguating the difference between a never-functional artwork and a once-functional artifact (whose museum placement would usually mark a one-way transit from functional use to symbolic display). The dreamwork continually operates to *straddle* these differences and transits. This straddling is not static but slides along as an ongoing foreclosure of foreclosure through a linked series of switches at which it must always go both ways and still cohere—both a kind of track and a kind of train: home/no-home...home/museum...museum/museum...art-museum/artifact museum. The question of "mobility versus fixity" is intimately related to the question of "functional space versus symbolic or specular space," especially insofar as both questions thematize the relation between dream and waking life in the important sense that muscular movement is neurologically off-line in sleep. The next ambiguity ("connected...or freestanding") functions as a qualification that continues to ambiguate the car's status (its functionality and/or dysfunctionality) as a home or a train, but, more important, it thematizes the question of *articulation* foregrounded by the image series that constitutes the dream (are they connected? one thing or many things? does the dream move or not?). The finally problematic "gap" elegantly elaborates this same question along x and y axes (that is, it throws into question the vertical and horizontal distance between platform and car), the car's questionable mobility and linear connectedness having already problematized the z axis (lateral distance).

The Gordian knot proposed by Einstein's famous thought experiments with relativity—featuring a moving train and an observer on a platform (Einstein 1961, 9–34)—may be cut by the famous blues standard where the narrator is poised "with one foot on the platform and the other foot on the train," but the dream goes a step further, deftly and continuously solving the problem of how to avoid being shorn in two along any number of axes. For the dreamer, a woman who has always intimately juggled multiple lives, cultures, and ethnicities and for whom "home" has always been problematic, it is easy to see how success may consist not in assimilation or difference but in maintaining indeterminacy or betweenness. The dreamwork, a perseverance of perversity, allows her to be between (neither/both marked/unmarked) without either being shorn in two or rendered invisible, a privilege (maybe *the* privilege) that none of her cultures fully enough allows her.

The dream enacts a logic in the spirit of Donna Haraway's qualification of Julian Huxley's definition of biological individuality ("indivisibility — the quality of being sufficiently heterogeneous in form to be rendered non-functional if cut in half"): Haraway adds the reminder that someone may be "an individual for some purposes, but not for others" (1991, 216). Just as the Barthesian text that always participates in multiple trajectories in multiple and irreconcilable frameworks, coherent agency and mushy abjection are not simply opposed but productively interpenetrating.

The following dream, reported to me by another friend, develops the implications of dreamwork:

I was standing in front of a house at dusk; the silhouette of a person was visible on the translucent curtain of an upper room. It was as if a tour guide were telling me, or as if I were remembering something I didn't know I knew: that a deformed man lived in the house, and that he never left the upper rooms but liked to oversee what was going on in the street below. It reminded me of a passage in The Stranger *where Mersault sits on his balcony, watching the street scene change. Then I was in the basement of the house, a long, cavelike passageway. The walls were made out of some translucent white plastic, uniformly lit from behind and bathing the hallway in a white light. I was following a woman, apparently my tour guide, down the hall. All the light made it hard to see. I kept following the woman, who never turned around and always stayed at the same distance in front of me, but she seemed to be getting smaller or maybe the hall was getting narrower, or maybe it was just a trick of perspective. Then the woman was gone; although I hadn't taken my eyes off her, I couldn't remember her disappearing. I kept walking. Then I had to stoop, then crawl, and finally the passage became so small I had to pull myself along on my stomach. At the end was a kind of opening, like a mail slot, with a hinged flap with a little chain attached. I managed to squeeze my arm around my shoulder and grab the chain. The end of the tunnel began to deform as I pulled it toward me. It was as if I was pulling the chain through my own body, until the slot began to get pulled open around my face. As my face squeezed through, I slowly began to open my eyes — in the dream* and *in real life: that was what was weird; it was such a seamless transition.*

This dream picks up the theme and strategy of transition and nontransition elaborated in the first dream. Its opening indeterminacy of remembering or being told (interior cognition or exterior perception? alone or in someone else's presence?) appears in conjunction with the dreamer's problematic relation to the house and its strange occupant (a mirror or Other to the dreamer?), echoed again in the split between upper room and basement passage in the house itself. The elided passage into the passage and the disappeared disappearance of the guide develop the aporetic logic that drove the first dream. Even when ambiguity among shrinking woman, narrowing hall, and shifting perspective is, in fact, resolved as a narrowing, it is in turn not noticed by the dreamer that this resolution would have foreclosed the perceptual possibility that the woman might have been shrinking (since a narrowing hall would have made her seem larger—not smaller—as she goes): provisional certainty is purchased only at the price of further contradiction. Likewise, the distance between the (male) dreamer and the female guide and the size of the dreamer's body remain constants, as if these consistencies were purchased relativistically at the cost of troubling all other perspectival frameworks, as if a certain relational continuity of self had been established *against* physio/psychological developmental scenarios that mandate that the relative size of the dreamer's body and his distance from a mother or from the feminine must *change* in a normative direction.

 The dream offers just enough anatomical specificity to render it radically ambiguous. The basement (as opposed to the overseeing "mental" space of the upper floor) certainly suggests some kind of bodily site, but what? The long, sphincteric passage, apparently connected at one end to the house, and with a slot that leads "outside" at the far end, suggests maybe an anus, a urethra, a vagina, a penis, or even a throat (which finally "speaks" the dreamer by deforming its otherwise slotlike mouth) or an eye (with its sphincteric pupil). The mail slot—as "male" slot—suggests the opening at the end of a penis, but arbitrarily to select this pun or another feature as definitive is to miss the ecology of indeterminacy that the dream works to maintain. By keeping these multiple passages open to each other—keeping them in question by neither conflating nor isolating them—the dream keeps the disciplinary and developmental body at bay.

 Verbal and figurative echoes that run through the dream also bind and ambiguate upper and lower: translucent curtains above and translucent passage below, the deformed man upstairs and the deformation of the passage below, the balcony "passage" from *The Stranger* and the basement "passageway." What the dreamer remembered most specifically about the Camus passage was that Mersault, just after his mother dies, watches the street all day from his balcony, realizing only after the fact that the day had ended, when "a cat, the first of the evening, crossed, unhurrying, the deserted street" (Camus 1954, 29). This retroactivity (that the day had ended without Mersault noticing, even though he had been watching it continuously), in conjunction with the mother's death, correlates with the disappearance of the female guide and the ongoing question of presence/absence in the dream. But if this disappearance marks a necessary separation, the dream's end again works to resituate this separation in a narrative whose ongoing origin, means, and end are not separation/individuation or return/assimilation but *betweenness* in an ongoing ecology of closure and openness.

The birth or expulsion scene that ends the dream meticulously deconstructs the passage from interior to exterior by situating the opening of the eyes as, simultaneously, both a dreamed and a waking action. Unlike cases where some real sensory input is incorporated into the dream, this maneuver questions the framework of interpretation and incorporation: as if the body were the dream that opens its eyes onto the world, as if the body were the eyes (since the slot is pulled open around the head as the eyelids are pulled back around the eyeballs, equating the body's head with the head's eyes). The interpenetrative topology of the dreamer pulling his body through the passage and then pulling the passage through his body is finally and even more succinctly enacted in this single eye-opening gesture. Far from bracketing the dream safely away from waking life, it makes the dreamer's day begin with an eye opening that is not an emergence into a categorically different world (an Enlightenment awakening to knowledge and vigilance) but an ironic quotation mark that articulates dream and waking life in a simple horizontal series, like an interlinked chain or the cars of a train.

Like the two dream-ends, the final paragraph of Derrida's *Of Grammatology* employs a complex strategy to level differences:

The opposition of the dream to wakefulness, is not that a representation of metaphysics as well? And what should dream or writing be if, as we know now, one may dream while writing? And if the scene of dream is always the scene of writing? At the bottom of a page of Emile, *after having once more cautioned us against books, writing . . . , Rousseau adds a note: ". . . the dreams of a bad night are given to us as philosophy. You will say I too am a dreamer; I admit it, but I do what others fail to do, I give my dreams as dreams, and leave the reader to discover whether there is anything in them which may prove useful to those who are awake" [p. 76]. (Derrida 1974, 316)*

Syntactically at least, Derrida's text echoes the famous final question of Shelley's "Mont Blanc" ("And what were thou, and earth, and stars, and sea, / If to the human mind's imaginings / Silence and solitude were vacancy?" [1977, 93]) and, thematically at least, the famous final question of Keats's "Ode to a Nightingale" ("do I wake or sleep?"). By embedding Romantic echoes alongside the "original" Romantic intertexts of Rousseau, by letting Rousseau have the last word and letting Rousseau's words seem to "speak for" the author, and by aligning "the bottom of a page of *Emile*" with the final paragraph of his book, Derrida's text deforms the relation between a "primary" and a "secondary" text (and between Romanticism and poststructuralism) by making it an interpenetrative one aligned with the ambiguous relation between dreams and writing and, by extension, of dreams and waking. The trick is again to write from, through, and toward a betweenness that simultaneously refuses to be configured *as* or *by* either an Enlightenment modernity or an anti-Enlightenment Romanticism. The passage activates the inertial or simply disingenuous assertion of self-identity ("dreams as dreams") with and against oppositional difference ("the opposition of the dream to wakefulness") in a combinatory of alignments and oppositions, so that self-difference becomes the ongoing condition of possibility and impossibility of a self.

Conceptual artist and text theorist Joseph Grigely works similar problematics of alignment and opposition in his 1993 diptych, *Guardian Angel*, an enlarged frontispiece and title page of a 1917 eugenics textbook. In the book, the

THE GUARDIAN ANGEL.

Nature's Secrets Revealed

SCIENTIFIC KNOWLEDGE OF

THE LAWS OF SEX LIFE and HEREDITY

OR

EUGENICS

Vital Information for the Married and Marriageable of All Ages;
a Word at the Right Time to the Boy, Girl, Young Man,
Young Woman, Husband, Wife, Father and Mother;
Also, Timely Help, Counsel and Instruction
for Every Member of Every Home

TOGETHER WITH IMPORTANT HINTS ON

**SOCIAL PURITY, HEREDITY,
PHYSICAL MANHOOD AND WOMANHOOD**
BY NOTED SPECIALISTS

Embracing a Department on Ethics of the Unmarried
by
PROFESSOR T. W. SHANNON, A. M.
International Lecturer; Editor Eugenics Department, Uplift Magazine; President Single
Standard Eugenic Movement; Author of Self-Knowledge, Perfect Manhood,
Perfect Womanhood, Heredity Explained, Guide to Sex Instruction, etc.

INTRODUCED BY
BISHOP SAMUEL FALLOWS, D. D., LL. D.

MEDICAL DEPARTMENT BY
W. J. TRUITT, M. D.
Formerly Associate Professor of Obstetrics, National Medical College, Chicago,
Assisted by Celebrated Specialists

PROFUSELY ILLUSTRATED

PUBLISHED BY
THE S. A. MULLIKIN COMPANY
MULLIKIN BUILDING
MARIETTA, - - - OHIO

1917

Guardian Angel. Conceptual artist Joseph Grigely reversed the position of this frontispiece and title page for his 1993 painting.

frontispiece would have been on the reader's left, making the cliff in the picture stand at the outer edge of the text. A boy reaches out to the scary void beyond and before the text, while an angel, her wings spread over the boy and girl like an open book, beckons them back to the safe ground of the text. Grigely has transposed the title page and frontispiece, revealing by this single gesture the *sinister* aspect of the text. The cliff that stood between book and world now divides text from picture and painting from itself. The boy's hands and gaze now reach out to the title page's cloudy promise of EUGENICS as his feet approach the abyss. It's hard to tell, now, whether the angel is beckoning the children back or pushing them toward the cliff. Where the world had been (the dangerous world that eugenics invents in order to save us from it) is now a strip of wall between the canvases, and where image and text had been bound together is now the open space around the canvas. By the single gesture of transposition (very like the eye-opening topology at the end of the dream), *Guardian Angel* asks what happens to the reader of the book in becoming the viewer of the painting, seeing as how the book has been turned inside out. Rather than offer a refuge, the artwork now seeks to infect the world.

The ambiguous closure of Freud's essay on the psychotic Judge Schreber ("On the Mechanism of Paranoia") performs a similar maneuver on the relation of analyst to analysand and, more generally, of psychoanalytic knowledge to paranoia and madness:

Since I neither fear the criticism of others nor shrink from criticizing myself, I have no motive for avoiding the mention of a similarity which may possibly damage our libido theory in the estimation of many of my readers. Schreber's "rays of God," which are made up of a condensation of the sun's rays, of nerve-fibres, and of spermatozoa, are in reality nothing else than a concrete representation and external projection of libidinal cathexes; and they thus lend his delusions a striking similarity with our theory. . . . I can nevertheless call a friend and fellow-specialist to witness that I had developed my theory of paranoia before I became acquainted with the contents of Schreber's book. It remains for the future to decide whether there is more delusion in my theory than I should like to admit, or whether there is more truth in Schreber's delusion than other people are as yet prepared to believe. (1963b, 48)

The Romantic opposition between science as a referential and objective experimentation on an Other and art as a recursively subjective self-experimentation (i.e., with the artist as both doctor and patient) is revealed here not simply as a fixed structure but as a machine that produces permutations, by the end of the nineteenth century, in the gothic Jekyll-and-Hyde scenario and in a psychoanalysis whose strength and weakness is that it can never quite shake its engagement in self-analysis, never unambiguously distinguish its method from its object. Schreber's paranoia differs from Freud's theory, apparently, not simply by externalizing what psychoanalysis internalizes, but because its "concrete representations" are at once too metaphorical and too concrete. That which Freud calls "libido," in other words, cannot be reduced to discrete "representations" or embodiments, functioning instead to infiltrate various embodiments or cut across realms of experience; it is mandated to assume "a thousand shapes and forms" without being reducible to any of them.

A final dream text demonstrates how the unresolvable dialectic of openness and closure observed in all of the above texts operates to make the text available for recoding while attempting (and by definition, always succeeding and failing) to control the terms by which it is received.

She was reading a book—but it was as if it were also a movie she was watching—called *The Song of Roland*. It was a kind of eighteenth-century novel, about the lord of an estate who would cross-dress (in gender and class) in order to have sex with various partners, but it turns out that the couples were always (apparently) heterosexual, but *both* partners were switching genders to get there— that is, the gardener was dressed as a man so Roland dressed as a scullery maid to make love to him, but the gardener also turned up as a lady and Roland wore *his* best (male) finery to make love to her.

She found the book/movie very funny, and (still in the dream) went off to tell it to a man (with whom she'd been flirting in real life), but instead of enjoying it with her, he launched into a humorless semiotic analysis, much to her disappointment.

I noticed two important changes between the time she first reported the dream (in 1990) and the account she reconstructed for me three years later. Her first account had ended with the revelation that the same heterosexual couple had been beneath all the outfits and impersonations all along; the second account (excerpted above) ambiguates the identity and sexual identity of the couples beneath the outfits by stressing that *the outfits* are continually shifted and coordinated to make an "(apparently) heterosexual" couple each time. A preliminary explanation for this slight but dramatic change may involve the fact that the first time the dreamer reported her dream to me, she had been flirting with the possibility of a romance with the man depicted as the "analyst" in her dream, so it is understandable that the denouement and desired telos of the dream would be, for her at that moment, the single coupling. But since she had become engaged with the man who appeared in the dream (shortly after—perhaps partly as a result of—reporting the dream to him) and had lived with him for the past three years, the balance of her narrative understandably shifted toward problematizing this (now boringly predictable) account by emphasizing the extent to which each partner may not be stably "the same" to begin with, and the extent to which each has to engage in "switching genders to get there." "There" is still a heterosexual telos, but switched from a matter of naked truth to dress performance. One might say that the dream and its tellings work to "balance" indeterminacy and heterosexual certainty; what sexualizes and narrativizes it is an indeterminacy between determinacy and indeterminacy. The move from a "truth" standard to a "performance" standard enacts a predictably post-modern historical logic, a topological turning-inside-out around a heterosexual axis that remains curiously intact. The dream's ongoing openness to renarrativization is also its openness to — and foreclosure of — closure.

Another significant event occurred in the interval between tell-ings: the movie *Orlando* had been released. At the beginning of her 1993 account, in fact, the dreamer cautioned me that "it's starting to get mixed up with images from the movie *Orlando,* as were images from the book mixed up in it." The release of the movie can only reperform for the dreamer the temporal and generic knot that constituted dream and book in the first place. Again, the knot is constituted as a com-binatory of multiple alignments and oppositions between a series of shifts ("switch-ings"): the shifts *within* the dream between the book/movie and its telling and then between its telling and analysis, the shift *between* the dream and its telling, and then between the two tellings of the dream, and then between the book and movie of *Orlando.* The relation of the real movie of *Orlando* to the book reperforms a version of the ongoing problematic of the dream: as Peter Stokes has observed (1996, 312), Virginia Woolf's Orlando "enjoyed the love of both sexes equally," while the movie's Orlando mutates from man to woman but remains unambiguously heterosexual in each case.

The dream's book/movie title is a textbook case of overdetermi-nation and condensation, combining the medieval *Song of Roland* (which the dreamer knew of, but had never read), the novel *Orlando* (which she'd read), the pop song "Roland the Headless Thompson Gunner," and the "semiotic analysis" of Roland Barthes (both of which she knew). The book and movie *Tom Jones,* another primary association she made with the picaresque dream narrative, was also obliquely grafted into the dream's web of Rolands, via the "Thompson" of the song title: in fact, Tom was the name of the man to whom she told the dream and became engaged. This knot of names, especially the transposition that links "Orlando" and "Roland," en-acts in the signifier what has already been established in the signified: a point of caption that is not simply a fixation but a strange attractor that generates permutations to cover the field in which it operates.

So what, if anything, makes the series of texts, of odds and ends of dreams that constitute this section, add up to anything but anecdotes? What kinds of claims can be authorized by such a series, about postmodernism or anything else, simply because its elements have been chosen to resonate with a certain coherent logic or because the dreamers happen to live in postmodern North America? In other words, what makes this series or its logic representative of anything? Or if not representative as such (able to stand for something else), perhaps then it can be called performative, since performative statements enact rather than represent but depend for what Austin called their "happiness" on a structure of authority they cannot in themselves constitute. In the classic example, the christening of a ship is a performative act, but the "happiness" of the gesture—the extent to which the christened name "sticks"—depends on a ceremonial structure that authorizes the christener to act as such.

The dream produces a certain kind of performative agency for itself: by being told, it makes something happen. By being divided into two sections, book and narration, the dream deftly makes any subsequent telling a retelling or re-performance; it attempts to ensure its priority over anything that can be said about it. In fact, the dream gave the dreamer a real "pick-up line," the success of which depended on the response *not* being the one represented in the dream (my response, on the other hand, fit then and now, a bit uncomfortably, into the role of humorless semiotic analyst that the dream had written for "Tom"). Rather than simply validating the dream, its success (the "engagement" of its respondents) necessitated that the dream be rewritten. The dream poses a question, written into which is a selection mechanism for organizing respondents, but the dream is not Diogenes looking for truth or a sphinx awaiting its Oedipus; it operates finally not to make the world into its own image or its Other (in fact, it seems to ask, ambivalently, to be resisted) but only to be a player in an ongoing intrigue that it sustains and that sustains it. The performativity of a question, its purchase on the world, is beyond both criteria of "truth" and "happiness": what it wants is to conserve itself as a question.

Some Semiotic Panoctopi

Lacan found a model of syntactic recursion in the fact that "the mere recoil of a 'but'" may utterly change the meaning of a previous sentence, "from which we can say that it is in the chain of the signifier that meaning 'insists' but that none of its elements 'consists' in the signification of which it is at that moment capable" (1977,

153). Freud's "Rat Man" had, long before, perfected to a neurotic fault the retroactive and nonlinear structuring force of the return of the repressed: "Something always inserted itself into his pious phrases and turned them into their opposite. For instance, if he said, 'May God protect him,' an evil spirit would hurriedly insinuate a 'not.' (Freud 1963b, 51). As it turns out, American popular culture (via *Saturday Night Live*'s Wayne and Garth) would later adopt the Rat Man's tic of adding, at the end of facetious assertions, an ironic *not.*

Lacan elaborated the otherwise still largely linear image of the "signifying chain" into a kind of fractal chain mail: "rings of a necklace that is a ring in another necklace made of rings" (1977, 153). This maneuver twists the image of the linear chain of recursive links into a recursive chain of recursive links, but at the expense of putting linearity *en abîme* in the form of an infinite linear regress in *scale*. Insufficient in itself to factor out Saussure's "linearity of the signifier," this maneuver only necessitates another that transforms the fractal chain mail into an even shiftier play of similarity and difference. This time Lacan takes off from Saussure's model of the linguistic sign, showing the word "tree" separated from its signified (a picture of a tree) by a bar:

Let us take our word "tree" again . . . and see how it crosses the bar of the Saussurian algorithm. (The anagram of "arbre" and "barre" should be noted.)

For even broken down into the double spectre of its vowels and consonants, it can still call up with the robur and the plane tree the significations it takes on, in the context of our flora, of strength and majesty. Drawing on all the symbolic contexts suggested in the Hebrew of the bible, it erects on a barren hill the shadow of the cross. Then reduces to the capital Y, the sign of the dichotomy which, except for the illustration used by heraldry, would owe nothing to the tree however genealogical we may think it. (1977, 154)

The anagram of "*arbre*" and "*barre*" begins the chain of images by suggesting one version of the dichotomy or splitting (that is, between vowels and consonants in variant arrangements) upon which the possibility of signification is based. Freud had observed his grandson repeatedly throwing a spool of thread and pulling it back, uttering the words "*fort*" (gone) and "*da*" (here) as he did so. Freud found in the game the child's attempt to master, by repetition and fantasy, his mother's otherwise uncontrollable absences and returns. Lacan may have thought that Freud had acted more as a proud grandparent when he understood the articulate words "*fort*" and "*da*" in the "long, drawn-out o-o-o-o'" and "joyful '*da*'" that he reports having heard (1961, 8–9). Nonetheless, Lacan finds that the incident marks the beginning of the construction of a subject by language, through the mere opposition of "two phonemes" and, apparently, the regularized sphincterization of throat and mouth that form them; that is, by their very abstraction or formality and its purchase on the body.

In Lacan's elaboration, the signifier "tree" splits into the two categories of its constitutive letters no less than its signified branches into two taxonomic categories (*robur,* plane tree) and these into emblematic qualities (strength, majesty), but the form of this branching cannot detach itself from the "tree-ness" it was meant to describe. Likewise, the reduced form of the tree, the capital letter Y, bears no inherent relation to live trees except by the simplified heraldic emblem, the question of genealogical relation and derivation again being unthinkable apart from its embodiment in the figure of the tree, the point here being that similarity (more likely than difference to be regarded as self-evident, natural, or given) is also produced by the sign as a result of what are selected as "essential" features. Lacan's multiplication of trees derives from but runs counter to Saussure's insistence on the arbitrarity of the relation between signifier and signified, producing instead a resemblance that roots itself in the bar between them, a resemblance signaled by the anagram that marks a metonymic slide. The sign, then, is always a kind of catachresis: the relation of "tree" to tree is itself a kind of tree, but this redoubling simultaneously flowers into a self-similar metatree (i.e., a metametaphor) and turns back on itself so as to preclude the possibility of tree-ness at all, becoming a rhizome of metonymically sprawling categories (marked by the empurpling of Lacan's prose at this juncture).

Umberto Eco recurs to the "tree of trees" figure in modeling semiotic relations:

The real problem is that every semantic unit used in order to analyze a sememe is in its turn a sememe to be analyzed. . . . *Each of them should constitute, inside the tree, a sort of* embedded sememe *generating its own tree, and so on* ad infinitum, *each of their semantic markers in turn generating another tree. The graphic representation of such a landscape of everlasting recursivity cannot be imagined.* (Eco 1976, 121–22)

As it turns out, "graphic representations" of Eco's old problem of trees and metatrees are now a dime a dozen: since Mandelbrot's 1977 *Fractal Geometry of Nature,* fractal "landscapes of everlasting recursivity" generated by elaboration of simple "feedback loop" functions have become widely available—in coffee-table books, make-your-own computer programs, studies of Romanticism and postmodernity, and so on. Eco's tree of trees is structured around the same contradiction as Lacan's "ring of rings," only reversed: the metatree models infinite recursion, while the tree (or tree-ness itself) is a model of *non*recursion (its branches cleave apart but never back together).

This contradiction achieves its avatar in a new generation of fractal paradigms, where trees and rings miscegenate and lose their rigidity, becoming fractal "cascades," or, in Floyd Merrell's more recent model of the semiotic universe, a roiling cluster of octopi:

Consider each sign possibility to be a point . . . with an infinite set of lines connecting it to all other points in the universe. . . . Each sign-point is like a chimerical octopus whose body is the point and whose tentacles are the infinite number of lines emanating from that point ready to suck in one or more of all the other sign points. (Merrell 1988, 260)

If Merrell's semiotic panoctopus illustrates the interdependence of each sign with every other sign, it is unclear how such thoroughly cross-connected structures could be flexible or move at all. Rather than forming a giant adamantine crystal, though, Merrell's semiotic universe is a squirmy, squishy, shifty, swarmy,

"A Landscape of Everlasting Recursivity": a "tree of trees"

skeletonless thing, a snake pit whose mode is a violent carnivorous flux in which each member is "ready to suck in" or incorporate its neighbors (a universe made for a decade of corporate, national, and transnational restructurings). This recursive flux is often aestheticized (against the "bad" linearity or fixity of obsolete models) by association with what David Bohm calls an "implicate order" (see Merrell 1991, 55), a model that describes musical sequence after the fashion of Lacan's syntactic recursion.

In his AIDS memoir, *Close to the Knives: A Memoir of Disintegration*, David Wojnarowicz develops a related octopal image in the visionary tradition of Ezekiel, Blake, and Ginsberg. Here, though, semiotic violence and embodiment are irreducibly implicated, beyond aestheticization, in a world where chaos everywhere underlies both "our order and disorder":

My arms sometimes feel twelve feet long and I get consumed by the emptiness and void surrounding and lying beneath each and every action I witness of others and myself. Each little gesture in the movements of the planet in its canyons and arroyos, in its suburbs and cities, in the motions of wind and light, each little action continuing, helping to continue the slow death of ourselves, the slow motion approach of the unveiling of our order and disorder in its ultimate climax beginning with a spark so subtle and beautiful that to trust it is to trust our own stupidity; it sparks in the inversion of wind and then flowers out momentarily in black petals of smoke and light and then extends vertically in an enlargement of a minute vision. In the very center, if one could withstand the light, it would appear to be octopal in its appendages. Wormlike tentacles thousands of feet long vibrate stroboscopically in the bluish mist that exudes from its center. The center is something outside of what we know as visual, more a sensation: a huge fat clockwork of civilizations; the whole onward crush of the world as we know it; all the walking swastikas yap-yapping cartoon video death language; a malfunctioning cannonball filled with bone and gristle and gearwheels and knives and bullets and animals rotting with skeletal remains and pistons and smokestacks pump-pumping cinders and lightning and shreds of flesh, spewing language and motions and shit and entrails in its wake. It's all swirling in every direction simultaneously so that it's neither going forward nor backward, not from side to side, embracing stasis beyond the ordinary sense of stillness one witnesses in death, in a decaying corpse that lasts millions of years in comparison to the sense of time that this thing operates within. This is the vision I see beneath the tiniest gesture of wiping one's lips after a meal or observing a traffic light. (1991, 68–69)

For Wojnarowicz, living with AIDS makes the world speed up *and* slow down simultaneously, as a game does for someone who's gotten very good at it or who must compensate for a slowing body with intelligence, with something that operates at the border of perception and cognition, where history

and futurity are compressed and "downloaded" into the present. Treelike models —
for example, the move in a chess game from which a thousand paths fork (a rough
model of the "many universes" interpretation of quantum theory) — leave off where
Wojnarowicz's recursive temporality begins. Subsequent moves in such a game may
make an earlier move turn out to have been a brilliant stratagem or a fatal mis-
step (or to have been one by virtue of having seemed to be the other). But this
process enacts more than a simple recontextualization of the past, since presumably
the players choose each move, to begin with, by evaluating its place in multiple
possible series of moves it may participate in producing. Even so, the "implicate
order" of games offers only a heuristic model that must be displaced in turn to enter a life politicized far more thoroughly than it could be with win-lose-or-draw
outcomes.

Wojnarowicz's universe operates by "somenesses," always between
infinitude and finitude, totality and locality, history and futurity; where all differences are split and split again, not only into a dust from whence we came and to which
we must return but into the ongoing whirlwind where they are partners. If the danger of this "leveling" is that it precludes simplistic oppositions or alignments between "general good" and particular interests (how can the relative importance or
"scale" of anything be evaluated?), it assumes this danger — and with it, the thoroughly political nature of the universe — as its condition.

Wojnarowicz's octopal vision links his own proprioception ("my
arms sometimes feel twelve feet long") with the fractal branchings of many-armed
"canyons and arroyos," as if Blake's wormlike worldline of the fallen human life, by
being multiplied in its extension in time and space, can no longer be distinguished
from the indiscretion or mystical participation of predisciplinary bodies and their
implicate worlds. What happens in the process is not simply that linearity is abolished
or compromised or rectified with mystical flux, the solid ground of matter and vitalist Enlightenment energy reduced to that which underlies them both, a wormhole-
ridden quantum foam of constantly reconfiguring possibilities. Instead, fractal re-
cursions and interpenetrations of the two reveal or produce an even more virulent
form of linearity, the juggernaut of "the whole onward crush of the world as we
know it," and with it the recognition that an adequate politics, of life and death, can
only be drawn in multiple caduceus-like diagonals.

The insistence of the vision in "the tiniest gesture of wiping one's
lips after a meal or observing a traffic light" serves to indicate how meaning insists
in a configuration always located somewhere between randomness and system or
between language and brute fact (i.e., in gesture or simple machinic sequence). What

is at stake at each figurative location is the policing and rhythming of canalization; here, the timing and placing of the flow of traffic and pedestrians, and the timing (mealtime) and placing of the entry of food (by mouth) into the body. It is not merely *meaning* that insists in these canalizations but also futility and absurdity in the face of the irreducible messiness of a universe where all provisional orderings are subsumed by a larger disorder ("rearranging the deck chairs on the Titanic") or built on the shifting sands of a ubiquitous microdisorder, a continual tyranny as they try and fail and try to stabilize arbitrariness and necessity, sex, and violence, themselves. Wojnarowicz's discourse is driven by ongoing refusal to cop a generic attitude about these insistences (e.g., meditative detachment, picaresque carpe diem, righteous indignation, clinical high seriousness, or elegiac heroism).

But rage. Not for order or apocalypse, beauty or justice, but to live and die in the fractal borderlands between, where the unbearable intensity of a too short life and the pathos whereby "too long a sacrifice can make a stone of the heart" always intersect, where "Being Queer in America" means to live out and to sustain in the world by any means necessary the monstrous knowledge that comes with having "a little less future."

Chinese Romanticism, Postmodernity, and "Obscure Poetry"

If Romanticism is ongoing "opposition to capitalism in the name of precapitalist values" (Sayre and Löwy 1990, 26), what kinds of Romanticism might accompany shifts toward a market economy in China? How would a "postsocialist" Romanticism resemble and differ from more or less "postfeudal" Romanticisms of late-eighteenth-century Europe, and how would it inhabit the postmodernity in which it would find itself?

It is relatively easy to see how reactionary fascist and/or ethnic-nationalist Romanticisms can be generated in the wake of the collapse of a state such as the Soviet Union. It may be more difficult to discern what more progressive forms of Romanticism might also accompany such a collapse or the more gradual changes in China. Such a Romanticism, arguably, already emerged in the wake of the collapse of the Chinese Empire. Student antigovernment protests in Beijing on May 4, 1919, inaugurated what became a national cultural movement to reject Confucianist tradition and to democratize Chinese culture. Profoundly nationalist *and* internationalist, the May Fourth Movement's commitment to Chinese political and cultural independence was combined with heightened engagement with Western literature, philosophy, and theory. The Chinese Communist Party, founded in 1921, was an offspring of these commitments and engagements.

This period is the subject of Leo Ou-fan Lee's *The Romantic Generation of Modern Chinese Writers* (1973). Lee's modernist Romanticism is an "outlook" that often accompanies a period of transition, the view of life as "a process of individual and subjective experience" and of reality as "a fragmented flow" (295). For Lee, Chinese Romanticism of the 1920s is especially marked by "dynamism" as a particular legacy of European influence. Lee follows the process whereby "a whole century of European romanticism — especially its French and English varieties — was swallowed up enthusiastically by one generation of Chinese literary men in one decade" (294). This characterization of cross-cultural engagement as a kind of transhistorical binge (with Romanticism cast as a new type of cultural opium addiction fostered by the British in China) implies a corollary belief in a chronologically normative literary development. Indeed, Lee describes how the belief in an organically deterministic and linear literary development "through the stages of classicism, romanticism, realism, naturalism, and neo-romanticism" (276) was widespread among Chinese literati of the period.

If, like Chinese critic Liang Shih-ch'iu's 1926 "Romantic Tendencies in Modern Chinese Literature," Lee's title marks the simultaneity of Romanticism and modernism in China as a temporal problematic, forms of Imagism can be said to enact this simultaneity both in Chinese and Western poetry of the period. Ezra Pound's modernist anti-Romanticism was as virulent as his Romantic anticapitalism, the latter in the name of a fascist-inflected medievalism. Pound shaped Imagism under the influence of Chinese poetry in translation, and Chinese poet Hu Shi's reading of Pound's 1913 Imagist manifesto strongly influenced his own manifestos of 1917 and 1918, which in turn played an important role in the May Fourth Movement. Eliot Weinberger calls this sequence "one of the neater symmetries of modernism: the East discovering in the West what the West had found in the East" (1986, 73); Sean Golden and John Minford call it "a circle turned full" (124). While the narrative of reciprocal exchange may be generous by Western standards, it can be downright rude under Chinese protocols, whereby the Gift (if cross-cultural appropriation can be so designated) tends to function more to produce differences as it circulates, to be by definition impossible to reciprocate in kind. The circle will, in fact, turn out to be eccentrically nested amid messier asymmetries and Möbius half-turns, the global yin-yang of cross-cultural interaction an incurably viral "difference engine" (e.g., see Weinberger's "Paz in Asia") as well as a vision of pacific wholeness and completion.

Perhaps the most obvious illustration of this is found in the various ways in which the agendas of the May Fourth Movement were taken up and altered by Chinese socialism. While Lee could still wonder stagily, in 1973, "whether the recent Cultural Revolution cannot be regarded as the resurgence of a kind of collective romantic spirit," he sets the stage for the inevitable sequel: "the problem of romanticism in a socialist setting will certainly be a most intriguing theme for another act in the drama" (296). Twenty years later, Liu Kang stresses a narrative of "interrupted development," whereby post-Mao literature and cultural theory take up "the recovery and continuation of the incomplete cultural enlightenment of the May Fourth Movement" (24), especially the humanism and subjectivism that Mao struggled so tragically finally to displace. By evoking "enlightenment," Liu Kang takes up a popular May Fourth Movement term for its own project. Likewise, Liu Kang implicitly extends Chinese poet-critic Sun Shaozhen's 1980 revaluation of the May Fourth poets as well as his recuperation of the May Fourth modernist argument that "art has its internal laws of development" (quoted in Tay 1985, 146).

Among the most coherent movements in post-Mao Chinese literature has been *menglong shi*, usually translated as "Obscure Poetry" (a critic's epithet that stuck, ironically or not). Like the Chinese filmmakers now achieving international recognition, the leading Obscure Poets were children and adolescents during the Cultural Revolution and came of age as artists in its aftermath. Director Chen Kaige (an old schoolmate of Obscure Poet Bei Dao) offers in *Farewell My Concubine* a symbolic account of the liberatory promise that the Cultural Revolution held, in its inception, for students subject to the rigors of Soviet-style education. Accordingly, it is difficult to say whether the humanism and subjectivism of this generation is more of a "recovery and continuation" or a backlash—or how they will be recast in turn by "another act in the drama."

While its "debt" to Imagism has been noted too often, several characteristic features of Obscure Poetry also suggest its complex relations to Romanticism, especially its new emphases on subjectivity and on subjective experience, and along with these, the tendency to endorse a mutual opposition between aesthetic and political discourse. Paradoxically or not, this tendency can remain a radical one in China only as long as the opposition itself continues to be thoroughly politicized; this observation also illustrates the danger of mistaking Romantic "features" as definitive when they signify very differently in different historical contexts. In any case, as we will see, Obscure Poetry, like Romantic poetry, tends also to accord special privilege to "poeticity" or self-reference, to symbolism over allegory, and to fragmentation and dynamism, although what these features mean in Chinese postmodernity is up for grabs.

Another problem with such a comparatist account, however, is that it tends to underwrite an Orientalist masternarrative of development, according to which modernization, for the East, always amounts to Westernization, an account that places the East always a step behind the West-becoming-itself.

Even sympathetic accounts of Obscure Poetry seem unable to shake this narrative. William Tay's early (1985) article is a case in point (although I should add that my use of it as a foil in what follows belies its importance in championing Obscure Poetry against critical opprobrium and neglect). Citing as exemplary a Gu Cheng poem that works by juxtaposing a flash of red and green against repeated images of grayness, Tay considers that, in the West, such "imagist experiments... can no longer elicit the kind of 'defamiliarizing' effect which they once had." (Curiously, the 1993 black-and-white U.S. film *Schindler's List* was hailed as innovative for including a flash of red that, just as in Gu Cheng's poem, occurs as the color of a child's clothing.) Tay drives home his point with particular emphasis: "Even in the modernist poetry from Taiwan, which was once heavily indebted to various avant-garde movements of the West, such concentrated color imagery has long been considered passé" (1985, 137). Likewise, Golden and Mitford, writing on Obscure Poet Yang Lian, characterize the post-Mao era of Chinese literature by its "great deal of interest in modernism (which in most cases has been long obsolete in the West)" (1990, 124). By these accounts, then, shabby Western Imagism and threadbare modernism are still welcome as hand-me-downs to the West's poor and backward cultural relations in the East, whom they still have the power to shock and delight. Alternatively, these accounts would have West say to East, as William Wordsworth said to his sister (in "Tintern Abbey"), with that Romantic mix of nostalgia and condescension: "in thy voice I catch / The language of my former heart, and read / My former pleasures in the shooting lights / Of thy wild eyes" (Wordsworth 1969, 165). It seems, then, that these accounts have just as much to say about the eternal return of Romantic narratives in the West as about the recurrent beginning of modernity in China that they construct.

By a related but different temporal shell game, East-West symmetry can also begin to look more like the West selling the East back its "true" and "unchanging" heritage. For example, Tay characterizes Gu Cheng's two short poems "Red Coral" and "Pearl Oyster" as "concrete, concentrated descriptions embodying no particular message"; this "lack of message," he speculates, may have prompted one Chinese critic to complain that "the themes are befuddling." The critic, Tay replies, "has probably forgotten that *yong wu shi* (thing-describing poems) abound in classical Chinese poetry" (156). This more-reactionary-than-thou response seems to situate politicized poetry as merely a relatively recent socialist aberration, against which a long, seemingly apolitical tradition can still reassert itself, essentially unchanged. As we will see, the poets themselves offer a different account.

To put Obscure Poetry into more adequate comparatist narratives requires first an engagement in the ways in which the poems in question themselves work to produce, authorize, and ambiguate certain kinds of narratives.

Gu Cheng's "Curve" ("Huxian") is identified by Tay as a typically Imagist poem "in its use of unconnected, montage-like juxtaposition of images" (139):

> A bird in the gusty wind
> Deftly changes direction
>
> A youth tries to pick up
> A penny
>
> The grapevine in fantasy
> Stretches its tentacle
>
> The wave in retreat
> Arches its back
> (Tay 1985, 138)

If modernist "juxtaposition" can end only with a kind of stasis that constitutes, at most, a dynamic equilibrium in which differences among images vibrate within a stabilizing sameness, characteristically postmodern "recursion" tends to generate unresolvable and metastasizing series. To investigate how the poem works the intersection of these strategies is also, as I hope to show, to begin to engage the logic of what Xudong Zhang, describing "contemporary Chinese cultural reflection," identifies as "a dialectic historically positioned within the historical conjuncture of premodern, modern, and postmodern" (1994, 140).

The first half of the poem enacts a critical trajectory. The first stanza posits an actor both autonomous from but dynamically "in" its dynamic environment; this positing is possible because the word "in" (*zai*) makes it radically indeterminate whether the bird turns *because of, in spite of,* or *regardless of* the wind. The second stanza counterposes to the bird's dynamic agency the humbler image of an action not much more than a conditioned reflex, the halting and stooping motion of the youth to pick up a coin. From the heroic acrobatics of the bird, its confidently executed revolution in the midst of perhaps countervailing forces, the poem swoops or stoops to earth, to the stooping to earth, to the gravity-binding reflex. If juxtaposition of images asks the reader to find patterns of similarity and/or difference, here the reader is challenged to discover or invent active syntaxes that can relate the images. Passing from the first to the second image, then, one may find either the enactment of a demystification or the temporal progress of a narrative that itself curves from the official version or original energy of the Cultural Revolution to its effect, especially on the young, of offering sudden access, if one would only stoop (and one always does) to the flash or promise of new power and liberty. Remarkably, this stooping for the coin might also be taken, proleptically, to characterize critically economic and cultural openings that have since arisen in the wake of the Cultural Revolution. This single double-edged image can be read as the emblem of a Chinese postmodernism that, as Xiaobing Tang has described it, "has to include at once a rejection of the repressive political order and a critique of the rapid process of commodification," a double rejection that works to "create a new field of uncompromising demystification" (1993, 296).

But the second half of the poem changes this trajectory dramatically. Not surprisingly, Tay translates the third and fourth stanzas to heighten the effect of juxtaposition by making them syntactically parallel to the first: "in the gusty wind" is echoed by "in fantasy" and "in retreat." A more literal translation would have to stress that it is *because* (*yin*) it is a fantasy that the grapevine stretches as it does, and *because* it is recoiling that the wave behaves as it does. This new and repeated construction tends to set the last two stanzas in parallel and *against* the first. Instead of privileging one translation over another, though, this observation only serves to demonstrate that the differences that the poem generates among its translations are not separate from it but an extension of its own logic, its own nonequivalence to itself, the articulative tension among the dynamically ambivalent or shifty alliances and oppositions that constitute the poem's affect and effect in the first place. (See also the very different version translated as "Arc" in Gu Cheng's *Selected Poems* [1990], 27).

More substantively, Tay's translation substitutes a menacing "tentacle" for Gu's "chrysalis-thread," but again, the translator's poetic decision serves to highlight what is posited in either case: that fantasy overattributes individual agency (i.e., by making a plant into an animal), whether the fantasy is of intervening more decisively and aggressively than one's power allows (i.e., of being a tentacle instead of a tendril) or of more thorough withdrawal and self-enclosure than the world affords (i.e., of cocoonlike involution rather than vinelike sprawl). Gu's "because" does counterpose more forcefully the real to the fantasized: because it is a fantasy, the otherwise rhizomic and parasitic sprawl of the grapevine is transformed into a gesture of cocooning and self-enclosure, with the implied end of self-metamorphosis to come, a precise account of how the fantasy of "self-organizing" Romantic or humanist subject-formation operates. At the same time, insofar as the "chrysalis-thread" suggests silk production, the organic metamorphosis that it enables is situated almost entirely in the literal "framework" of human (agri)culture and commodification, a critical connotation that Tay's "tentacle" fails to grasp.

The fantastic logic that shifts grapevine into chrysalis repeats, at a "smaller" scale, the shift from extensive to intensive action that characterizes the shift from the first half of the poem to the last. This sense of withdrawal links the third stanza, in turn, with the final stanza's image of retreat or recoil. In other words, the poem not only juxtaposes the four curves described by the stanzas but embeds curves recursively within and between the stanzas as well, continuing *both to progress and to recoil* at several scales as it moves from the image of the turn to the halting and stooping, to withdrawal and self-enclosure, and finally into retreat.

The final stanza confirms this contradictory recursive progress. "Rears up" might be a more literal translation than "arches," but the choice again indicates a productive ambiguity in the poem: are we to imagine, here, a wave that swells and falls back as the pattern in which it participates moves forward (ongoing condition of ocean waves, or of subjects in history), or the vertical swell of a wave that rears up as it pushes against an insurmountable obstacle, precipitating a retreat? Business as usual, or the crash against an absolute limit and a dramatic turnaround? The image of the wave's back (a doubled term, *bei ji*, literally "back-spine") seems also to work at two scales, making the wave not only a spine in itself but also the vertebra of a metaspine of successive waves — at any scale, a curvature that aligns the straining of the upright-evolved human form against gravity with the ocean's straining against horizontality as it is pushed by winds and pulled by the moon.

The poem's juxtaposition of curves that each must be in some sense "the same" nonetheless make up a metacurve whose thrust is to differ as it goes, enacting an overall movement from reality to fantasy, extension to withdrawal, evolutionary progress to reactionary backlash. This movement, in turn — a syntax or trajectory or logic that the poem challenges us to invent to account for the series of images — is not a simple two-stage process, for it remains pointedly ambiguous, ambivalent, and irreconcilable with itself as it goes. Is it possible, then, to find or invent a metasyntax that could hold its irreconcilable possibilities together, could validate the recognition that progress and backlash, the Cultural Revolution and post-Mao period, and Romanticism and postmodernity are movements that are always somehow simultaneous, if only because their temporal extension cannot simply constitute what they "are" but what they *make happen*? If juxtaposition produces a challenge to construct a context for disjoint images, and then a metacontext that can contextualize irreconcilable contexts, recursion describes the way this process does not simply yield transcendent syntheses but, at every step and in total, keeps falling back onto itself. This description enables the central problematics of Imagism to be linked with the problem of translation generally, since the multiple connotations, conventions, and literary histories in which an individual word or image or syntax is associated in one language can never be reproduced in another without producing multiple—often unpredictable or radically contingent, and sometimes definitive—excesses and lacks. As it turns out, this problem is also more specifically the problem of translating Chinese poetry into English, since Chinese allows syntactic ambiguity to play a much more integral role than English will allow. If Obscure Poetry in exile posits as a question whether it is possible to produce a metalanguage or metaculture in which Chinese and English would be accommodated and reconciled, it simultaneously enacts the way in which the impossibility of this project has recursive and extensive effects in both Chinese and English. The global yin-yang or "circle turned full" enters its postmodern avatar as a spiral or "strange attractor" in which symmetry and asymmetry are always simultaneous and coextensive.

Like "Curve," Bei Dao's "Gains" elaborates an ambivalently recursive economy:

> A single mosquito
> has enlarged night's size
> taking a drop
> of my blood
>
> I am a mosquito
> reduced by night's size
> taking a drop
> of night's blood
>
> I am a sizeless
> hovering night
> taking a drop
> of heaven's blood
> (1991, 63)

"Gains" offers a series of three developing propositions about two actors—a mosquito and a presumably human narrator—and their stage, the night; or to put it more pointedly, two local agents and the global corporation or state they work for and/or against. In the first stanza, a mosquito acting as night's agent adds incrementally to it by taking blood from an individual narrator. Secondly, narrator and mosquito are equated rather than opposed and set as one against the night, the vastness of which seems to reduce the individual to a petty thief who must steal back some of its own blood. In place of the first stanza's simple zero-sum game or parasitical one-way expropriation, the second stanza offers a properly dialectical (although still antagonistic or cross-parasitical) relationship between individual and collective formations; the third stanza seems to resolve the dialectic and to produce a new antithesis. Finally, then, the features of narrator, mosquito, and night (actors and stage, dancers and dance) are conflated in the denouement of a process that might be called (after Keats's caricature of Wordsworth) "egotistical sublimation": over the course of the poem, "I" is repeatedly dislocated in order that the subject (i.e., that subjectivity) can transcend scale by embodying both local and global (by being both mosquito and night; by being "sizeless"), while autonomizing itself as a continual and dynamic motion independent of any ground or context ("hovering"), since it has become its own invisible yet all-subsuming context ("night"). Whether this process should be identified as the logic of Romantic subject formation or of postmodern capital circulation is, typically, up for grabs. In any case, the new "gain," which the poem itself attempts self-referentially to perform, requires and produces a new Other, here called "heaven"—the poem's "surplus value." Significantly, though, it is unclear whether this development should be regarded as the subject's gain at the expense of parasitical predation on this Other (the despoiling or commodification of what now seems to be "heaven," of what had previously been allowed to be unreifiable, unnameable), or as the subject's unprecedented access to an inexhaustible surplus that its own metamorphosis has produced—money for nothing. Insofar as the poem can be read as a possibly critical rehearsal of Romantic/humanist subject formation (with "heaven" inserted in place of the proletariat?), Bei Dao's mosquito-subject is both smaller and larger, more parasitical and more autonomous, more frenetic and more stable than Wordsworth's sluggish leech-subject of "Resolution and Independence." In that poem, Wordsworth had used the images of leech and leech-gatherer as proxies in his meditation on the problematic status of the writer as both parasite and healing agent, but Wordsworth's meditation is "resolved" by the specular "help and stay secure" to be found in a mystified self-sufficiency, a resolution Bei Dao profoundly ambiguates. Wordsworth completed his hymn to heroic self-sufficiency on having just received his substantial patrimony, while Bei Dao wrote "Gains" in the economic and cultural "hovering" of his post-Tiananmen exile to the vagaries of the international culture-circuit. These biographical details index the kinds of economic and cultural contradictions that characterize the status of the writer in postfeudal and postsocialist/postmodern Romanticisms.

In identifying the process of "Gains" more explicitly with the writing process, Bei Dao's "Composition" further elaborates a subject that is both dissolved and produced by textuality:

Composition

starts in the stream and stops at the source

diamond rain
is ruthlessly dissecting
the glass world

it opens the sluice, opens
a woman's lips
pricked on a man's arm

opens the book
the words have decomposed, the ruins
have imperial integrity
(1991, 75)

Like "Gains," "Composition" enacts a series of dislocations in order to produce a final image that offers a paradoxical payoff: here, a new kind of power. The leading characteristic of textual power, the power of words and of the book, is that its abjection and fragmentation *is* its power; it achieves integrity by being dissected, dislocated, decomposed, and in ruins; its postmodern empire can and must be neither/both Chinese/English.

The otherwise stereotypically Romantic figure of ruins runs through Obscure Poetry. Explaining, in 1981, that "the old kind of poetry has always propagandized about a 'non-individual' 'I' or 'self,' an 'I' that is self-denying and self-destructive," Gu Cheng caricatures such a self as "a grain of sand, a road-paving pebble, a cogwheel, a steel screw." Once such a self "has eradicated his most concrete, individual being, he himself finally loses control and is destroyed. The new kind of 'self' is born on this heap of ruins" (quoted in Tay 1985, 147). A decade or so later, Bei Dao repeats this topos when asked about his relation to traditional Chinese poetry: "Tradition today is like a house in ruins; we can't live in it; it must be reconstructed. But it must be reconstructed on the foundation of that ruin" (1994a, 8).

Between them, in other words, Gu Cheng and Bei Dao found *menglong shi* on the ruins of *both* "tradition" and socialist "modernity." In a similar spirit, Bei Dao and his fellow editors of the early democracy-movement literary journal *Today* trenchantly chose the ruins of the Qianlong emperor's European palaces as the site, in 1979, for two now-legendary poetry readings where (as Bei Dao later described it), "under very close surveillance by the police, a thousand people appreciated difficult works of poetry with enthusiasm" (1994b, 13). The European-style palaces on the outskirts of Beijing, vengefully destroyed in 1860 by English troops during the Second Opium War, pointedly mark China's ongoingly problematic and ironic relation with Western culture and imperialism. Typically, as in Western academic accounts of Chinese "Imagism," this irony is suppressed in most Western mass-media accounts of the democracy movement, which prefer to focus on such icons as the papier-mâché Statue of Liberty paraded in Tiananmen in 1989.

For Xiaobing Tang, it is the "peculiar, but historically wrought absence of cultural normativity" in China that "makes irony the dominant mode of writing and reading" (1993, 294). While "such a disintegrative cultural environment certainly reminds one of the historical background from which Western modernism emerged" (and, one might add, of Chinese modernism in the 1920s),

> it is postmodernism, however, as a general description of being simultaneously modernist and modernist manqué, that best characterizes contemporary Chinese culture which, due to the lack of any legitimate normativity or rather because of a synchronic juxtaposition of different, if indeed incompatible, modes of production, gives continuous rise to irony and displaces all efforts to stabilize meaning. (295)

Heterochrony and interpenetration of modes of production cannot now characterize China against the West, except to situate it as exemplary, since these have become definitive postmodern characteristics. If there is a (typically Orientalist) distinction to be made between a China where starker temporal and modal contradictions prevail and a West in which the mix of times and modes approaches a kind of pixilated puree, it is in either case only in the play of resonances and disjunctions across scale between pixel and "big picture" that the course of postmodernity can be charted.

Like postempire China of the 1920s, post-Mao Chinese culture has been marked by a stepped-up engagement with Western texts, especially those of cultural theory. During the so-called Culture Fever, as Xudong Zhang describes it, the "flood of 'texts' was overwhelming, and indeed constituted a world exhibition of discourses,"

from Max Weber to Habermas; Nietzsche and Heidegger to Derrida and Foucault; from Russian
thinkers such as Berdyaev and Shestov to "Western Marxists" ranging from Adorno and
Marcuse to Althusser and Fredric Jameson; and from Freud and Lacan to
the so-called logical empiricism. The picture is slightly different if we keep in mind that these
are not names conjoined in a carnival of the presentiment of the hegemonic modern,
but rather images standing for a "nonhegemonic universality" provided by a diversified
collective experience, by an unconscious project in its mosaic form. (1994, 144)

  While terms like "Fever" and "flood" recall the logic of pathological excess by which Lee characterized Chinese appetite for Western texts in the 1920s, the difference between Lee's modernist account of modernism and Zhang's postmodernist account of postmodernism is, again, that simultaneity or temporal interpenetration—and the permeability of cultural boundaries in space—are postmodern *norms*, aberrant only with respect to modernity's account of itself. Zhang's "world exhibition of discourses" does, of course, retain its own irony toward global colonization by the shopping-mall culture of postmodern capital, perhaps recalling some of its antecedents: the great Victorian exhibitions in which capitalist technologies and images of its Others were sold to the folks at home and, before these, the almost archetypical exhibit of Western science and technology that an English expedition brought to Qianlong's China in the Romantic year 1793, the failure of which led to English imperialist enterprises to "open the market" by force. The recognition that the narrative of colonization by capitalism, by technology—and even by "Westernness" itself—from Romanticism to postmodernity, was and is and will prove to be a perpetually incomplete project *in the West itself*, as well as in the East, is a definitive one for the project of "nonhegemonic universality" (the syllabic if not dialectic partner of Xiaobing Tang's "uncompromising demystification").

  If demystification or temporal irony gets played out as the double rejection of a past characterized by "political repression" and a future characterized by "commodification," this rejection must also paradoxically include the rejection of Romantic narratives that characterize temporal progress as ongoing liberation and ongoing commodification in the first place. This temporal multiple rejection is itself matched, in Chinese postmodernism, by another double negation of the spatial metonyms "West" and "East": "The logic of the 'great cultural discussion' can be explained away neither as a tacit or outright sinification complex nor as a faithful or twisted interpretation of foreign texts, but rather as the dialectic presentation of itself under the guise of either of the former two and through the critical negation of both of them" (Zhang 1994, 140).

These two double negations, one could say, are what enable Xiao-bing Tang to make an optimistic distinction between the rise of capitalism in post-feudal Europe and postsocialist China; Tang's distinction can be characterized as "optimistic" if only because, this time,

any humanist optimism about laissez-faire capitalism and the market is a historically precluded illusion. Unless shielding themselves with bad faith, the advocates of free enterprise and its legitimizing ideology of liberalism, even though they may represent an emergent and productive social force in a national context, will never enjoy the same masterful confidence as those Enlightenment giants who, in revolt against political absolutism, resolutely stood up to call for an age of reason and individual freedom. In short, any form of utopia, within the boundaries of a nation-state, now becomes a categorical impossibility. (1993, 293)

While Liu Kang deployed "Enlightenment" as a term of approbation to index a resumed continuity with an interrupted organic development in China, Tang deploys it as a term of opprobrium to establish China's new break from a (Western) continuist history. In either case, the choice of "Enlightenment" as the definitive trope is prejudicial at least insofar as, always already on the heels of Enlightenment, it is Romanticism that sets itself up as both a new break and a renewed continuity with organic development, that constitutes a falling away from the "masterful confidence" in "an age of reason," and that, finally, may best be described as the apotropaic enterprise of "shielding...with bad faith." It was precisely in these terms that Paul de Man described Romanticism as a poetics whereby the doctrine of the "symbol" is "substituted for that of 'allegory' in an act of ontological bad faith," attempting thereby to repress "a conception of the self seen in its authentically temporal predicament" by "a defensive strategy that tries to hide from this negative self-knowledge" (de Man 1983, 211, 208). In the United States, at any rate, Tang's "bad faith" is still very much the creed of corporate politicians and their cultural counterparts (e.g., in films such as *Schindler's List*), who seem never to tire of repeating that entrepreneurship and venture capitalism will indeed save the world and liberate the oppressed.

Xudong Zhang associates a Chinese dialectic operating in "the historical conjuncture of premodern, modern, and postmodern" with the hovering site of spatial coordinations and displacements in scale between local and global (i.e., "fractal") phenomena: "In the 1980s, the Chinese situation is characterized by the fact that a new domestic social space opened by the resumed and speeded national project of modernity coincides and intertwines with the globalization of market and cultural life often called 'postmodern'" (1994, 154).

To say that versions of this conjuncture, the site of maximal be-tweenness rather than a "leading edge" in cultural time or space, have been and are ongoing and definitive in both China and the West from Romanticism through post-modernity is not to belie historical and cultural discontinuity and contradiction but to insist that, in the last instance, the embodiment of discontinuity, contradiction, and heterochrony is the ongoing work of cultures — no less than of the subcultures and metacultures they mediate.

The perverse and Romantic heterochrony that inspired William Blake to announce (in 1793, the year of the McCartney expedition) that "Empire is no more!" — at the moment when English imperialism was cranking up — is in some sense only an echo of more thoroughly heterochronous postmodern annunciations. Singer-poet Leonard Cohen's recent announcement of a molecular revolution be-ing enacted in everything from power struggles in kitchens to megacorporations and "from those nights in Tiananmen Square" — the announcement that "Democracy is coming to the U.S.A." — is, likewise, doubly an anachronism because officially too late and, realistically, premature. Cohen's whimsical hope (or "wild patience," as Adrienne Rich put it) is conjoined to a problematically Romantic mock nostalgia (for "the Berlin Wall" and for "Stalin and St. Paul") in the face of a "Future" where "things are gonna slide in all directions" under the relentless "blizzard of the world" (Cohen 1993, 367–72). This imagistic and temporal configuration is curiously affirmed and negated by Bei Dao's reminders that "old snow comes constantly, new snow comes not at all" and that "the upward path of the future / is a gigantic slippery slide" (1991, 31, 65).

After this rhetorical blizzard, a typically postmodern argument from the science of evolution makes a fittingly polemical epigraph (and a fittingly perverse epitaph for Romantic Orientalism). Gould argues that "a *general, temporal retardation of development has clearly characterized human evolution*" and that "*this re-tardation establishe[s] a matrix within which all trends in the evolution of human morphol-ogy must be assessed*" (1977, 365; emphasis in orginal); in other words, apes (for exam-ple) are born less fully developed than fish, and humans are born less fully developed than apes, but by virtue of this retardation they gain more flexibility in engaging their changing environments. A similar heterochrony may dictate that latecomers to "modernity" gain thereby the power dynamically to orient the postmodern.

Works Cited

Abrams, M. H. 1971. *Natural Supernaturalism*. New York: Norton.

Althusser, Louis. 1971. "Ideology and Ideological State Apparatuses: Notes toward an Investigation." In *Lenin and Philosophy, and Other Essays*, translated by Ben Brewster. New York: Monthly Review Press.

The Anti-Jacobin. 1797. "Prospectus of *The Anti-Jacobin*." London: Wright.

Bakhtin, M. M. 1981. *The Dialogic Imagination*. Translated by Caryl Emerson and Michael Holquist. Austin: University of Texas Press.

Barthes, Roland. 1977. *Image, Music, Text*. Translated by Stephen Heath. New York: Hill and Wang.

Baudrillard, Jean. 1975. *The Mirror of Production*. Translated by Mark Poster. St. Louis, Mo.: Telos Press.

——. 1980. "Forgetting Foucault." Translated by Nicole Dufresne. *Humanities in Society* 3, no. 1 (Winter): 87–111.

——. 1983. *In the Shadow of the Silent Majorities*. Translated by Paul Foss, Paul Patton, and John Johnston. New York: Semiotext(e).

Bei Dao. 1991. *Old Snow*. Translated by Bonnie S. McDougall and Chen Maiping. New York: New Directions.

——. 1994a. Interview with Chantal Chen-Andro and Claude Mouchard. Translated by Esther Allen. *Sulfur* 34 (Spring): 8–11.

——. 1994b. "The Purposes of the Magazine *Today* (*Jintian*)." Translated from Chinese by Chantal Chen-Andro and from French by Esther Allen. *Sulfur* 34 (Spring): 12–14.

Bella, David. 1987. "Organizations and Systematic Distortion of Information." *Journal of Professional Issues in Engineering* 113, no. 4 (October): 360–70.

Benjamin, Walter. 1969. *Illuminations*. Edited by Hannah Arendt and translated by Harry Zohn. New York: Schocken Books.

Berman, Marshall. 1982. *All That Is Solid Melts into Air: The Experience of Modernity*. New York: Penguin.

Blake, William. 1969. *Blake's "Job."* Introduction by S. F. Damon. New York: Dutton.

——. 1982. *The Complete Poetry and Prose*. New rev. ed. Edited by D. V. Erdman. Garden City, N.Y.: Doubleday, Anchor Press.

Bourdieu, Pierre. 1984. *Distinction: A Social Critique of the Judgment of Taste*. Translated by Richard Nice. Cambridge, Mass.: Harvard University Press.

Burke, Edmund. 1973. *Reflections on the Revolution in France*. Joint edition with Thomas Paine, *The Rights of Man*. New York: Doubleday, Anchor Press.

Byron, George Gordon. 1986. *Byron*. Oxford Authors. Edited by Jerome McGann. Oxford: Oxford University Press.

Camus, Albert. 1954. *The Stranger*. Translated by Stuart Gilbert. New York: Random House, Vintage.

Cardwell, D. S. L. 1971. *From Watt to Clausius: The Rise of Thermodynamics in the Early Industrial Age*. Ithaca, N.Y.: Cornell University Press.

Carlyle, Thomas. 1937. *Sartor Resartus*. Edited by C. F. Harrold. Indianapolis: Bobbs-Merrill, Odyssey.

Cartwright, Lisa, and Brian Goldfarb. 1992. "Radiography, Cinematography and the Decline of the Lens." In *Incorporations*, edited by Jonathan Crary and Sanford Kwinter, 190–202. New York: Zone.

Cohen, Leonard. 1993. *Stranger Music: Selected Poems and Songs*. New York: Pantheon.

Coleridge, Samuel Taylor. 1985. *Samuel Taylor Coleridge*. Oxford Authors. Edited by H. J. Jackson. Oxford: Oxford University Press.

Critchley, Macdonald, ed. 1955. *James Parkinson* (includes facsimile of Parkinson's 1817 *Essay on the Shaking Palsy*). London: Macmillan.

De Landa, Manuel. 1991. *War in the Age of Intelligent Machines*. New York: Zone.

Deleuze, Gilles, and Félix Guattari. 1987. *A Thousand Plateaus: Capitalism and Schizophrenia*. Translated by Brian Massumi. Minneapolis: University of Minnesota Press.

de Man, Paul. 1983. *Blindness and Insight*. 2nd ed., rev. Minneapolis: University of Minnesota Press.

———. 1984. *The Rhetoric of Romanticism*. New York: Columbia University Press.

De Quincey, Thomas. 1950. *Confessions of an English Opium Eater, together with Selections from the Autobiography of Thomas De Quincey*. Edited by Edward Sackville-West. London: Cresset Press.

Derrida, Jacques. 1974. *Of Grammatology*. Translated by Gayatri Chakravorty Spivak. Baltimore, Md.: Johns Hopkins University Press.

———. 1978. *Writing and Difference*. Translated by Alan Bass. Chicago: University of Chicago Press.

Duck, Stephen. 1985. *The Thresher's Labour*. Published with Mary Collier, *The Woman's Labour*. Augustan Reprint Society Publication no. 230. Los Angeles, Calif.: UCLA, William Andrews Clark Memorial Library.

Duden, Barbara. 1991. *The Woman beneath the Skin: A Doctor's Patients in Eighteenth-Century Germany*. Translated by Thomas Dunlap. Cambridge, Mass.: Harvard University Press.

Eastwood, David. 1989. "'Amplifying the Province of the Legislature': The Flow of Information and the English State in the Early Nineteenth Century." *Historical Research* 62: 276–94.

Eco, Umberto. 1976. *A Theory of Semiotics*. Bloomington: Indiana University Press.

1811 Dictionary of the Vulgar Tongue. 1971. Adelaide, Australia: Bibliophile Books.

Einstein, Albert. 1961. *Relativity: The Special and General Theory*. Translated by Robert W. Lawson. New York: Crown.

Erdman, David. 1954. *Blake: Prophet against Empire*. Princeton, N.J.: Princeton University Press.

Fausto-Sterling, Anne. 1985. *Myths of Gender*. 2nd ed. New York: BasicBooks.

Foucault, Michel. 1975. *The Birth of the Clinic*. Translated by A. M. S. Smith. New York: Vintage.

———. 1976. *The Archaeology of Knowledge*. Translated by A. M. S. Smith. New York: Harper and Row.

———. 1984. *The Foucault Reader*. Edited by Paul Rabinow. New York: Pantheon.

Freud, Sigmund. 1961. *Beyond the Pleasure Principle*. Translated and edited by James Strachey. New York: Norton.

———. 1963a. *Character and Culture*. Edited by Philip Rieff. New York: Collier.

———. 1963b. *General Psychological Theory*. Edited by Philip Rieff. New York: Collier.

———. 1963c. *Three Case Histories*. Edited by Philip Rieff. New York: Macmillan, Collier.

———. 1965. *The Interpretation of Dreams*. Translated and edited by James Strachey. New York: Avon Books.

Gallagher, Catherine. 1987. "The Body Versus the Social Body in the Works of Thomas Malthus and Henry Mayhew." In *The Making of the Modern Body*, edited by Catherine Gallagher and Thomas Laqueur, 83–106. Berkeley: University of California Press.

Gans, Carl. 1972. "How Snakes Move." In *Vertebrate Structures and Functions*, 38–47. San Francisco, Calif.: Freeman.

Gleckner, Robert, and Gerald Ensoe, eds. 1975. *Romanticism: Points of View*. 2nd ed. Detroit, Mich.: Wayne State University Press.

Godwin, William. 1946. *An Enquiry Concerning Political Justice*. 3 vols. Toronto: University of Toronto Press.

———. 1988. *Things as They Are; or, The Adventures of Caleb Williams*. London: Penguin.

Golden, Sean, and John Mitford. 1990. "Yang Lian and the Chinese Tradition." In *Worlds Apart: Recent Chinese Writing and Its Audiences*, edited by Howard Goldblatt, 119–37. London: Sharpe.

Gould, Stephen Jay. 1977. *Ontogeny and Phylogeny*. Cambridge, Mass.: Harvard University Press, Belknap Press.

———. 1987. *Time's Arrow, Time's Cycle: Myth and Metaphor in the Discovery of Geological Time*. Cambridge, Mass.: Harvard University Press.

Gu Cheng. 1990. *Selected Poems*. Edited by Sean Golden and Chu Chiyu. Hong Kong: Renditions Paperbacks, Research Centre for Translation, Chinese University of Hong Kong.

Halberstam, Judith, and Ira Livingston. 1995. Introduction to *Posthuman Bodies*, edited by Halberstam and Livingston, 1–19. Bloomington: Indiana University Press.

Haraway, Donna. 1991. *Simians, Cyborgs, and Women: The Reinvention of Nature*. New York: Routledge.

Harvey, David. 1990. *The Condition of Postmodernity*. Cambridge, Mass.: Blackwell.

Hayles, N. Katherine. 1995. "Embodied Virtuality; or, How to Put Bodies Back into the Picture." Paper delivered at State University of New York at Stony Brook, 1995.

Hills, Richard L. 1989. *Power from Steam: A History of the Stationary Steam Engine*. Cambridge: Cambridge University Press.

Huet, Marie-Hélène. 1993. *Monstrous Imagination*. Cambridge, Mass.: Harvard University Press.

Jakobson, Roman. 1960. "Linguistics and Poetics." In *Style In Language*, edited by Thomas Sebeok, 350–77. Cambridge, Mass.: MIT Press.

Jameson, Fredric. 1981. *The Political Unconscious*. Ithaca, N.Y.: Cornell University Press.

Johnson, Samuel. 1963. *Johnson's Dictionary: A Modern Selection*. Edited by E. L. McAdam Jr. and George Milne. New York: Random House, Pantheon.

Keats, John. 1958. *Letters of John Keats*. Edited by Hyder Rollins. Vol. 1 (1814–1821). Cambridge, Mass.: Harvard University Press.

———. 1970. *Letters of John Keats*. Selected and edited by Robert Gittings. Oxford: Oxford University Press.

———. 1978. *The Poems of John Keats*. Edited by Jack Stillinger. Cambridge, Mass.: Harvard University Press.

Kincaid, Jamaica. 1990a. *Lucy*. New York: Farrar Straus Giroux.

———. 1990b. "An Interview with Jamaica Kincaid," by Donna Perry. In *Reading Black Literature*, edited by Henry Louis Gates Jr., 492–509. New York: Penguin.

Klancher, Jon. 1987. *The Making of English Reading Audiences, 1790–1832*. Madison: University of Wisconsin Press.

Kristeva, Julia. 1984. *The Revolution in Poetic Language*. Translated by Margaret Walker. New York: Columbia University Press.

Kuhn, Thomas. 1970. *The Structure of Scientific Revolutions*. 2nd ed., enlarged. Chicago: University of Chicago Press.

Lacan, Jacques. 1977. *Ecrits*. Translated by Alan Sheridan. New York: Norton.

Laqueur, Thomas. 1987. "Orgasm, Generation, and the Politics of Reproductive Biology." In *The Making of the Modern Body*, edited by Catherine Gallagher and Thomas Laqueur, 1–41. Berkeley: University of California Press.

Latour, Bruno. 1993. *We Have Never Been Modern*. Cambridge, Mass.: Harvard University Press.

Latour, Bruno, and Steve Woolgar. 1986. *Laboratory Life: The Construction of Scientific Facts*. Princeton, N.J.: Princeton University Press.

Lee, Leo Ou-fan. 1973. *The Romantic Generation of Modern Chinese Writers*. Cambridge, Mass.: Harvard University Press.

Lenhoff, Sylvia G., and Howard M. Lenhoff. 1986. *Hydra and the Birth of Experimental Biology — 1794*. Pacific Grove, Calif.: Boxwood Press.

Levinson, Marjorie. 1988. *Keats's Life of Allegory*. New York: Blackwell.

Linkin, Harriet Kramer. 1991. "The Current Canon in British Romantics Studies." *College English* 53, no. 5 (September): 548–70.

Lonsdale, Roger, ed. 1990. *Eighteenth-Century Women Poets*. Oxford: Oxford University Press.

Lorde, Audre. 1984. *Sister Outsider*. Freedom, Calif.: Crossing Press.

Liu Kang. 1993. "Subjectivity, Marxism, and Cultural Theory in China." In *Politics, Ideology, and Literary Discourse in Modern China*, edited by Liu Kang and Xiaobing Tang, 23–55. Durham, N.C.: Duke University Press.

Lyotard, Jean-François. 1984. *The Postmodern Condition: A Report on Knowledge*. Translated by Geoff Bennington and Brian Massumi. Minneapolis: University of Minnesota Press.

Mandelbrot, Benoit. 1983. *The Fractal Geometry of Nature*. Updated and augmented. San Francisco, Calif.: Freeman.

Marx, Karl. 1972. *The Marx-Engels Reader*. 2nd ed. New York: Norton.

McGann, Jerome. 1985. *The Beauty of Inflections.* Oxford: Clarendon.

Mellor, Anne K. 1980. *English Romantic Irony.* Cambridge, Mass.: Harvard University Press.

Mellow, James R. 1980. *Nathaniel Hawthorne in His Times.* Boston: Houghton Mifflin.

Merrell, Floyd. 1988. "An Uncertain Semiotic." In *The Current in Criticism: Essays on the Present and Future of Literary Theory,* edited by Clayton Koelb and Virgil Lokke, 243–64. West Lafayette, Ind.: Purdue University Press.

———. 1991. *Signs Becoming Signs.* Bloomington: Indiana University Press.

Miller, D. A. 1988. *The Novel and the Police.* Berkeley: University of California Press.

Muecke, D. C. 1969. *The Compass of Irony.* London: Methuen.

The Norton Anthology of English Literature. 1986. 5th ed. Vol. 2. New York: Norton.

Olalquiaga, Celeste. 1992. *Megalopolis: Contemporary Cultural Sensibilities.* Minneapolis: University of Minnesota Press.

Olby, Robert C. 1966. *Origins of Mendelism.* New York: Schocken Books.

Paine, Thomas. 1973. *The Rights of Man.* Joint edition with Edmund Burke, *Reflections on the Revolution in France.* New York: Doubleday, Anchor Press.

Pateman, Carole. 1989. *The Disorder of Women: Democracy, Feminism and Political Theory.* Stanford, Calif.: Stanford University Press.

Peirce, Charles S. 1955. *Philosophical Writings of Peirce.* Selected and edited by J. Buchler. New York: Dover.

Peitgen, Heinz-Otto, and Peter H. Richter. 1986. *The Beauty of Fractals.* Berlin: Springer.

Perkins, David, ed. 1967. *English Romantic Writers.* New York: Harcourt Brace Jovanovich.

Perry, Ruth. 1991. "Colonizing the Breast: Sexuality and Maternity in Eighteenth-Century England." *Journal of the History of Sexuality* 2, no. 2 (October): 204–34.

Reynolds, Craig W. 1987. "Flocks, Herds, and Schools: A Distributed Behavioral Model." *Computer Graphics* 21 no. 4 (July): 25–34.

Russell, Nicholas. 1986. *Like Engend'ring Like: Heredity and Animal Breeding in Early Modern England.* Cambridge: Cambridge University Press.

Sacks, Oliver. 1987. *The Man Who Mistook His Wife for a Hat and Other Clinical Tales.* New York: HarperCollins.

———. 1990. *Awakenings.* Rev. ed. New York: HarperCollins.

Said, Edward. 1978. *Orientalism.* New York: Random House, Vintage.

Sagan, Dorion. 1992. "Metametazoa: Biology and Multiplicity." In *Incorporations,* edited by Jonathan Crary and Sanford Kwinter, 362–85. New York: Zone.

Sayre, Robert, and Michael Löwy. 1990. "Figures of Romantic Anticapitalism." In *Spirits of Fire: English Romantic Writers and Contemporary Historical Methods,* edited by G. A. Rosso and Daniel P. Watkins, 23–68. London: Associated University Presses.

Scott, Wilson. 1970. *The Conflict between Atomism and Conservation Theory, 1644–1860.* London: Macdonald.

Sedgwick, Eve Kosofsky. 1990. *Epistemology of the Closet.* Berkeley: University of California Press.

Serres, Michel. 1982. *Hermes: Literature, Science, Philosophy.* Edited by Josué V. Harari and David F. Bell. Baltimore, Md.: Johns Hopkins University Press.

Shaviro, Steven. 1993. *The Cinematic Body.* Minneapolis: University of Minnesota Press.

Shaw, Evelyn. 1962. "The Schooling of Fishes." *Scientific American* 206 no. 6 (June): 128–39.

Shelley, Mary. 1974. *Frankenstein; or, The Modern Prometheus: The 1818 Text.* Edited by James Rieger. Chicago: University of Chicago Press.

Shelley, Percy Bysshe. 1977. *Shelley's Poetry and Prose.* Selected and edited by Donald H. Reiman and Sharon B. Powers. New York: Norton.

Simpson, David. 1993. *Romanticism, Nationalism, and the Revolt against Theory.* Chicago: University of Chicago Press.

Siskin, Clifford. 1988. *The Historicity of Romantic Discourse.* Oxford: Oxford University Press.

Stevens, Wallace. 1972. *The Palm at the End of the Mind.* Edited by Holly Stevens. New York: Vintage.

Stokes, Peter. 1996. "Literature and Apocalypse: Writing, Gender and the Discourse of Catastrophe." Ph. D. diss. State University of New York at Stony Brook.

Tang, Xiaobing. 1993. "The Function of New Theory: What Does It Mean to Talk about Postmodernism in China?" In *Politics, Ideology, and Literary Discourse in Modern China,* edited by Liu Kang and Xiaobing Tang, 278–99. Durham, N.C.: Duke University Press.

Tay, William. 1985. "'Obscure Poetry': A Controversy in Post-Mao China." In *After Mao: Chinese Literature and Society, 1978–1981,* edited by Jeffrey C. Kinkley, 133–57. Cambridge, Mass.: Harvard University, Council on East Asian Studies.

Theweleit, Klaus. 1987. *Male Fantasies.* Vol. 1. Translated by Stephen Conway. Minneapolis: University of Minnesota Press.

Thompson, E. P. 1966. *The Making of the English Working Class*. New York: Vintage Books.

———. 1993. *Customs in Common: Studies in Traditional Popular Culture*. New York: New Press.

Thorpe, Clarence D. 1926. *The Mind of John Keats*. New York: Russell and Russell.

Todorov, Tzvetan. 1977. *The Poetics of Prose*. Translated by Richard Howard. Ithaca, N.Y.: Cornell University Press.

Valéry, Paul. 1973. *Monsieur Teste*. Translated by Jackson Mathews. Vol. 6 of *Collected Works of Paul Valéry*. Princeton, N.J.: Princeton University Press.

Wehl, Hermann. 1952. *Symmetry*. Princeton, N.J.: Princeton University Press.

Weinberger, Eliot. 1986. *Works on Paper*. New York: New Directions.

———. 1992. "Paz in Asia." In *Outside Stories*, 17–45. New York: New Directions.

Whitaker, C. S. 1970. *The Politics of Tradition, Continuity and Change in Northern Nigeria, 1946–1966*. Princeton, N.J.: Princeton University Press.

Wilson, Mona. 1971. *The Life of William Blake*. New ed. Edited by Geoffrey Keynes. Oxford: Oxford University Press.

Winner, Langdon. 1993. "If You Liked Chaos, You'll Love Complexity." *New York Times Book Review*, February 14, 1993, 12.

Wojnarowicz, David. 1991. *Close to the Knives: A Memoir of Disintegration*. New York: Vintage.

Wollstonecraft, Mary. 1989. *A Vindication of the Rights of Woman*. In *The Works of Mary Wollstonecraft*, edited by Janet Todd and Marilyn Butler, vol. 5. New York: New York University Press.

Wordsworth, Dorothy. 1941. *Journals of Dorothy Wordsworth*. Vol. 1. Edited by Ernest de Selincourt. New York: Macmillan.

Wordsworth, Dorthy, and William Wordsworth. 1967. *The Early Years: 1787–1805*. Revised by C. L. Shaver. Vol. 1 of *Letters of William and Dorothy Wordsworth*, edited by Ernest de Selincourt. 2nd ed. 8 vols. Oxford: Oxford University Press, 1967–93.

———. 1969. *The Middle Years, Part 1: 1806–1811*. Revised by M. Moorman. Vol. 2 of *Letters of William and Dorothy Wordsworth*, edited by Ernest de Selincourt. Oxford: Oxford University Press, 1967–93.

———. 1979. *The Later Years, Part 2: 1829–1834*. Revised and edited by A. G. Hill. Vol. 5 of *Letters of William and Dorthy Wordsworth*, edited by Ernest de Selincourt. Oxford: Oxford University Press, 1967–93.

Wordsworth, William. 1969. *Poetical Works*. Edited by Thomas Hutchinson and revised by Ernest de Selincourt. Oxford: Oxford University Press.

———. 1974. *Prose Works of William Wordsworth*. Edited by W. J. B. Owen and J. W. Smyser. Oxford: Oxford University Press.

———. 1979. *The Prelude, 1799, 1805, 1850*. Edited by J. Wordsworth, M. H. Abrams, and S. Gill. New York: Norton.

Yeats, W. B. 1956. *Collected Poems of W. B. Yeats*. Definitive ed. with author's final revisions. New York: Macmillan.

———. 1966. *A Vision*. New York: Collier.

Zhang, Xudong. 1994. "On Some Motifs in the Chinese 'Cultural Fever' of the Late 1980s: Social Change, Ideology, and Theory." *Social Text* 39 (Summer): 129–56.

Zirkle, Conway. 1952. "Early Ideas on Inbreeding and Crossbreeding." In *Heterosis*, edited by John W. Gowen. Ames: Iowa State College Press.

Žižek, Slavoj. 1989. *The Sublime Object of Ideology*. London: Verso.

Index

Ira Livingston is assistant professor of English at the State University of New York at Stony Brook. He is coeditor, with Judith Halberstam, of *Posthuman Bodies* (1995) and has published assorted essays, artwork, and poetry.